The Media i

NATIONAL MEDIAS

Series editor: Brian McNair, University of Strathclyde

National Medias is a series of textbooks designed to give readers an insight into some of the most important media systems throughout the world. Each book in the series provides a comprehensive overview of the media of a particular country or a geographical group of countries or nation states.

Titles in the series

The Media in Italy: Press, Cinema and Broadcasting from Unification to Digital

Matthew Hibberd

The Media in Latin America

Ed. Jairo Lugo

THE MEDIA IN ITALY

Press, Cinema and Broadcasting from Unification to Digital

Matthew Hibberd

Mc Graw Hill Open University Press

Open University Press
McGraw-Hill Education
McGraw-Hill House
Shoppenhangers Road
Maidenhead
Berkshire
England
SL6 2QL

email: enquiries@openup.co.uk
world wide web: www.openup.co.uk

and Two Penn Plaza, New York, NY 10121—2289, USA

First published 2008

A catalogue record of this book is available from the British Library

ISBN-13: 978 0 335 22285 8 (pb) 978 0 335 22286 5 (hb)
ISBN-10: 0 335 222 854 (pb) 0335 222 862 (hb)

Typeset by Kerrypress, Luton, Bedfordshire
Printed in Great Britain by Bell and Bain Ltd, Glasgow

CONTENTS

ACKNOWLEDGEMENTS

This book was commissioned by Chris Cudmore, Open University Press, and Professor Brian McNair, University of Strathclyde, in June 2006. The manuscript was prepared between July 2006 and May 2007. Revisions were made in June 2007. My sincere thanks go to Brian, Chris and staff at OUP for their kind advice and support.

Producing this book required the help and support of numerous people. Some of the ideas contained here date to my Ph.D. research completed in March 1999 and subsequent published articles. My colleagues in the Department of Film and Media Studies, University of Stirling, Scotland, assisted me in the successful completion of this research. My thanks go to all members of the department, both academic and secretarial, but especially to my Head of Department, Professor Neil Blain, my supervisor, Richard Kilborn and to the late Professor Mauro Wolf, University of Bologna. His premature death in 1996, at just 48 years old, robbed Italy and Europe of a fine academic and scholar. The former Director of the Stirling Media Research Institute, Professor Philip Schlesinger, has been instrumental in providing intellectual support for more than a decade. My sincere thanks go to him. My colleagues at the Pontifical Gregorian University have been very kind in allowing me to develop two journalism courses in the past three years. My thanks go to the director of CICS, Fr Jacob Srampickal, and to my good friend Michele Sorice. I would also like to thank the British Academy and Carnegie Trust for the Universities of Scotland for their financial help.

Various libraries and librarians have helped me research this topic in the past 15 years. My thanks go to the following libraries and their staff: RAI library, Via Col di Lana, Via Teulada and Viale Mazzini, Rome; Il Mulino Library, Bologna; the Universities of Bologna and Rome, *La Sapienza*; the University of Stirling, Scotland; University College, London; the London School of Economics; and the University of London (Senate House). My thanks go also to Louise Womersley, Jane Campbell and Karen Forrest for their administrative support.

Some of the ideas and concepts discussed in this volume have benefited from critical comments from colleagues in Italy and the UK. The late Jader Jacobelli, RAI, was very supportive in discussing issues under debate in this book. He was a very fine scholar and trenchant supporter of public service broadcasting who will be sadly missed by friends and colleagues. My thanks go also to Raymond Boyle, Martin Bull, Nico Carpentier, Fausto Colombo, Luca Cocciolo, Vincent Dalla Sala, Emiliana De Blasio, Francesco De Vescovi, Gillian Doyle, David Forgacs, Sergio Fabbrini, Enrico Manca, Enrico Menduni, Paolo Pedullà, Martin Rhodes, Giuseppe Richeri, Franco Rositi, Bruno Somalvico, Carlo Sorrentino, Beatrice Ugolini, David Ward and Maria Way. It goes without saying that all errors remain the sole responsibility of the author.

My sincere thanks go also to family and friends in the UK and Italy for providing me with peace and quiet to conduct this work. My thanks go to my brothers Mark, Mike and Neil, as well as Heidi, Susy, Lisa, Isabel and Christopher. In Italy, Fiorenzo and Giovanna Pederzoli provided me with peaceful surrounds during spring and summer 2005 and 2006 to undertake writing and editing work. My thanks go also to Daniele, Rita, Carolina and Edoardo Ricci and Flaminio, Ada and Silvana Marata. This book would not have been possible without the support of my loving wife, Roberta, and our children, Thomas and Victoria. I apologise to them for my frequent absences during evenings and weekends while working on this book.

I dedicate this book to my loving parents, Thomas William Hibberd and Patricia Margaret Hibberd.

Matthew Hibberd

Dunrossil House, Dunblane 19 October 2007

INTRODUCTION

- Citizenship, democracy and the media
- Italian historiography and mass media research
- Book structure

The main aim of this book is to provide an introductory overview to Italian media development from Unification in 1861 to the present day. The book is designed to give readers an insight into the Italian media system, which is one of the largest but also most controversial of its kind in mainland Europe. The book will focus on the key events in the development of the country's main media – press, cinema, radio and television – and will examine the impact of economic, political, sociocultural and technological processes on media expansion. The time period under examination covers successive waves of industrialization and migration and different systems of government, including fascism and democratic rule. It charts Italy's rise from a sub-literate, dialect-speaking, rural-based society emerging from centuries of foreign occupation to a leading industrialized and urbanized European power, which has spearheaded key economic and political changes in the postwar years including the formation of the European Economic Community (EEC) (today the European Union – EU). The book outlines the development of the media in a country which has undergone massive transformations but which, at the same time, retains a very strong political culture associated with the past. In Paul Ginsborg's words: 'Italy has been transformed, but the continuities of history are not easily set aside' (1990: 1).

The media have played a key role in these great transformations, in good times and bad. Benito Mussolini's rise to power and the subsequent period of fascism relied in part on the exploitation of the mass media, especially newspapers and then radio and cinema and, by 1945, years of dictatorship and war had reduced the country to a political, social and economic mess. But Italy's remarkable postwar recovery, and the development of democratic institutions, laws and processes, however imperfectly they might work in practice, can be attributed in no small part to the development of a successful and pluralistic media system. The media have played a central part in promoting the postwar ideals of hope and renewal, allowing Italians to recognize themselves as leading European citizens.

Silvio Berlusconi's rise to power since the mid-1990s has led to fierce criticisms both nationally and internationally that Italy's hard-earned freedoms have been jeopardized by the emergence of its richest person to high political office. Some respected international organizations, including the Council of Europe and the American political pressure group, Freedom House, now argue that Berlusconi wields too much media and political power, harming Italy's international reputation for good economic and political governance. This book argues that Berlusconi's political rise can only be understood by examining recurring themes in Italian political culture and the increasing importance of mass media in advanced capitalist societies.

Important recurring themes that will be discussed in this book include: how governing parties and individuals in Italy have traditionally been able to assert strong influence over media institutions and companies as well as other key social and economic institutions; the close relationship between political elites and media professionals; the weakness of the Italian state that has led to a lack of consensus over key media reforms; and the importance of the Catholic Church and other social and political institutions to media development. The book therefore takes a long view by examining the historical development of Italian broadcasting, cinema and press and how these media have been shaped by Italy's political culture, history and events, as well as key concepts which are vital to our understanding of contemporary Europe: citizenship; democracy; nation-state; and globalization. The book also seeks to give broad indications of how media institutions have helped educate and socialize Italians about their fellow citizens and the wider world.

Citizenship, democracy and the media

In advanced capitalist societies like Italy, the media act as a vital means of communication between political elites and wider society. They therefore function as central institutions of political life. The media also promote human understanding, encouraging sets of values and ideas that facilitate discussion and talk in the wider society and therefore have an equally important role as cultural or social mediators. There is little doubt that the media constitute an important commercial sector in the twenty-first century. It is generally agreed therefore that in fulfilling a public interest or general welfare role, the mass media are actually contributing towards the promotion and maintenance of democratic processes and institutions.

Raymond Williams, drawing on the Greek origins of the word, defined democracy as 'government by the people'. Citing Weekley, Williams points out that the term 'democracy' only assumed renewed political meaning in the late eighteenth century. He also points out that the term was often used pejoratively in relation to the hated Jacobins or mob-rule. Finally, Williams argues that the term has been interpreted in a number of different ways (1959: xiv). Therefore, for this book, I will use Norberto Bobbio's minimalist definition of democracy (1987: 25): 'The basic rule of democracy is the rule of the majority; in other words the rule according to which decisions are considered collective, and thus binding on the whole group, if they are approved by at least the majority of those entrusted with taking the decision'.

Democratic rights have traditionally been upheld by a state apparatus, known as the liberal state. The liberal or minimal state was originally conceptualized as part of a wider rebellion in the seventeenth and eighteenth centuries against the twin powers of feudal Europe: monarchy and Christianity. Political liberalism was the attempt to prise the governing institutions from absolutist rulers and religious powers, and hand them to newly-elected chambers. The liberal state, which was also conceived as a lay state, entrenched political rights for new emerging economic and social classes. For this condition to be realized, the public required certain rights, defined as 'basic rights', to be upheld. Such rights included the freedom of expression, speech, opinion, association, assembly, etc. In order to uphold these basic rights, the doctrine of *Rechtstaat*, or judicial state, was applied whereby the state not only exercised power *sub lege*, but exercised power within these inviolable rights (Bobbio 1987: 25–6).

The term 'public sphere' is intimately linked to the rise of the liberal state, founded upon the basic or inviolable rights accorded to male property owners. It was as a result of these new-found rights and the extension of the political franchise to the emerging property-owning class that new public institutions were founded within civil society. The growth of newspapers, libraries, universities and debating societies in turn led to the formation of a new form of political power: public opinion. And the growth of public opinion inevitably reconfigured the nature and shape of political debate. The formation of these institutions collectively represented a public sphere (Habermas 1989: 14–23). For Habermas, the characteristics of this new political space included protection from traditional public authorities, the Church and the state, and the accessibility of the new institutions due to the low operating costs. Such a public sphere promoted a whole series of debates as to the nature and direction of society. The rational nature of this debate, in line with the wider beliefs of the Enlightenment movement, emphasized human progress in all spheres of life. This book will examine how the Italian media have developed historically in relation to Habermas' concept of the public sphere.

The gradual transfer of powers from the absolutist state to parliamentary assemblies involved the gradual progression of political rights to the point where the concept of universal suffrage became widely accepted. At this point, as the late Italian political theorist Norberto Bobbio argues, the liberal or minimal state transformed itself into the representative or democratic state (1987: 110–11). The liberal state, which itself was a condemnation of paternalistic and enlightened despots, was replaced by a new democratic state that gradually renewed the belief in, and desire for, interventionist approaches in the form of social measures related to education, health, pensions and unemployment, in order to promote democratic forms and practices. Bobbio (1987: 25–6) therefore argues that:

The liberal state is not only the historical but the legal premise of the democratic state. The liberal state and the democratic state are doubly independent: if liberalism provides those liberties necessary for the proper exercise of democratic power, democracy guarantees the existence and persistence of fundamental liberties.

The persistence of fundamental liberties based on the exercise of democratic power requires the empowerment of the public as citizens (Dahlgren 1995: 19). Full membership of nation-states in postwar Western Europe has depended on three elements of citizenship being firmly entrenched within society. The first is the civil aspect of citizenship which includes freedom of speech and property rights. The second aspect is its political dimension which entails the right to take an active part in the political process, voting rights and rights of association. The third strand, which belongs squarely in the twentieth century, is the concept of social citizenship. The ideal of the social citizen has been closely associated with the development of welfare provisions in the postwar years, providing for greater economic security and social improvements (Golding 1990: 99).

The resurgence of liberalism in the late 1970s revived the idea of economic independence from political interference. Where the ideas of political liberalism had been used in the Cold War period to entrench basic rights (in part against the communist East), the brand of economic liberalism now being espoused saw as its natural enemy the social-democratic state promoted in the postwar period. Economic liberalism was premised on reducing the level of state intervention in economic and social issues and on the emancipation of economic activity from political power (Bobbio 1987: 104–6). The mechanism by which economic activity would become regulated was the hidden hand of the free market. The reemergence of economic liberalism therefore constituted the desire on the part of many intellectuals and politicians to move back towards the minimal or lay state. This book will examine how Italian media in the postwar period contributed to the empowerment of Italian citizenship, but how also the application of free market economics since the 1970s has led some to accuse the media of undermining serious political debate in favour of celebrity-led gossip and 'infotainment'.

The idea of citizenship also has other dimensions, which are relevant for our purposes in this book. Citizenship is not only a manifestation of political and macro-social circumstances, defined by universal rights; it is also a constituent feature of individual and collective identity. While the establishment of a formal institutional footing for universal rights is an essential prerequisite for citizenship, those same ideals must be internalized as a value system, providing a common civil and political bond in order to create a durable and stable platform for citizenship to thrive. In his book on the media and democracy, Peter Dahlgren (1995: 20) cogently argues this point by adding that:

The nature of what the social bond should be between citizens has been a point of contention within political philosophy, but it is clear that some minimal form of collective identity, what Vico called the *sensus communis*, is required. Even if it is de-emphasised, no democratic order will work without some shared sense of commonality among its members. Talk both manifests and presupposes some kinds of social bond between citizens.

The whole notion of citizenship is therefore dependent on the realization of a *sensus communis*. It can be argued that there are two essential prerequisites to creating a *sensus communis* – culture and social organization: culture in its broadest sense meaning 'a way of life', shared sets of symbols and beliefs codified through a common language; social organization meaning the association of human individuals with stratified categories (Gellner 1997: 1–4). Of course, a shared sense of commonality does not describe the nature only of democratic societies; it describes all communities throughout the ages. Indeed, the term *sensus communis* is primordial in so far as human societies have always grouped themselves into tribes, communities and societies extending beyond the immediate familial or primary group.

While social bonding is undoubtedly primordial in nature, I think there is one hallmark of *sensus communis* that can be more clearly identified with modernity; that is the idea of culture and social organization coinciding with political organization. In many pre-industrial societies, cultural and social association rarely coincided with political legitimation. In short, communities were rarely masters of their own culture and polity contemporaneously. For example, feudal society was based on an explicit cultural stratification of serfs and their masters into fiefdoms. Social mobility between groups was extremely limited and opportunities for mobility were restricted to conquests, crusades or wars. Technical ability or the shrewd use of land resources were rarely reciprocated with personal advancement or promotion. Political power was therefore mediated through, and despite, cultural difference. Authority was normally associated with different cultural elites in a far-off and distant land (Gellner 1997: 14–21).

This point is stressed here because in the pre-industrial world, the term 'citizenship' did not exist in the sense ascribed to it today. In the modern age, citizenship is firmly rooted to the practice of political and cultural coherence. Under the conditions of modernity, citizenship encompasses a mixture of political rights combined with membership of a wider cultural and social organization. On the one hand, participation of members is universal: formal political and civic statutes (declarations or constitutions) that emphasize full individual rights (liberty) irrespective of sex, race or social status (equity). Yet, on the other hand, to enjoy these full rights requires full membership or recognition of membership of a social unit with a broadly defined culture (fraternity). The concept of citizenship therefore denotes the process of political and cultural integration. This clearly differs to a pre-industrial age defined by its political exclusivity and cultural stratification.

The political and social unit which has served as a conduit to realize and entrench the modern condition of citizenship is the nation-state. The essential prerequisites of nationalism were a unitary political authority (the state) and a unitary or national culture. Nationhood also favoured those societies that had evolved a broadly defined culture through the slow sedimentation of multiculturalism and through the emergence of a single political authority (Gellner 1997: 50–2). These nation-states constituted the first wave of nations in the sixteenth century (France, Britain, Spain and Portugal). The second wave of nation-building took place in the nineteenth century and involved those societies with a broadly-defined cultural heritage that required political cohesion (Germany, Italy). There was, however, a key difference between Germany and Italy that will be explored in this book. Germany, arguably, developed a broad-based cultural heritage, shared by the rural masses, whereas Italy developed a national culture shared by a minority of urban and political elites. The third wave of nation-building resulted from the break-up of the Ottoman and Austro-Hungarian Empires and the promotion of Wilsonian principles of self-determination (Gellner 1997: 54–6). Finally, the fourth stage of nation-building was constituted by the reemergence of the nation-states formerly controlled by communism or the Soviet Union (Gellner 1997: 56–8).

There are a number of cultural agencies that contribute towards the functioning of the nation-state and citizenship. The key ideological apparatuses in which collective memory is constructed are social agencies of state and civil society. The major social agencies in modern industrial countries are the state education system and the family. It is within these key sectors that 'cultural capital' is initially acquired. But another set of key institutions that also contributes towards the reconstruction of the collective self is the media. The media play a central role in shaping public attitudes and opinions, in reconfirming preexisting values and beliefs, and therefore have an important role to play in promoting citizenship. This is especially evident where social bonds are weak, and the role of the media becomes more important for the cohesion of the public (Rosen 1986, quoted in Dahlgren 1995: 134–5).

The chronic features of national identities include the construction of a reflexive self by communities using signs provided by their culture, which operate via a call to traditional values and the remembrance of the glorious past (popular memory), and generate a sense of nostalgia and moral well-being. Such traditions are not God-given, but are manufactured, and involve the 'selective interpretation of history' and some conception of a Them and Us. But to point to indefinite versions of interpretation would be wrong. Interpretations of traditions are invented largely within ideological frameworks. Additonally, for nations, there is some conception of a territorial boundary (Schlesinger 1991: 168–71).

Many political scientists and socialists have stressed the importance of early mass media to the development of nation-state building and nationalism. Benedict Anderson (1991), for example, highlights the critical importance of newspapers for creating 'imagined communities' or nation-states. Habermas' concept of the public sphere is also central to many discussions of democracy and citizenship, and ascribes a key role to the rise of newspaper readership among the middle classes in eighteenth-century Britain. Some theorists have placed emphasis on other key public institutions for the rise of nationalism. Ernest Gellner (1983), for example, stressed the importance of public education systems for the diffusion of nationalist ideas. These issues will be examined in relation to Italian historical development. For the purposes of this book, I will argue that although newspapers played an important role in spreading Italian nationalism in the pre-Unification period, Italian media played a far more important role in disseminating national cultural traits – language, culture and values – after the Second World War, when the majority of Italians still lived in rural areas, worked on the land, and spoke in dialect.

The nation-state has also suffered from sporadic bouts of self-destruction. This is because nationalism is premised not only on reason but also on feeling and the sense of belonging. The advent of Romanticism, initially an eighteenth-century literature-based reaction against the cold, harsh logic of reason, promoted the cause of nationalism but also spawned a new ethno- and cultural-centrism that brought about successive international conflicts. The promotion of citizenship-through-roots (ethnos) at the expense of citizenship-through-rights (demos) has been at the root of two global wars this century and a host of regional conflicts. As a result, there are those that have passionately advocated the replacement of the nation-state with supranational bodies (Pinder 1991: 18). In many ways, such thinkers can be seen as the modern torch-carriers of Enlightenment practices: the reassertion of the rational over the irrational, the faith of reason over feeling and belonging. For example, the growth of the European institutions can be interpreted broadly along the following lines: the reaction of nation-states against their own nihilistic excesses (two European wars), built on the promise of a better future (Enlightenment), underpinned by common decision-making institutions (political union) and a customs union (economic growth). Yet, the emergence of European institutions has been hampered by a lack of political accountability (the democratic deficit) and national cultural specificity (Burgelman 1997: 129–35; Schlesinger 1997: 369–88).

In addition to the nihilistic tendencies outlined above, the continued survival of the nation-state has been threatened by the vagaries of modern life (Schlesinger 1992: 12–14). If citizenship is promoted by the nation-state, and the latter is a political configuration of modernity, the advent of a postmodern condition warrants an urgent rethink on how citizenship can be hypothesized outwith the nation-state. Giddens argues that in the period of modernity – defined broadly as the age of industrial capitalism – the concept of time-space distanciation has occurred: the separation of time and space through the intensification of worldwide social relations. Social relationships have to an extent become disembedded and disconnected from traditional face-to-face interactions. Instead, social relationships via communications and the mass media have become reembedded across different social places and physical spaces (Giddens 1991: 3).

The jump to a postmodern condition has occurred through an acceleration in the globalizing and unifying tendencies of monopoly capitalism. The rapid expansion of global capital accumulation, aided by instant telecommunications and a supply of cheap international labour, has resulted in a further distribution of social relationships across time and space. This has created conditions in which new social orders can emerge. The postmodernist claim is that this new economic, social and technological revolution has impacted on how culture is made and remade, with the explicit assumption that the old concept of a 'high' or national culture has been largely superseded by a vast multiplicity of cultural identities as we consume more commercial and international media content. It is this dissolution and fragmentation of culture, it is argued, that threatens the very stability of the nation-state. Some theorists have emphasized the increasing political importance of economic, social and special interest movements, effectively bypassing the nation-state: multinational conglomerates, environmentalists, etc., as evidence that economic and political activity is moving away from the sphere of the traditional institutions of the nation-state, such as political parties, to new corporate entities or non-governmental movements that best reflect the emergence of global issues: free trade, the nuclear threat, environmental damage, etc. (Melucci 1990, quoted in Schlesinger 1992: 13).

Yet, where history demonstrates the extent to which a nation-state has been affected by the vagaries of modern life, it shows that its status has grown in importance, not diminished. The collapse of the Soviet bloc and the bloody fragmentation of the former Yugoslavia saw the tide of history turn towards a period of renewed nation-state building. These countries have also witnessed attempted 'short cuts' in the achievement of nationhood that deny basic human rights. The 'slow sedimentation of multiculturalism' common in more organic developments of nationhood has been replaced by a quicker recipe in order to guarantee cultural homogeneity and political compliancy: ethnic cleansing. So although the nation-state has been affected by globalizing tendencies and (ongoing) regional conflicts, it still constitutes the basic social and political unit that promotes and nurtures citizenship.

This book will examine the ways in which Italian media have been shaped by the nation-state and Italian political culture. Italy has often been characterized as an unstable or weak nation-state in semi-perpetual crisis due to political and social divisions. We will explore how these divisions have impacted on media development and examine whether Italian media have helped strengthen national identity and bridge political and social divides or merely reinforced preexisting differences, thus weakening national identity.

Italian historiography and mass media research

The deep political and social divisions in Italian society have also been highlighted by its historiography. Italian history writing since the 1870s can be defined as 'corporate history' (Clark 1984: 2). That is to say, Italian historians have often belonged to one of several historical schools – nationalist, liberal, Catholic, Marxist and radical – and this has had a determining impact. Edward Carr's (1962: 44) maxim is particularly pertinent in this case: 'Before you study the history study the historian ... study his historical and social environment. The historian, being an individual, is also a product of history; and it is in this light that the student must come to regard him'.

More specific to this book is the fact that historical studies of Italian media have displayed the hallmarks of committed historiography. Some accounts, written principally by media executives or journalists from a broadly liberal perspective, have sought to defend and stress the important role the media have played in promoting a new democratic Italy (Monteleone 1980: 8–10). Other accounts, especially those written from a Marxist perspective, stress the role played by the media in giving legitimacy to the capitalist system (Cesareo 1974). In part, such historiography can be traced to the influence of two diametrically opposed schools of thought on Italian research. The two most important schools were functionalist and Marxist, both of which reinforced the political and social divide in a postwar (and Cold War) Italy.

Broad theoretical schools of historiography have existed for some time, and continue to do so, if only in residual form, and they provide a useful starting point to approach questions relating to mass media research. The last 40 years have seen great diversification of media research in Italy and the systematic development of many specialized branches of media knowledge. What has occurred is a move away from the 'corporate' school of historiography to specialized areas of research which analyse the multifaceted complexities of the Italian mass media. This can be demonstrated with a very brief analysis of media research in Italy.

In Italy, mass media research, as we would understand it, was not conducted until the 1950s. This was relatively late when compared to the USA and other European countries. In part, this can be explained by the slow development of Italian media in the postwar years and by the lack of interest shown by academic institutions in media research until the 1950s (Monteleone 1992: xiii). Giovanni Bechelloni argues that media research has developed in three historical stages (1995: 268–75). The first stage lasted from the 1950s through to 1968. It coincided with the arrival of key media texts from abroad and gave Italian researchers the methodological and bibliographic know-how to conduct media research. The kind of subjects put under the media microscope were the problems of mass society and the role of the media, the connection between empiricism and theoretical debates, and the development of specific Italian features in the wider context of macro-sociological and comparative approaches (Monteleone 1992: xiii).

A second phase of media research came in the aftermath of 1968 and lasted until the early 1980s. The political and social upheavals of 1968 resulted in the growth and development of academic studies relating to the analysis of social and political phenomena, including the mass media.

Academic groups formed throughout Italy. The period also saw the increasing influence of Marxist sociology and the crisis of American mainstream sociology. In the 1970s, this momentum and interest was maintained by the rapid transformation of the media industries in Italy, especially the growth of new national newspapers and the emergence of commercial broadcasting in the post-1976 period. As a result, the number of research topics continued to grow to cover a whole range of political, economic, social and cultural questions. This period also saw the publication of empirical studies in new academic publications. *Problemi dell' Informazione*, started by Paolo Murialdi in 1976 and *IKON* were two such journals.

Finally, the 1980s and 1990s saw the emergence of a third phase of media research. The direction of research interests further diversified to include: the development of stronger interdisciplinary fields, and a reduction in specialized research; bridge-building between 'administrative' (industry-led) research and 'academic' (university-led) research; and the expansion of vocational courses (e.g. journalist schools). There was also the rapid growth of research into audience and cultural studies, marketing and related topics on the back of the expansion of national commercial television channels in the early 1980s. As a result of these developments, the role of industrial bodies increased.

Academic institutes devoted to media research exist throughout the peninsula, producing very useful material for this book. I have used numerous Italian and international studies of politics, culture and mass media in Italy to help bridge my own knowledge gaps. Key texts used in this book include: Murialdi (2000, 2003) and Forgacs (1990a) for newspapers; Grasso (1992), Monteleone (1992) and Sorice (2002) (for broadcasting); and Forgacs (1990a) and Sorlin (1996) (for film).

Book structure

The book is structured into 10 chapters including this introduction, and a conclusion. Until 1861, Italy was ruled by different European powers: the Austro-Hungarian Empire, France, Spain and the Papal Territories as well as by city-states (Venice, Florence, etc). Chapter 1 presents a brief overview of media development in Italy from the Roman period to Unification. The second and third chapters focus on the key events in the historical development of the country's main media – press, cinema and radio – in the liberal and fascist years. These chapters explore the development of the Italian press in the post-Unification period, examining the difficulties of media development in an illiterate, rural-based society emerging from centuries of foreign occupation. In Chapters 4 and 5, I analyse the role of the media in rebuilding Italy in the post-Second World War period. These chapters also detail the key regulations relating to the media in Italy, for example, constitutional provisions and other legislation up until 1990. Chapter 6 examines the development of commercial media in Italy, discussing their impact on key media debates. Chapters 7 and 8 examine the development of the media in the aftermath of the collapse of the First Italian Republic, following financial scandals and political meltdown in 1992–3. Chapter 8, in particular, looks at the issue of media ownership in Italy, tackling the accusations levelled against Berlusconi of holding a 'conflict of interest'. This chapter also details the key legislation that has affected Italian media development since 1990. Chapter 9 examines the rise of digital media in the past decade.

1 THE MEDIA AND THE UNIFICATION OF ITALY

● **The development of early media in Italy**

The concept of a united Italy is more ancient than that of England, Scotland or France (Hearder 1983: 156). In the third century BC, the Italian peninsula up to the River Arno was unified by the Romans into a political confederation. Between 220 BC and 118 BC, the Ligurian peninsula was conquered. The whole of Italy, south of the River Po, was incorporated into part of the Roman state by 89 BC. Finally, in 27 BC, the Emperor Augustus incorporated the rest of Gallia Cisalpina as far north as the Alpine foothills. Although political unity did not survive the fall of the Roman Empire, its legacy did (Hearder 1983: 156). The idea of a united Italy as a political concept (roughly encompassing its current geographical borders) and as a unitary linguistic culture was understood by Dante in the twelfth century. Dante was a key figure in shaping the idea of Italy as a nation based on a homogeneous language and culture (both heavily Florentine in influence) (Hearder 1983: 156). If the Age of Dante and the subsequent period of the Renaissance did not lead to the direct Italianization of Europe, it left a considerable cultural and artistic legacy and certainly contributed to the Italianization of the towns and villages within Italy itself (Burke 1990: 14).

Yet, while the country enjoyed such breathtaking cultural and artistic developments, the political climate actually took a turn for the worse. Dante certainly despaired of the constant civil wars, especially in contrast to the cultural development. His own pessimistic oratory on the state of thirteenth-century Italy is summed up by some famous lines from Canto VI of *Il Purgatorio*:

Ah! servile Italy, grief's hostelry!
A ship without a pilot in great tempest!
No Lady thou of Provinces, but brothel!

That noble soul was so impatient, only
At the sweet sound of his own native land,
To make its citizen glad welcome there;

And now within thee are not without war
Thy living ones, and one doth gnaw the other
Of those whom one wall and one fosse shut in!

Search, wretched one, all round about the shores
Thy seaboard, and then look within thy bosom,
If any part of thee enjoyeth peace!

The situation had not improved nearly 200 years later when Machiavelli wrote *The Prince*. For Machiavelli, the date of the French invasion in 1494 marked the beginning of a new period of foreign despotism in Italy. When he wrote *The Prince* in 1513, Machiavelli wanted the foreign barbarians expelled from Italy and saw the possibility of greater unity of Italian states. In the final chapter, he advises Giuliano dei Medici to lead an Italian army to force the invading French out of Italy (Hearder 1983: 157; Machiavelli [1513] 1991: 223–31). This was, at least, an advance on Dante's earlier notion that a German prince, as the then leader of the Holy Roman Empire, should unite the country. The idea of seeking help from a foreign monarch was anathema to Machiavelli. Neither could he foresee intervention from the papacy in the cause of wider political unity, hence his call for Florence to spearhead the charge. But Machiavelli talked more about the possibility of unitary political action rather than any concept of nationality. Also, he never proposed (unlike Dante) that Florence should become subjected to a higher political authority (i.e. an Italian state) (Hearder 1983: 158–9).

The sixteenth and seventeenth centuries also saw the idea of a united Italy lose ground to the rise of 'a scientific and philosophical movement espousing universal, immutable truths and ideals' (Berlin 1956: 17). The Enlightenment movement was international in both membership and outlook. It was most closely associated with the philosopher Descartes, who urged that Enlightenment thinking should purge human societies of everything that was irrational, built on superstition, or reliant on groundless foundations, and replace it by reconstituting human thought and practice on rational foundations. But while European monarchs from Catherine the Great of Russia to Frederick the Great of Prussia promoted the use of the French language and a cosmopolitan culture, the seeds of a nationalist push in the eighteenth and nineteenth centuries were being sown. The ideas of this period ultimately undermined the whole basis of government across Europe, questioning the absolute right of monarchs to rule in the name of God, and brought into the public sphere ideas supporting rational and truthful debate. In line with this strand of thinking, key Italian writers of the Enlightenment – for example, Cesare Beccaria and the Verri brothers, Pietro and Alessandro – identified themselves more with their European counterparts rather than with the peasant masses spread along the peninsula, and promoted the idea of reforms in Lombardy under the Austro-Hungarians rather than independence from empire. They were important in translating Diderot and D'Alembert, and in publishing key Enlightenment ideas in the *Il Caffe* newsletter (Murialdi 2000: 15).

The nationalist movement of the eighteenth and nineteenth centuries was a reaction against much of the Enlightenment thinking (Hearder 1983: 160). While the Enlightenment emphasized the limitless potential of

Man through scientific observation and experiment, the Romantic movement retreated into local and subjective cultures; the feeling of instinctively belonging to a group, community or nation. The movement owes much of strength to the writings of Rousseau, but he also included elements of Enlightenment thinking in his philosophy, including the belief in human goodness and in a social contract. In Germany, the nationalist movement was associated with promoting a language- and rural-based 'Volk' culture inspired through the writings of Johann Gottfried Herder. It is true to say that Herder was the most influential exponent of Romanticism; this was certainly the case in Italy, where Giuseppe Mazzini was later heavily influenced by his writings. But even Herder was not exempt from the attitudes of the previous age. He was strongly anti-militarist and anti-Prussian. He developed his ideas in a theory of language arguing that a diversity of languages embodies a diversity of forms of common life among human identities (Gray 1995: 130–3).

Italian writers of the period were less concerned with thoughts of nationalism or political independence. So when a nascent Italian nationalist movement did develop, it is not surprising that it was very different to its German equivalent. The main difference was that the construction of Italianism as a cultural identity was based on the social customs of a small minority of people. For one thing, Italian was only spoken by educated elites. The majority of Italian people spoke in the vernacular, lived in rural and remote areas, were tied to a feudal farming agreement of tenant and landlord, and enjoyed different social customs. Therefore, the Italian movement was not born out of the vestiges of feudalism, as in Germany. In many ways, the problem of Italian-ness or *Italianità*, what it constitutes and who actually possesses it, has remained a salient one throughout the period of Italian unity. Commentators have often claimed that the Italian media created a national identity in the post-Second World War period, and we will return to this subject later, in Chapters 4 and 5.

The first push towards a unified Italy came through the efforts of Napoleon Bonaparte in the 1790s. Napoleon's march through the peninsula resulted in the creation of the Cisalpine Republic in 1797. Although the size and name of the Republic chopped and changed (according to which country France was at war with at any given time), the majority of northern Italians were organized into a unitary political state. In the areas covered by the Republic, Napoleon's appointees imposed the French system of government: a highly centralized administrative and legal system. During the years of Napoleon's reign, the Republic benefitted from the many material improvements carried out: road and transport links, bridges, buildings, schools, etc. In addition, a new financial regime was organized (taxes, banking). Finally, the implementation of a new administrative system and the *Code Napoléon* centralized the system of law-making, introducing the idea of equality for all before the law. In effect, therefore, the period of French rule swept away some of the vestiges of feudal society.

The development of early media in Italy

The Italian peninsula has long been at the forefront of media innovations. This legacy dates back to the Romans who had a sophisticated system for circulating news called *acta* – handwritten news-sheets, filled with news of political developments and military campaigns, etc., which were published daily or weekly, and posted in the Roman Forum from 59 BC to AD 222, and then distributed throughout the Empire. There were at least two different kinds of *acta*: the *acta senatus* detailed the business of the Senate and the *acta divina populi romani*, also known as *acta urbana*, contained general news. Senate records were kept as early as 449 BC , but these were only made public in 59 BC during Julius Caesar's reign. Some Roman journalism was also sourced from market-place gossip and Cicero, then proconsul to Cilicia in Asia Minor (southern Turkey) complained of excessive 'tittle-tattle' in the *acta* he read: 'Reports of gladiatorial pairs, the adjournment of trials ... and such tittle-tattle as nobody would have the impertinence to repeat to me when I am in Rome' (quoted in Stephens 1988: 62).

No copies of *acta* have survived but they were used and quoted extensively in letters to construct historical records. Quoting from Cicero's letter sent to his friend (and then governor in Africa), Cornificius, after Caesar's assassination in 44 BC: 'I am well aware that the record of transactions in the city [*rerum urbanarum acta*] is being sent to you. Did I not think so, I should myself write a full account of them, and especially of the attempt by Caesar Octavian [to have Antony murdered]' (quoted in Stephens 1988: 64). Eight months later in a letter to Caesar's assassin, Cassius, Cicero wrote: 'The scandalous conduct of your relative Lepidus [who allied himself with their enemy Antony] and his amazing fickleness and inconstancy I imagine you have already learnt from the daily gazette [*ex actis*] which I am assured is being sent to you' (quoted in Stephens 1988: 65).

Scandal was a prominent feature of the *acta* and there is evidence that news was manipulated to serve the interests of those in power against their enemies. One example of this was Caesar's decision to publish the *acta senatus* in 59 BC. These early publications, like newspapers in the industrialized world, would have the twin purpose of helping to coordinate society through the production and dissemination of information and to socialize members in the Empire (Stephens 1988: 67).

In the Middle Ages, too, the Italian peninsula played a formative role in developing a primitive form of news journalism. Among the oldest direct ancestors of the modern newspaper appear to have been the handwritten news-sheets that circulated widely in Venice in the sixteenth century. Venice, like most of the cities that played a major role in the early history of the newspaper, was a centre for trade and therefore for information. These Venetian news-sheets, known as *gazette*, were filled with information on wars and politics in Italy and Europe. They were distributed weekly as early as 1550 onwards and were seen as far away as London. They employed a style of journalism that would later be used by early newspapers: short sets of news items, forwarded from a particular city with the date on which they were sent (Stephens 1988: 151–5; Murialdi 2000: 9–19). Salvatore Bongi's discussion of early Venetian journalism noted that:

> The first Italian gazettes were written without any special instrument. They consisted of a sheet of paper written by hand with a simple style of handwriting and the use of abbreviations. The papers were distributed every week, almost all on Saturday ... It is said that no respectable writer of the time ever mentioned their authors.
>
> (*Bongi 1869, quoted in Stephens 1988: 152*)

In Italy, other early recorded news-sheets were produced in Florence and Genoa in 1636 and 1639 respectively. News-sheets, many with no formal name, and containing a mix of international and local news, gradually spread around the major towns and cities in seventeenth-century Italy. The first example of literary journalism aimed at educated readers was the Rome-based quarterly, *Giornale di Letterati*, published from 1668. Again, Venice quickly took over as the main centre for this specialist form of journalism, publishing the *Giornale dei letterati d'Italia*. Italians would also be influenced by the writings of seventeenth- and eighteenth-century British and Irish writers such as Burke, Dafoe, Milton, Payne and Swift. But it was the 1789 French Revolution that would have the most direct and long-lasting impact on newspaper production across the peninsula (Stephens 1988: 193–8). With the overthrow of the ancient regime in France, the newly appointed National Assembly of France passed a Declaration of the Rights of Man in August 1789, with Article 11 declaring: 'The free communication of ideas and opinions is one of the most precious of the rights of man. Every citizen may, accordingly, speak, write, and print with freedom, but shall be responsible for such abuses of this freedom as shall be defined by law'.

Parts of northern Italy were French-controlled, so reaction to regime change was swift. Many Italian-based news-sheets advocated the early phase of revolution in France. Among those reacting most positively were the *Gazzetta Universale* in Florence and the *Notizie del Mondo* in Venice. Some 2,500 copies of the *Gazzetta Universale* were printed in the decade before 1789, but little evidence remains to indicate how many copies of this paper were sold after 1789. In some places, like Milan, papers remained unpopular because they were controlled by the Church, with the result that foreign newspapers from France and Switzerland also sold in limited numbers.

One of the early benefits of the French Revolution was the reduction in the amount of censorship faced by news-sheets across some parts of the Italian peninsula. The amount of censorship varied from state to state, although rules were relaxed in many places after 1789, as governments digested events in France. But the relaxation of censorship rules proved short-lived. Many governments began reintroducing tight restrictions, especially after the execution of Louis XVI of France in 1792 and the ensuing reign of terror. The kingdoms of Sardinia and Naples, the latter under Bourbon control, turned anti-French. In Milan, the authorities brought back strict censorship of news-sheets after 1791, curtailing circulation of foreign-produced sheets and keeping Italian-based news-sheets, like *Il Caffe* and *Gazzetta Universale* under tight control or by forcing a change in editorial policy to a less radical position. Leading this 'counter-revolution' and the reassertion of strict censorship rules were Church-backed books and periodicals denouncing the libertarian and egalitarian ideas of the Revolution. The most important of these, the *Giornales ecclesiastico di Roma*, was published between 1785 and 1798. The Church also maintained close contacts with the literary press and sought to promote its reactionary ideology through such publications (Capra 1976; Murialdi 2000: 21–2).

Napoleon's push through northern Italy and the creation of the Cisalpine Republic had an immediate effect on news. Some censorship restrictions were lifted and, in parts of the North, there was a recognizable freedom of the press for a limited period after 23 May 1796. Article 354 of the Cisalpine Republic's constitution also guaranteed freedom of expression and excluded prior censorship. The impact of these provisions was a sharp growth in the number of news-sheets and papers. By the end of the eighteenth century, 40 papers were being published in Milan; 20 in Genoa; but only 10 in Venice, Rome and Naples, where some restrictions remained. Milan therefore became the news capital of Italy. The city attracted exiles and refugees from across the peninsula. Yet, tensions quickly surfaced. Some newspapers were suspended due to anti-French satire and gossip, but such content produced popular news-papers. One publisher, Carlo Barelle, neither named nor dated his publication for fear of French suppression, but quickly sold 4,000 copies on the back of its satirical and tabloid content. The most famous newspapers of the Cisalpine Republic were the *Monitori* series published in Bologna, Genoa, Florence, Milan, Naples, Rome and Venice, with the titles taking their name from the *Moniteur Universel*, which was founded in Paris in 1789 and was Napoleon's preferred newspaper. In Milan, two versions of the *Monitore* were published. One was moderate in tone and protected and financed by the French. The other was more radical (Murialdi 2000: 23–4).

As a result of the Austro-Russian war of 1799, Napoleon was forced temporally to abandon the Italian peninsula and the Cisalpine Republic fell. The legacy of those three years of benign liberal rule was to inspire Italian nationalists of the *Risorgimento* (the Resurgence) until unification was finally achieved in 1861. Most of the liberal-supporting newspapers disappeared after 1799. Napoleon's victory at the battle of Marengo on 14 June 1800 opened up the second period of Napoleonic domination across the North and Centre of the peninsula. This time, however, Napoleon was seen not as a liberator from the Austrians, but as a dictator. The main difference second time round was that the French authorities stamped down heavily on Italian nationalist sentiment and encouraged bilingual or French-only language publications. Across the peninsula, books and newspapers faced the unenviable choice of either compromising with various governments in order to survive, or going elsewhere. Opposition voices were forced offshore to Sicily, Sardinia or even Malta, which was under British control. Most of the remaining papers were run on similar lines to the *Moniteur di Paris*. A new generation of newspapers started, of which one of the most successful was the *Giornale Italiano*, which despite its use of the adjective *Italiano*, and its explicit intention to 'form a national public spirit', followed a rather conformist political line, increasing its sales from 2,240 copies per day in 1808 to 3,671 copies in 1814. It is no coincidence that sales of this paper peaked at the time of major defeats for Napoleon. Away from political journalism, the Napoleonic period coincided with the rise in publications focused towards women. The year 1791 saw the first publication of *Giornale delle Dame* and in 1804 the Milanese-based *Corriere delle Dame* was founded (Murialdi 2000: 28).

The 1815 Congress of Vienna restored continental Europe to the old, pre-Napoleon powers and provided the main European political settle- ment until 1848. Italy was once again divided between France and Austro-Hungary in the North and the Papal Territories and the Kingdom of Naples in the Central-South. Absolutist states were therefore restored their lands and powers. While strict censorship remained (although varying from state to state), the newspaper sector was very different compared to the pre-Napoleonic period (Galante Garrone 1979: 6; Murialdi 2000: 35). Newspapers had grown along the Italian peninsula as they had in the rest of Europe. In Italy this growth was stunted by slow technological change and the unfavourable political and social climate (absolutism and lack of an educated population). After the 1815 Restora- tion, Milan became the journalistic and cultural capital of the peninsula. The formation of a more nationalist intellectual class during the early years of Napoleon's rule ensured that these people were drawn to ideas of nationalism and liberty and remained hostile towards the Restoration. It would not take long for insurrections to start across the peninsula (Murialdi 2000: 36).

As noted above, the unfavourable political climate made life difficult for newspapers after 1815. Many publications folded quickly and those that did survive sold few copies. Publications rarely enjoyed circulation figures over 1,000. Non-political newspapers, magazines and journals fared better. Two journals which were central to Romance ideas were the Milanese-based *Il Conciliatore*, founded in September 1818 by Luigi Lambertenghi and Frederico Confalonieri, and which was also liberal in its outlook, and the *Antologia*, which was founded in Florence in 1821 by Gian Piero Vieusseux. The list of contributors in future years read like a *Who's Who* of great nineteenth-century Italians: Foscolo, Leopardi, Mazzini and Tommaseo. When Niccolò Tommaseo took over the editor's job in 1827, the journal gained a more forceful streak of Romanticism and, with it, of Italian nationalism (Hearder 1983: 73–4, 254).

The first major revolt against the Treaty of Vienna came in 1820 and 1821, when various European states experienced political unrest. In the papal-controlled Romagna, a new journal, *L'Illuminatore*, was published, deriding the power of the Church and the temporal powers of the Pope. The government in Naples and Sicily also faced insurrections and new underground papers emerged in other parts of Italy. The insurrections along with the underground press were quickly repressed and an air of normalcy resumed until 1831. The 1820s saw the emergence of key journalists and patriotic leaders who would later spearhead the *Risorgimento* movement. Notable among these were Carlo Cattaneo and Giuseppe Mazzini. Mazzini first came to public prominence writing for the *Indicatore Genovese*, which was founded in 1828. When this journal was repressed by despotic authorities, Mazzini and his colleagues switched to the *Indicatore Livornese* which was started in 1829 by Francesco Domenico Guerrazzi. In 1831, further insurrections broke out across the peninsula, although these were quickly repressed and new prior-censorial measures came into force. Mazzini went into political exile in Marseilles in 1832 and founded the seminal unification movement and journal, *Giovane Italia* (Murialdi 2000: 40–1). Mazzini moved on to Switzerland in 1833 before he found semi-permanent residence in London in 1837, where he spent most of his remaining years (he died in 1872). Journalism was central to Mazzini's life, both as a way of diffusing his ideas and for raising funds to stave off hardship while in exile. Mazzini's biographer, the historian Denis Mack Smith, quotes Mazzini as saying that journalism was 'rapidly becoming one of the great forces in the world'. Furthermore, Mack Smith argues that journalism 'was the only method for communicating his ideas about democracy, patriotism and internationalism to a wider public, and for the rest of his life it remained the chief weapon in his armoury' (Mack Smith 1996: 12).

After 1831, some states began promoting press modernization. Charles Albert of Piedmont was at the forefront of transforming the *Gazzetta Piemontese* from a thrice-weekly to a daily newspaper. Turin also imported the same make of printing presses that had been used by the London *Times* since 1814. The Kingdom of Naples saw a growth in the number of newspapers after 1833, coinciding with the reign of Ferdinand II. The 1830s also saw rudimentary attempts to develop a more popular press, targeting the poorer classes, despite the fact that most working classes and peasants spoke dialect and were illiterate. The most important newspaper of this kind was the *Letture popolari*, founded in Turin by Lorenzo Valerio in 1837. The paper was paternalistic, fought against poverty and called for social reforms.

Still in Turin, Carlo Cattaneo founded *Il Politecnico* in 1839. Although never selling more than 700 copies per month, the journal enjoyed notable critical acclaim. It closed in 1844, when Cattaneo joined the *Rivista Europeo*. The two Turin-based journals that best symbolized the political climate were the *Antologia italiana* and *Il Mondo illustrato*. Both were founded in 1846 and featured contributions from key 'moderate' *Risorgimento* figures and, in the case of Camillo Benso di Cavour and Massimo D'Azeglio, future Italian prime ministers. 'Radical' writers like Mazzini were still banned and censorship remained heavy. However, some signs of progress were noted. By February 1847, Carlo Cattaneo wrote of 'the potent, manifest and unexpected progress of journalism everywhere in Italy' (Murialdi 2000: 45).

According to Murialdi (2000: 45), the whole Italian peninsula was gradually introducing clearer rules on press censorship. These began in the Papal Territories on 15 March 1847 and concluded with the Piedmontese 'Albertine' constitution on 28 March 1848 (Article 28). The Turin-based *Risorgimento* was founded by Count Cesare Balbo and Cavour in 1848 and advocated a representative parliamentary system. In his biography of Cavour, Denis Mack Smith (1985: 32) notes how journalism was central to Cavour's plans to achieve greater (economic) unity across the Italian peninsula in 1848:

> Cavour soon learnt that slight distortions and exaggerations were needed in journalism to strike the imagination of readers. To gain a sympathetic hearing from ministers he bestowed excessive and presumably not altogether sincere praise on Charles Albert. In his articles he was conciliatory towards the Church, because only if the parish clergy were prised loose from the two extremes of radicalism and traditional authoritarianism would moderates have much chance of winning broad appeal. His special responsibility on the paper was foreign policy, and here he argued against all interference by foreign governments in Italian affairs. Yet in private he explained that he saw danger in the growing popular excitement against Austria because the extremists – and this included or perhaps meant Mazzini – might exploit it for their own revolutionary purposes.

The 1848 Five Day Revolution in Milan also led temporarily to greater press freedoms in Lombardy. But the revolutionary uprisings of 1848 failed to change political systems across the peninsula and bring unification. The so-called war of independence declared by Charles Albert ended in defeat by the Austrians at Novara and he soon abdicated in favour of his son, Victor Emmanuel II. The iron fist of absolutism reasserted itself in many parts of the peninsula, except for Genoa, Sardinia and Turin. In Genoa, radical and republican ideals were put forward by Mazzini and his followers. In Sardinia and Turin, the press would instead be influenced by moderate nationalist leaders like Cavour. In the 1850s press freedoms only really existed in the Kingdom of Sardinia under Victor Emmanuel II. When Italy unified in 1861, the Albertine Constitution and press laws were extended to the rest of the peninsula, apart from those areas that remained outside the new state's reach until 1866 (Venice) and 1870 (Rome) (Murialdi 2000: 50).

In conclusion, the media played, as Giuseppe Mazzini argued, a vital role in the diffusion of radical ideas among political and economic elites relating to Italian nationalism. In turn, these ideas were debated and discussed among people across the breadth and length of the Italian peninsula. But it is worth stating again that the Italian media had a limited audience. It has been calculated that at the time of Unification only 2.5 to 10 per cent of the Italian people spoke the national language, based on the literary dialects of Tuscany and Rome (Forgacs 1990a: 17). While there is little doubt that nationalist ideas were diffused through oral cultures and traditions, Italy remained a country of localities, regions and dialects.

2 THE LIBERAL YEARS, 1861–1922

- • **Newspapers in the liberal years**
- • **The birth of cinema in Italy**

When Italy achieved Unification in 1861, the Italian state became an extension of the Piedmontese state and the 1848 Albertine Constitution, which was modelled on the British political system: a constitutional monarchy with a Parliament composed of members of the upper classes. The administrative system however was French-inspired. It was a highly centralized system based on the *Code Napoléon*. The system introduced French-style penal and civil codes and an administrative system where local prefects were appointed by the government. Few powers were therefore devolved to the regions and provinces. The political franchise was limited until 1913, and there were no mass parties in the new Italian Parliament, only loose political formations. In 1882, there were further reforms which extended the vote to about 2 million citizens out of a total of 30 million living in the united Italy.

The problem of Unification was that it had resulted in the creation of two Italys (Seton-Watson 1968: 96). Firstly there was the 'legal' Italy: the centralized political state put in place by the Piedmontese. The second Italy formed after Unification was the 'real' Italy, corresponding to the wide social and economic disparities which existed along the peninsula and islands and to the vast majority of Italians who enjoyed no formal civil or political rights. Massimo d'Azeglio, the Piedmontese statesman, declared in the aftermath of Unification that 'the *Risorgimento* has made Italy, the task now is to make Italians' (Clark 1984: 2). It was a sentiment echoed half a century later by Antonio Gramsci in his famous prison notebooks. For Gramsci, the *Risorgimento* was a revolution *passiva* and *mancata*; it was not a truly nationalist revolution since large swathes of the agricultural masses had been bypassed completely in the process of unification. Essentially, the *Risorgimento* had produced a political union, a state, before it had created a nation (Clark 1984: 2).

Therefore, the main problem was how to reconcile state to society and instil a minimum of *sensus communis* – a common civil and political culture. Minority groups found themselves on the wrong side of the border after Unification, and these groups continued to live and work along the length and breadth of the country: there were, and remain, Germans, French, Greeks, Albanians and Slovenians. Geographically, southern Sicily is as far south as Tunis and Algiers (36 N), while in the North, Milan is closer to London than it is to Reggio Calabria (45.5 N). With such disparate social conditions, exacerbated by the long periods of foreign domination, international partition or isolation preceding Unification, it is not surprising that 'making Italians' would become a long, difficult and drawn-out process.

The major task facing the Italian political establishment in the post-*Risorgimento* period therefore was to unite the country. The truth is however that in the immediate post-Unification period, social, cultural and economic differences became worse. This is made clear by examining the relationship between the North and South. Northern Italy, but especially Piedmont, had been home for many of the leading liberals of the *Risorgimento*. The North possessed many of the expanding industrial and agricultural sectors. It was an area rich in minerals and good quality farming land, so with the help of modern technology and the latest farming methods it became highly successful. And it was this development that influenced many progressive (liberal) thinkers who prescribed the same treatment for the South. The South however only had an abundance of sulphur mines in Sicily, which suffered from competition with the North after 1870. The farmland in the South was poor due to deforestation, erosion and neglect by absentee landowners.

There is also a similar picture in terms of cultural competence. In 1861, the first census undertaken in Italy confirmed the idea of the North/South divide. For example, the illiteracy rate for Italy as a whole was 74.7 per cent. In the South, the numbers of illiterates surpassed their northern counterparts: in Sardinia the figure was 90 per cent; in Sicily, 89 per cent; and in the mainland South, 86 per cent. This compared to the figure in Piedmont, 54 per cent; in Lombardy, 54 per cent; in Emilia-Romagna, 78 per cent; and in Latium, 68 per cent (Forgacs 1990a: 18). It is not surprising therefore that profound social and economic inequalities would lead to civil unrest and social turmoil. The post-1870 period saw sporadic outbreaks of civilian unrest which cost more lives than the *Risorgimento* itself. The Brigand Wars were the main example of southern rebellion against northern rule.

Government coalitions in the years after Unification tended to be fragmentary, due in part to this lack of social or economic cohesion. Political groups were therefore more interested in their own sectarian interests rather than the wider goal of parliamentary rule in the national interest. It was a system institutionalized and recognized by the term *trasformismo*, a term coined by the prime minister, Agostino Depretis, in 1876, who hoped for a 'fertile transformation of parties and the unification of all shades of liberal in Parliament in exchange for those old party labels so often abused' (Joll 1983: 124). The transformation did not end the fragmentary political process, since politicians found that to win and retain political power precluded any real possibility of dissolving political groups. These characteristics were developed and institutionalized into a liberal-democratic parliamentary government in the postwar period, generally defined as 'bargained pluralist democracy' 'with power dispersed across a wide range of areas. Although in appearance the system is based on a strong version of party government, the ability of the parties to aggregate demands and respond to them by offering voters clear policy is limited' (Hine 1993: 1).

Indeed, *trasformismo* resulted in a system of politics where the retention of power was an end in itself. Any parliamentary action required a large degree of consensus, or failing that, corruption. Difficult social and economic measures were often too difficult to introduce without numerous concessions being made. This meant that vital economic and social reforms central to the process of modernization and encouraging the development of Italian cohesion were watered down or not implemented. Education provision is a prime example of this. The first and second Education Acts (1877 and 1911) were neither properly considered nor ever fully implemented (Clark 1984: 50; Forgacs 1990a: 19). This in turn hampered the development of linguistic and cultural advances. For example, illiteracy levels remained high and associated benefits, like newspaper reading, never properly developed (see next section). Other social reforms, while forthcoming, tended to be voluntary measures or piecemeal. Only major investments made in railways mitigated the lack of social development. The result bred public apathy towards the parliamentary system and discontent throughout the peninsula. The cumulative effect of corruption on such a grand scale and of such an ineffective legislature was, in the words of one historian, highly detrimental: 'The result in the generation which grew up after the achievements of the *Risorgimento* was a growing disillusionment about Italian life and politics and a growing desire for a radical change, whether by revolution or by a war for national expansion' (Joll 1983: 126).

If radical change or revolution was unlikely, national renewal through warfare resulted in further misery for Italy. The development of a belligerent Italian nationalism in the post-Unification period mirrored the wider rise of national demands at the end of the nineteenth century. In the Italian case, however, plans to expand and create an empire were intimately linked with internal problems and social discontent. The defeat at Adowa in 1896 frustrated Italian plans for expansion along northern Africa for years. Italy's inclusion in the First World War on the side of the Alliance powers proved disastrous (even though the Alliance won the war). The Battle of Caporetto in 1917 was a national humiliation and the subsequent peace treaty, which denied Italy the spoils of war promised by the Alliance, compounded that humiliation. There were none of the African colonies nor expansion along the Istrian coast as promised by the Alliance; it was called the 'mutilated peace' (*vittoria mutilata*). The question of the *vittoria mutilata* was a continuous thorn in the side of successive governments in the postwar period. Indeed, it was one reason for the failure of liberal democracy in Italy. The campaign by the leading poet Gabriele d'Annunzio led to the occupation of Trieste in direct contravention of the peace accord. It was left to the fascists to exploit national insecurity to the full: the African campaign in 1936 ended with a victory in Abyssinia that secured Italian national pride for a short period prior to the calamitous war (1940–3) and civil war between 1943 and 1945.

Newspapers in the liberal years

In the newly-unified Italy, newspaper reading, one associated benefit of increased literacy rates, tended to be relatively rare, with pronounced social and regional differences in newspaper sales due to major socioeconomic disparities. Their subsequent development, even in the twentieth century and post-Second World War period, was comparatively slow. Indeed, the newspaper industry in Italy has always had a small circulation in comparison to its northern European partners. This has traditionally hampered investment in plant and expansion of operations (Forgacs 1990a: 23, 33).

The development of newspapers in Italy was also affected by political upheavals in the 1860s and, specifically, the continuous change of capital city in those years. Italy's capital changed three times in little more than a decade, moving from Turin to Florence in 1865 and then, finally, to Rome in 1871. One early success was the rise of the *La Nazione* newspaper which had been founded by Bettino Ricasoli in Florence in 1859. Other key newspapers were founded in the period 1861–87 including *Il Secolo* and *Corriere della Sera* (see below). Rome's leading newspaper, *Il Messaggero*, was launched by Luigi Cesana in 1878 and this was followed by three other important regional titles: Bologna's *Resto Del Carlino* in 1885; *Il Secolo XIX* in Genoa in 1886; and *Il Gazzettino* in Venice in 1887 (Murialdi 2000: 76–80).

A key period of growth for the Italian newspaper industry came at the end of the nineteenth century. At that time, few newspapers sold more than 50,000 copies daily. The market leader in the post-Unification period was *Il Secolo*, which was founded in 1866. Like its competitors, the newspaper was sold cheaply with extra income coming through advertising. But by the turn of the century, newspapers sought extra capital to expand their operations. Forging the path to modernization was the Milan-based *Corriere della Sera*, which was set up in 1876. The *Corriere* became Italy's leading newspaper at the turn of the century and remains so today. Luigi Albertini was editor of the paper from 1900–21, a very creative period, when a range of editorial and technological developments were introduced. Under Albertini, profits were ploughed back into the company and key changes took place. More journalists were hired and weekly and monthly supplements were introduced, including *Domenica del Corriere*, which was launched in 1898. While the paper was owned by key Italian industrialists (including Crespi, Pirelli and De Angeli), Albertini made key staff appointments and retained editorial control. The paper espoused the liberal-conservative values of the Lombard industrialists, but was against the powerful Giolitti government because of its deals with Socialists and Catholics (the so-called *connubio* or wedding, a term which dates back to Cavour who formed a *connubio* between the centre-left and centre-right in the Piedmontese Parliament in 1852 which, in Harry Hearder's words prevented 'a choice between two parties based on clear-cut principles' (1983: 215)) (Forgacs 1990a: 36; Murialdi 2000: 61–73).

Italian journalism was also caught up in early financial scandals that rocked the Italian state in the 1890s. The main one was the collapse of the Banca Romana in 1893, which left thousands of investors penniless. The following inquiry in to the bank's demise uncovered illicit payments to journalists and newspapers by the bank in return for favourable news coverage. This scandal raised legitimate questions about relationships between journalists, newspapers, big business and politics. Newspapers, though, played an important and, arguably, more positive role in resisting government attempts to embark on a colonialist policy between 1892 and 1895. The defeat at Adowa proved that the newspapers had been right to question the government. Another key feature of Italian journalism at the turn of the century was the appearance and development of high profile writers like Scarfoglio: highly individualistic, partisan commentators who showed an extremely entrepreneurial spirit (Murialdi 2000: 73–83). The Italian press enjoyed a buoyant period as other papers followed the *Corriere della Sera*'s example and modernized their operations. Bologna's *Resto del Carlino* took on new investors and changed its political line. Politically, newspapers moved to the right in the early years of the twentieth century and began espousing imperialist policies in the pre-First World War period, arguably shaping Italian political opinion – which would prove important when deciding whether to intervene in the Great War.

The industrialization of the newpaper industry also affected the Catholic press in Italy. Since Unification, the Church had always encouraged an extensive diocesan press and although most Catholic papers were little more than parish bulletins, some sold very well. In 1907, Giovanni Grosoli formed a Catholic newspaper trust, bringing together the *Corriere d'Italia*, *L'Italia*, *Il Momento* and *Il Messaggero Toscano*. These papers played a key role in organizing support for Catholic candidates at the general elections of 1909 and 1913. Financial support came from Catholic banks (Forgacs 1990a: 37–8). The turn of the century also saw the development of a more active labour press in Italy. *Avanti!* was the paper of the Italian Socialist Party and was set up in 1896. Wealthy socialists paid for the newspaper and by 1914 it was selling 400,000 copies each day. The paper was also able to modernize thanks to additional support from the Party and saved important distribution costs by entrusting this to the Party's own organizational network (Forgacs 1990a: 39; Murialdi 2000: 82–3). Newspaper sales remained remarkably stable (but still low by international standards) between 1915 and 1980. The development of education policy, however imperfect, and a rise in adult literacy levels, offset the damaging effects of newer media on newspapers – namely cinema, radio and television. I will now start our examination of cinema.

The birth of cinema in Italy

The advent of cinema, as Pierre Sorlin argues, allowed Italians across the peninsula to watch national events 'almost simultaneously' (1996: 19). Whether it was footage of the king or of Mount Etna erupting, the cinema would help teach Italians about each other and the rapidly developing world around them. Cinema would become the most important mass medium in Italy from the late 1930s until the 1960s – both in terms of audience size and revenues generated, and film-going was responsible for promoting new collective forms of cultural consumption replacing, in some cases, variety and live theatre. But it should also be noted that apart from the golden age of Italian cinema in the 1960s, most Italians watched Hollywood films, which were entertainment-driven and promoted American cultural values. The cinema may well have taught Italians about themselves and the outside world, but the tools to achieve this were distinctly un-Italian, highlighting the importance of non-national and commercial media content in nation-building.

As we have already discussed in relation to newspapers, the start of cinema also coincided with major economic and social changes in Italy. Although still predominantly rural, Italy went through a phase of industrial development between 1895 and 1914 which saw social migration from South to North in the booming industries such as engineering, chemicals and car-making (Forgacs 1990a; Sorlin 1996: 19). One of the first major events in Italian cinematic life was Filateo Alberini's presentation of his new Alberini Kinetograph to local officials in Milan on 11 October 1895. Although Alberini's cinematic hardware would quickly be forgotten, he did go on to become a major film producer and owner in the early years of Italian cinema (Brunetta 1995a: 25). The first Italian picture show took place in Rome on 12 March 1896 and was staged by one of the Lumiere brothers' travelling salesmen. Thereafter, film shows took place in photo studios as the brothers were keen to sell their new 'camera equipment'. Content was a secondary consideration and tended to be street scenes, royal visits and so on; uncomplicated scenes due in part to the heavy camera equipment. Films quickly took on a life of their own and spectators found them an appealing form of escapism. Early cinema shows in Italy formed part of broader shows that included musicals, reviews, variety, etc., and were also linked to live performance and travelling shows. Theatre owners soon saw commercial potential in the new medium, but not as a freestanding form of entertainment.

Up until 1905, all these early films were shot by foreign companies (Sorlin 1996: 17–19). Domestic film production in Italy began in that year with the first Italian-made movie, *The Fall of Rome*, which retold the story of the 1870 conquest of Rome by Italian troops. The film was made by Alberini and was shown in squares up and down Italy, promoted by the use of early marketing techniques (such as personal appearances of actors) (Sorlin 1996: 19–20). In 1906, Alberini established Cines, Italy's leading film producer in the period around the First World War (Brunetta 1995a: 27). Films then expanded rapidly in Italy: 126 were made in 1906;

482 in 1908 and 867 in 1910. Most were short films lasting 5–10 minutes, but feature formats were eventually developed after 1911. Film production in the very early years was a piecemeal effort, with most companies producing one or two films and then going bankrupt (Sorlin 1996: 19–21).

By 1911, however, three Italian firms dominated domestic filmmaking: Itala Film, Societa Anonimà and Cines. These big three made 60 per cent of films at this time; 80 per cent of films were made by the top six companies (Sorlin 1996: 21). Itala Film was shooting one film every three days; Cines was filming one daily. These short films tended to be documentary, one-man shows or versions of foreign works, all aimed primarily at the domestic market. Italian producers also looked for ways of developing classic texts – Classicism – for domestic and foreign markets. Dante's *Inferno* was the first Italian feature film in 1911. Dante's poem was divided into simple scenes accompanied by sentences from the poem. Attempts were also made to bring great biblical, Greek and Latin stories to screen as well as Shakespeare and Italian writers such as Manzoni (Brunetta 1995a: 50–8).

An original feature of Italian filmmaking, and one invented by the main studios, was the idea or myth of *divismo*, the cult of female film stars – commonly known still as *dive* or divas. Stars like Francesca Bertini came to the fore as leading actresses able to demand high salaries. Film companies pampered their stars because, arguably, *dive* bought an essential element to Italian cinema: glamour. Audiences flocked to see their films. *Dive* roles usually entailed playing independent or working-class women, who were both vulnerable and tough at the same time (Sorlin 1996: 33). There were no male equivalents as such. The most famous pre-war actor was Mario Bonnard and he became a director. Instead, the studios cultivated men as *forzati* – hard men or tough guys, such as Bartolomeo Pagano who placed Maciste in *Cabiria* and who would go on to make a series of films based on this character in the war and postwar years (Brunetta 1995a: 97–118; Sorlin 1996: 34).

The most successful commercial prewar feature film was *Cabiria*, which was released in 1914 and directed by Giovanni Pastrone. *Cabiria* is set during the Punic Wars when Carthaginian pirates hunted the Italian coasts kidnapping Romans and selling them as slaves. Cabiria, a peasant slave girl, is bought by the high priest of Moloch. She is saved by a Roman slave Maciste, while the victorious Romans destroy the Carthaginians. Pierre Sorlin argues that the film acted as an allegory for the Italian colonial expansion at the turn of the century; firstly the disastrous Ethiopia War; but then the successful war in 1911–12 on Turkey that resulted in Italy conquering part of modern-day Libya. It was a nationalist and imperialist manifesto. But *Cabiria* also contained numerous filmic innovations, for example, in plot, camera movement and close-ups (Brunetta 1995a: 56–8; Sorlin 1996: 37).

The most popular film genre in prewar Italy was melodramas that sought to establish an open space in which spectators could insert their own wishes and fantasies rather than narrate a coherent plot. Women, like Cabiria, were placed at the heart of these films. They were seen as defenceless. Other films saw women in more cunning and devious guise. Some films, like those emerging from Elva Notari's production facilities in Naples, were more backward-looking: women were supposed to be obedient wives, and there were terrible consequences if they broke the rules applying to their station. While Italian studios introduced many innovative features relating to *mise-en-scene*, they also welcomed foreign influences and hired many professionals from abroad. The first director slated for *Cabiria* was a Frenchman, and the film was eventually shot by a Spaniard (Sorlin 1996: 38–9).

Censorship made a very early appearance in Italian films. At the release of the earliest films, groups and individuals decried the supposed negative effects of film on wider society. It was not long before governments and the Catholic Church became involved. A National Film Board of Censors was established in 1913 to curtail bad influences and moral corruption. The Italian film industry was able to take advantage of those criticisms, since its movies – unlike other European films – rarely attacked established authorities, especially the Church. Censorship, as it is today, was viewed by some as a form of protectionism (Sorlin 1996: 45).

The Italian government quickly recognized the importance of film for propaganda in time of war. The Libya campaign in 1911–12 saw cameramen follow the war, resulting in the production of some 40 newsreels. At the outset of Italy's involvement in the Great War, a military film crew was set up on the front line. Much of the surviving footage never made the cinema screens, however, due to the realistic portrayal of the harsh conditions faced by Italian soldiers. With the general collapse of the Italian army in 1917, following the disastrous Battle of Caporetto, orders were issued in July that year banning plays that dealt with war themes and restricting war-related newsreels to 20 per cent of any news bulletin. The main Italian war-related film, *The Italian War on the Adamello*, was released in 1916 at about the same time as the first full-length war documentary, *The Battle of the Somme* (Sorlin 1996: 45–7).

Early Italian film production was based primarily in four cities: Milan, Naples, Rome and, most importantly, Turin which, as Gian Piero Brunetta states, became known as *Filmopoli*: 'Filmsville' or the city of films. Italian production companies were also able to make films and, importantly for them, profits by selling movies to the ever-growing Italian diaspora resident in the USA. Italian filmmaking was widely admired from an aesthetic point of view: average shots were longer than in US films; there was extensive use of medium shots and simple editing techniques, with greater reliance on professional actors, lighting and camera-work. It was not Turin which imitated Hollywood in 1914, rather vice versa, although American producers often criticized Italian plots as being rather fantastic and improbable (Brunetta 1995a: 34–8; Sorlin 1996: 21–7).

By 1914, Italy had the largest film industry in Europe and was the third largest exporter of films in the world, demonstrated the country's close affinity with film production and consumption. Italians were among the leading world experts in film lighting and shooting large outdoor or panoramic scenes. Although the number of Italian films produced increased after 1914, major problems began to surface, which would eventually lead to the decline and collapse of the film industry in the 1920s. Italian studios made large investments after 1910 in equipment and plant, which could not be repaid while fighting a war. These investments led to debts which became unsustainable in the postwar period. Banks then refused loans, cutting short-term capital. The first reaction of the major film companies to these problems was to expand film production, but this hid underlying problems. As early as 1913 the key American market began importing fewer prints of Italian films, and between 1912 and 1914 British imports of Italian films dropped by 50 per cent, and American imports by 80 per cent. Italy's disastrous involvement in the Great War would also hasten the eventual downturn in fortunes for the Italian film industry and the ensuing financial crises and bankruptcies. No Italian exports were going to the USA or UK by 1917, despite the fact that these countries were wartime allies. And American distributors began cornering the domestic Italian market too. So many Italian companies went bankrupt or merged. Matters would then deteriorate further under fascism from 1922 until 1932 (Forgacs 1990a: 53; Sorlin 1996: 44).

In summary, there were numerous overlapping reasons for the decline of film in Italy and these were related to: Italian economic decline; a disorganized and disaggregated industry; an increase in production costs; the decline in foreign markets for Italian films; the increasing dominance of the American film industry; a certain lack of ambition in Italy; renewed competition from other forms of entertainment such as the theatre; the loss of key personnel to foreign film industries; and an unfavourable tax regime in Italy (Brunetta 1995a: 132–6).

3 THE MEDIA IN FASCIST ITALY

- Italian newspapers and fascism
- The fall and rise of cinema in Fascist Italy
- The development of radio in Italy

The meteoric rise of an ex-socialist newspaper editor, Benito Mussolini, was built on the widespread discontent felt by many Italians in the postwar years and also on the ideological battles taking place throughout Europe after the 1917 Russian Revolution. The failure of the political system to solve Italy's chronic economic and social problems led to the rise of new parties on both extremes of the political spectrum. In the aftermath of 1917, socialism made inroads into the northern Italian industrial areas. But the formation of the Fascist Party had a wider support base among Italians. Mussolini was backed by a disparate coalition of groups including big business and petit bourgeoisie. The inability of liberals to form a new government led to the so-called 'March on Rome' of October 1922, which brought the Fascists on an overnight train from Milan to Rome. The king appointed Mussolini head of a coalition little changed from its predecessor. But what followed was the erosion of the parliamentary system of government in Italy.

While essential political rights were abolished under the Fascists after 1925, one feature of Mussolini's political policy was his promise to modernize and renovate Italy in the style of the Roman Empire. It was this sense of *sacro egoismo* that drove Fascist nationalism. Plans to expand along the North African coast were a direct appeal to the greatness of a Roman past and the promise of a great Italian future. Yet, beyond the nationalist rhetoric of modernization and expansion, what Mussolini understood by the term 'modernity' remains somewhat ambiguous. He was suspicious of committing the regime to the urbanization or industrialization of society. Under the Fascists the structure of industrial output never altered significantly. One reason for the hostility towards pushing industrial production at the expense of agricultural production was the threat of communism. Yet, at the same time, the industrial north and the business community were important constituents for the Fascists. So the government was not totally against industrial growth partly for fear of losing powerful supporters. However, all this meant that the government turned away from the economic liberalism of the early years and became more interventionist in the 1930s (the years of autarky). The interventionist policy preached by Fascists was overtly militaristic rather than social (Clark 1984: 263–8). There was little productive social legislation and in many ways Italy remained a backward country.

In one aspect of industrial policy, however, the Fascist government had a longer and more enduring legacy. The move from a liberal economic policy to an interventionist policy with the onset of the Great Depression from 1929 brought about a rise in state involvement. In order to aid private companies struggling in the years of the Depression, Mussolini instituted a number of plans whereby state industries would take over ailing commercial companies. The IRI (*Istituto per la Ricostruzione Industriale* – Industrial Reconstruction Institute) was formed in 1931 and was the major body handed the task of reforming Italian industry. To enjoy full flexibility in its commercial operation, the IRI was classified as a state-holding company, part of a wider para-state: such companies would be wholly owned by the state but would enjoy company status in order to operate in commercial activities. The advantages of such companies were that state help could be sought in times of crisis. This happened to the radio company EIAR (*Ente Italiano per le Audizioni Radiofoniche*) in 1933 and the film studios at Cinecittà in 1938.

Before examining the relationship with the media in detail, it is worth noting what David Forgacs highlighted as a significant contradiction in Fascist cultural policies throughout the 1920s and 1930s. While Mussolini wanted to construct a 'national culture' based on Fascist doctrine and values, most cultural consumption in Italy under fascism was of non-national products such as films, novels and comic books. People enjoyed and demanded these products and the cultural industries were happy to supply them, ensuring a rapid turnover of films, books, etc. This meant that not enough Italian cultural goods were produced. How should this be interpreted? Communists would later highlight these cultural patterns in the postwar period, linking fascism firmly with American consumerist ideology, an argument premised on mass society models of media. The failure of the state to construct a national culture based on Italian-made media overestimates the role of the state in cultural production and consumption, and underestimates the role of private companies (Forgacs 1990a: 72–82).

Italian newspapers and fascism

Newspaper owners, by and large, welcomed the rise of fascism. Many had seen profits hit by economic downturn following the Great War. Also, newspaper costs had risen and damaging strikes, blamed on communist agitators, affected the printing and distribution of newspapers. The Fascists promised that most elusive of all commodities: stability. It is not surprising that Italian newspapers took a broadly pro-Fascist stance in the early years of Mussolini's rule (1921–4). Some leading Fascists, including Mussolini, had been journalists themselves and understood the political importance of newspapers. They understood how they worked. The other main forms of media were much younger. Radio broadcasting in Italy only started in 1924 and cinema was in decline by 1922. The press was controlled more closely than either radio or cinema (Forgacs 1990a: 72–3).

Between 1922 and 1926, Italian newspapers underwent what has been termed as the process of 'fascistization'. This meant suppressing opposition newspapers, and changing editorial staff on others in order to gain their compliance. It also meant vetting stories and proactively seeking a change of ownership at some newspapers. Newspapers remained private, and there was no attempt to nationalize the press under direct Fascist rule. The late newspaper historian, Paolo Murialdi, describes this process of subjugation as applying to four distinct newspaper groups. Firstly, opposition newspapers were simply suppressed and were forced underground by the end of 1926. A key example here was Mussolini's old newspaper, *Avanti!*, which faced the wrath of Fascists unhappy in the postwar years with the *vittoria mutilata*. *Avanti!* was subject to frequent attacks by Fascists and its offices were burned down in 1919. When the Fascists came to power, they carried out a series of sequestrations of equipment. *Avanti!* had its resources drained by continual sequestrations, lower circulation figures and resulting redundancy payments. The Communist Party-funded *L'Unità* also suffered a similar fate (Forgacs 1990a: 40).

The second group of newspapers in Murialdi's classification never needed coercing as they were already loyal supporters of the Fascist Party: newspapers like the *Popolo d'Italia* in Milan, *Il Tevere* in Rome and various smaller provincial newspapers. The third group was those newspapers that became 'fascistized' without coercion and aligned themselves to fascism spontaneously, as Mussolini rose to power. The Bologna-based *Resto Del Carlino* is a classic example. Owned by a consortium of industrialists – sugar trusts, engineering companies and local agrarian interests – *Il Carlino* became an ardent supporter of fascism in 1922.

The fourth and final group of newspapers became Fascist supporters only after some persuasion. Luigi Albertini's, *Corriere della Sera*, for example, initially supported fascism, judging it as necessary to tackle the communist left. But the paper turned against the Fascist Party and strongly denounced the murder in 1924 of the socialist parliamentarian, Giacomo Matteotti. Internal shareholders at the paper sought to persuade Albertini to tone down criticisms and Fascist newspapers turned against the paper, organizing a boycott of its distribution. In 1925, the pro-Fascist Crespi family bought out Albertini and installed a new editor, Piero Croci. Despite these changes in political direction, sales held up at around 430,000 copies per day (Forgacs 1990a: 72–5). There is evidence that Mussolini sought to downplay overt Fascist support by the *Corriere della Sera*, as it was Italy's leading foreign-selling newspaper and he feared that the paper would be ridiculed abroad. In fact *Corriere* was a success story. Advertising grew for the paper and by the 1930s it was attracting international advertisers.

The case of *La Stampa* was similar. Its opposition to fascism led to shareholder attempts to sack editors Alfredo Frassati and Luigi Salvatorelli. At the end of 1925 the editors were indeed removed and the Frassati family was bought out by Fiat. In 1926, Giovanni Agnelli appointed the pro-Fascist Andrea Torre as editor (Forgacs 1990a: 74–6).

Catholic papers, under Vatican alignment, broadly followed Mussolini's line. One notable exception was the *Eco di Bergamo* where the intervention of the local Fascist leader led to the editor's removal. The process of fascistization was complete by end of 1926 and any remaining anti-Fascist press was forced underground. Fascist control also extended to news agencies and the syndication of news was awarded to Fascist-controlled Agenzia Stefani. The Fascists also introduced a system of circulars known as *Veline*, which instructed papers to cover stories from a particular angle or recommended what stories to avoid. Editors became poodles of Fascist authorities; journalists were required to hold a Party card and belong to the *Albo dei Giornalisti* professional association (Forgacs 1990a: 41, 74).

The fall and rise of cinema in Fascist Italy

Like their newspaper colleagues, many filmmakers and producers initially backed fascism because they thought it would halt the political unrest of the times and, more importantly, halt the decline of the film industry. But unlike his approach to newspapers, Mussolini was never keen to intervene as he did not see many obvious political advantages. One area where he did intervene was in nationalizing the *Istituto Luce* (Light Institute) in 1926. The Institute specialized in producing documentaries and its nationalization, arguably, was recognition of cinema's importance as an instrument of propaganda and education. The Institute was entrusted with making newsreels and documentaries, informing the public about the achievements of fascism. The Institute articulated and reinforced Fascist policy, making some 900 films and newsreels between 1927 and 1931 and 2,000 between 1931 and 1943 (Brunetta 1995a: 167, 180). However, Fascist propaganda remained somewhat spasmodic and ill-organized, unlike in Nazi Germany. Instead, fascism was advertised primarily through Mussolini's speeches (Sorlin 1996: 51).

Apart from the Luce Institute, other film activity remained in the commercial sector. Studios wanted greater state help but not nationalization, especially as their fortunes sharply declined after 1920. The number of Italian-made movies demonstrates this downturn. In 1920, 371 feature-length films were made; this declined to 114 in 1923; and to just 8 in 1930. Film production was on the verge of extinction by 1930, accounting for less than 10 per cent of domestic cinema income. This is despite the fact that film attendance in Italy rose continuously after the mid-1920s. Part of the reason for this rapid decline was the rise of other media, such as radio. But Italian producers were also slow to exploit the success of talking movies, which were introduced to Italy with the release of *The Jazz Singer* in April 1929. Only Cines installed recording equipment immediately, allowing the company to release the first four Italian-made talking movies in 1930. Italy remained dependent on buying foreign equipment and films (Sorlin 1996: 55).

The switch to talking movies resulted in the closure of some Italian cinemas (due to added costs associated with installing sound equipment and also to the general economic downturn). There were 3,000 cinemas in Italy in 1929. By 1933 there were 2,500, but all were capable of showing talking pictures. Italian film production, distribution and exhibition remained a cottage industry in the 1920s and 1930s. The top four American studios increasingly dominated all three film sectors and Italian distributors became increasingly tied to American supply deals. This dominance provoked outrage across Europe with governments protecting their cultural heritage by introducing 'quota systems'. Italy offered the least amount of resistance to American dominance and restrictions remained light. Italian studios were not in a strong enough position economically to oppose US distributors. The Americans, along with Italy's leading film distributor, Pittalunga, lobbied hard against any import restrictions of American films (Sorlin 1996: 55–6).

America's hold over all aspects of the Italian film industry grew tighter. The Catholic Church and Communist Party would later denounce this 'Americanization' of Italian life. But the truth was that Italians enjoyed many US productions due, in part, to the poor quality of Italian cultural products. Furthermore, the regime did not promote Italian culture adequately and, arguably, used film infrequently as a propaganda tool. Sorlin argues that three Fascist feature films stand out from the 1930s: Forzano's *Black Shirt*, Simonelli's, *Dawn over the Sea*, and Blasetti's *Old Guard*. Alessandro Blasetti was a key filmmaker who made other Fascist-pleasing films including *1860* about Garibaldi and the *Risorgimento* and also *La Cena delle Beffe* which shocked audiences as it contained a semi-nude scene of actress Clara Calamai which avoided the censor's eye (Brunetta 1995a: 194; Sorlin 1996: 62–4).

The revival in the Italian film industry's fortunes dates from 1930 when Mussolini received a delegation from the Italian film industry. Delegates included Pittalunga and Lombardo, who lobbied the Fascist government for more state intervention. The result was Law 918 (18 June 1931), which sought to help Italian producers against American competition. But the law was weak and ineffectual and until 1938, 73 per cent of box office receipts were for US films (Brunetta 1995a: 166–8). Other, non-legal, measures enjoyed a more positive impact. One example was the start of the Venice Festival in 1932 as a means of promoting the Italian film industry. The institution of 'Italian-only' categories at the Festival in 1935 also gave Italian films a morale boost. Gallone's *Scipio the African* won best film in 1935. Film production also revived thanks to the rise of Italian comedy films. Of the 132 talking movies made between 1930 and 1935, 60 per cent were comedies. The main comedy star in Italy at this time was Vittorio de Sica, who would later become one of Italy's leading film directors. One of de Sica's early films, *What Rascals Men Are!*, was made in 1932. In Italy, de Sica was compared only to Chaplin and Welles

(Sorlin 1996: 65). Other actors and actresses that made their names in the 1930s and would become key figures in postwar cinema, including neorealism, were Aldo Fabrizi, Macario, Anna Magnani and Totò.

Italian film production was given a further boost by the opening of the Experimental Centre for Filmmakers in 1935, followed closely in 1937 by the huge film production unit opened in Cinecittà on the outskirts of Rome. Ownership of Cinecittà transferred to the state in 1938 and 50 per cent of Italian films were soon being made there. The tradition of *Filmopoli* was being revived, but in Rome not Turin (Brunetta 1995a: 175–8, 182, 188–90; Sorlin 1996: 65–70). Films also became more popular in the 1930s due to an official change in government policy after the rather ineffectual 1931 law. Economics was an important factor. Importing films was a costly use of foreign currency. When Mussolini first considered a ban on imports to help foreign trade and exchange rates, exhibitors, led by Mussolini's son, Vittorio, claimed that there was insufficient domestic production to fill cinema schedules. But by 1938, the policy of self-sufficiency – autarky – was firmly set out and film imports were strictly controlled. Despite this ban, US films still found their way to Italy. This was due to contradictions in Fascist policy, which saw the government cut back support for Italian filmmakers at the same time as restricting American imports (Sorlin 1996: 70–1).

But while the Fascist government cut funds available to Italian film producers, it began funding a new cinema-building scheme. Between 1937 and 1940, 1,000 cinemas opened in Italy. The main reason for this policy, it seems, was the often strained relationship between Church and state. The Church's moral authority was very strong along the length of the Italian peninsula. Italian clergy, rather than lay associations attached to the Church, sought to establish moral authority over congregations by showing movies to instruct the young. In the 1920s priests set up film projectors in parish halls to show 'good' and 'wholesome' films. By 1934 the Church had set up the Catholic Church for Cinema organization and started its own magazine, *Cinematic Information*. The Church was able to act as a film censor, determining which films were shown. The state was also slow in reacting to the power of the Church. The 1924 Gentile Education Act sought to allow students to gain the necessary skills for jobs, and media education, via the Luce Institute, was included as part of this policy. The state altered this strategy and decided to build up the numbers of 'lay' cinemas to counter Catholic influence (Sorlin 1996: 71–2).

The Italian film industry, helped by Fascist autarky, enjoyed a new productive age, which saw a sharp rise in film production and cinema attendance. In 1936, 260 million cinema tickets were sold, rising to 470 million in 1942, 662 million in 1950 and 819 million in 1955. Italian film production increased after 1938, helped by the ban on US film imports. In 1935, 30 Italian films were made and this figure rose to 87 in 1940 and 98 in 1941. And as already outlined, not all films were required to be Fascist-inspired. What were supposed to be key features of Fascist doctrine could also be seen in US films: reverence for leaders; importance of family life; recourse to nationalist rhetoric. However, unlike many Hollywood films, not all Italian films took an optimistic or positive outlook in the 1930s. Films such as *Luciano Serra Pilota* and *Giarabub* showed Italian soldiers in times of crisis and defeat. Despite this, most Fascist cinema was escapist, with comedies leading the way, followed by melodramas and historical movies. The 1930s was a period of depression and many people viewed the cinema as a means of escapism. Workers and peasants were also able to enjoy movies due to a freeze on ticket prices. Cinema-going was relatively cheap for those prepared to accept less expensive seats. It cost 2 lira in 1939 for the cheapest cinema seats and ticket prices remained very low throughout the 1940s and 1950s (Sorlin 1996: 75–83).

The growth of film's importance in the 1930s was also due to the regime's attempts to strengthen the state and future employees through education. University film societies developed from 1933. *Bianco and Nero* and *Cinema* magazines were launched in 1936. Cinema also became more of an academic or intellectual activity and an important centre of social life. All social classes were brought together when attending the cinema, in what remained a heavily segregated society (Sorlin 1996: 75). By 1942, Italy was the fifth largest country in the world for film production. Italians were fascinated by film and, postwar, the country would embark on one of its most productive periods, heralding the neorealism movement.

The development of radio in Italy

Radio broadcasting was developed in the early years of the twentieth century following Guglielmo Marconi's initial outdoor experiments in 1895 and his first transatlantic broadcast in 1901. While the medium was developed for military purposes during the First World War, various European governments began issuing radio licences for civilian purposes by the early 1920s. In the UK, for example, a consortium of radio operators formed the British Broadcasting Company in November 1922 and a month later recruited its first Director General, John Reith, later to become Lord Reith of Stonehaven. The BBC was charged with making radio programmes primarily in order to promote the sale of radio sets for consortium members. It was Reith himself who argued that radio programmes could be used as a new progressive force in society and, in the words of the broadcast historian, Paddy Scannell (1989: 140): 'the fundamentally democratic thrust of broadcasting lay in the new kind of access to virtually the whole spectrum of public life ... made available to all'. On the advice of two government-appointed committees, the BBC was nationalized on 1 January 1927, becoming the British Broadcasting Corporation (BBC).

Before examining the development of radio in Italy, it is worth briefly looking at Reith's ideas as these would have a direct impact on Italy in the postwar period. There were three basic ideas that shaped and informed

Reith's management of the BBC (Scannell and Cardiff 1982: 163). The first was the belief that a public service broadcaster should be a wholly public-owned entity but politically independent from the state. Reith stated his opposition to direct state control in an uncompromising manner: 'The BBC should be a public service not only in performance but in constitution – but certainly not as a department of state' (Reith 1949: 102; Briggs 1961: 235–6). In declaring his forthright opposition to state intervention, Reith was restating the basic premise of liberal thinking: the essential mistrust of state power and the classic liberal doctrine of the (press) media as the Fourth Estate carrying out its 'watchdog function' (Curran 1991: 29; Hibberd 2006).

Reith's second idea was that broadcasting should be independent of any direct commercial pressures. As general manager of the privately-owned British Broadcasting Company, Reith took the extraordinary step of privately advising the government-appointed Crawford Committee that broadcasting should be placed under the aegis of a public-owned company: 'the trade directors of the BBC knew my views; they had seen the rationality of the argument; had given me leave to speak my mind' (Reith 1949: 101). Reith had the advantage of looking at the problems facing the American system, which was wholly commercial. But he was not anti-commercial; his record of leading both public and private companies during his long career bears this out. Instead, Reith grasped the wider cultural and political importance of broadcasting; it was this, his third idea of exploring the wider pedagogic potential of the broadcast media, that appealed to him:

> ... broadcasting was a potential influence, national and interna-
> tional, of the highest import. It would have been a prostitution of its
> worth had the services been used solely for entertainment in the
> narrow sense. The informative and educational possibilities must be
> recognised and developed.
>
> *(1949: 99–100)*

But in espousing such strong views, Reith exposed himself to a potential backlash among government authorities, colleagues and other interest groups. In actively lobbying for a publicly-funded broadcasting corporation that was democratically accountable, but which remained independent of state and big business, Reith was effectively seeking a third way between state and private management of important utilities. In outlining this philosophy of political and market independence, Reith demonstrated a remarkable foresight in envisaging new forms of experimental ownership that was an 'outstanding example of the potentiality of a combination of private enterprise and of public control' (Briggs 1961: 237). The position adopted by Reith was therefore closer to the concept of the (Habermasian) public sphere than to classic liberal doctrines (see Introduction (Hibberd 2006)).

Radio broadcasting started in Italy in 1924 and, like the BBC, was developed by a consortium of radio manufacturers given an exclusive government concession: the *Unione Radiofonica Italiana* (URI). The similarities did not stop there. Revenues, like the BBC, were generated by a licence fee and a levy payable on the sale of radio sets. But the URI was also funded by advertising revenues and set up its own advertising arm in 1926, SIPRA – *Società Italiana Pubblicità Radioifonica Anonima* – which today remains one of Italy's largest and most important advertising companies. And like the BBC, the URI underwent a name change in 1928 when the state became more active in radio broadcasting. The new company, EIAR, was still heavily dominated by commercial interests but the government now had four seats on its governing board.

The Italian government showed less interest in the early years of radio broadcasting in intervening in programme-related issues with the result that the majority of programming in the early years was non-controversial, entertainment and music-led (of many types including classical, popular, military bands, etc.) followed by news and children programmes. Although Mussolini's speeches were broadcast by the radio company, fascism seldom made full use of radio as a means of propaganda. The lack of state intervention did have negative effects. Radio broadcasting was slow to develop in Italy primarily because there were little available monies to invest in the transmission infrastructure. This only changed after 1929 when the Turin-based electrical company, SIP – *Società Idroelettrica Piemonte* – bought a controlling share in EIAR, seeing greater economic potential in expanding the radio network and exploring synergies in the radio, telephone and electrical industries. Many of EIAR's operations moved to Turin.

Limited demand for radio services meant that sets remained expensive: new radio sets costs 3,000 lira in 1931. This compared to a new car which cost 10,000 lira. The new radio service in Italy did not constitute a universal service available to all. It was limited predominantly to the middle classes in urban areas. In addition, radio in Italy suffered severe reception problems – something that has never fully been solved – and technicians often lacked expert training. Programme standards were also compromised by the fact that actors often adapted badly to radio production conventions. Things did improve somewhat in the 1930s (Forgacs 1990a: 54–5); with the completion of new transmission sites early in that decade, more towns and cities became connected to the radio network. Attempts were also made to break foreign domination of the radio set market and introduce cheaper, domestic versions. By the mid-1930s, portable radio sets were available for less than 1,000 lire, the most popular being the Radioballila (Sorice 2002). This made radio more affordable for families. The state also helped the company in two ways. In response to the economic depression of the early 1930s, the Italian state-holding company IRI bought out SIP, which was suffering economic problems. The state also eased financial pressures on EIAR by reducing the amount the company paid for its radio licences, and introduced other protectionist measures to help radio broadcasting. Although EIAR's radio monopoly would be safeguarded, limited competition began in 1931 in the form of Radio Vaticano, which helped pioneer radio production techniques and content in the 1930s.

But with these positive moves came negative signals. Radio in Italy became more and more controlled by political elites. Like newspapers, radio gradually became fascistized. Firstly, members of EIAR's Administrative Council were appointed by IRI, which in turn was closely politically controlled. Secondly, radio programmes, primarily news services, became more directly politicized. Fascist organizations were given privileged access to the airwaves and radio was more actively promoted to schools and the rural masses. The increase in political control of EIAR led to increasing tensions with advertisers. A number of Fascists criticized the low standards of programmes, blaming advertising for lowering cultural standards. From July 1937 onwards, EIAR was ordered by the Ministry for Popular Culture to stop spot advertising, although programme sponsorship did continue.

The colonial war in Africa (1936), only Italy's second post-*Risorgimento* military success, and the defeat of the communist threat won Mussolini many admirers in Italy and abroad. But the political repression of opposition parties, the denial of basic civic and political rights, and the delay in implementing many vital economic and social policies, all ensured that large parts of Italian society would never become reconciled to the Fascist state. Under such circumstances, it was not surprising that Italy imploded into bitter internal fighting after the downfall of the Fascist regime in 1943. The subsequent invasion of a foreign army in the North (Germany) and South (the Armistice with the Allies) brought Italy back to the dark period of the Middle Ages – a country under foreign occupation with compatriots conducting a bitter civil war, split by irreconcilable differences: a bleak situation which Dante Alighieri would certainly have recognized.

4 THE FIRST ITALIAN REPUBLIC: CINEMA AND THE PRESS IN THE POSTWAR YEARS

- The 1948 Italian constitution and media regulation
- Political ideology and the struggle between Catholicism and communism
- The Communists: inheritors of the Gramscian spirit?
- Neorealism and the development of film in postwar Italy
- Rebuilding a free press in postwar Italy

Much of Italy lay in ruins at the end of the Second World War. The concept of nationhood entailed explicit overtones associated with the regime of the 1930s. The situation was further exacerbated by the sheer gravity of the war crimes committed during the war. Yet, there was also a strong desire to avoid a repetition of the mistakes made after the First World War. Any solutions would, however, require a clean break from the nationalist principles which had guided European political thought since the late nineteenth century. That is, postwar peace would only be maintained with the refusal to allow nationalist sentiments and suspicions to reemerge, since such feelings had been held responsible for the problems that had engulfed Europe, and were now viewed as wholly unacceptable.

Yet, at the same time, the reconstruction of Italy (along with the rest of Europe) would require the presence of strong social cohesion and a sense of collective identity. Ties of allegiance extending beyond familial bonds to wider cultural symbols were required for political and social bridge-building. The destruction wrought on France, Italy and Germany did not entail the dissolution of the nation as a political, economic and social reference point. Instead, their revival was deemed essential to the Allies in order to combat the newly-declared enemy, communism. Identity and allegiance in Rome, Paris and Bonn therefore became synonymous with differentiating against the communist enemy in the era of the Cold War. The question, therefore, was how to reconcile the need for the nation-state as the primary focus for collective identity with the danger of arousing the kind of jingoistic noises associated with nationalism that had done so much damage to Europe. The subsequent policies adopted included a mixture of the following three elements: reconciliation that required and promoted selected amnesia with regards to past events; promotion of 'founding myths' for hope and renewal; and enactment of state-led policy measures to encourage greater political, social and economic equity (Judt 1994: 1–4).[1]

In Italy, however, the situation was made even more difficult because the task of renewal was hampered by traditional problems, notably the struggle to reunite the diversity of groups and communities with the country's political institutions. The Italian people had suffered years of occupation, hunger and disease and there was much anger directed at state institutions for their collaboration with the Fascist Party. In 1946, for example, the monarchy was ousted in a popular referendum that brought in Italy's First Republic. So the problems facing the new postwar government required urgent attention if serious social unrest was to be avoided. The immediate postwar years saw the anti-Fascist alliance tending to the more urgent needs of the country while convening a Constituent Assembly to construct a new constitution. The restoration and reconstitution of basic political and civic rights denied by the previous regime constituted an improvement in itself. The provision of basic social and economic norms and responsibilities also represented a qualitative improvement in the formal rights of Italian citizens.

Once the work of the Constituent Assembly had been completed, few doubted that old battles would reemerge. When the Christian Democrats, aided by the Church and the Americans, gained victory in the 1948 elections, they were able to undermine the power of the many state and para-state institutions and turn them into fiefdoms of political patronage (Spotts and Wieser 1986: 2–4). The Christian Democrats were helped in this task because many elements of the pre-Republic state machinery still remained and because a majority of civil servants supported the party. There were a number of historic reasons why the civil service supported the Christian Democrats *en masse* in the postwar period. To start with, many civil servants originated from the South of Italy, one of the heartlands of Christian Democrat support. This was a legacy of the Giolitti government which used the civil service as a means of stimulating job prospects for the otherwise impoverished South. It was a system continued by the Fascists to gain political support. They were further helped because the average pay of the civil servant remained poor, dissuading northerners from entering into the profession. The rates of pay in the northern industrial zones were a lot higher in comparison to the civil service.

Furthermore, the policy of *epurazione* — the purging of the old Fascist state apparatus – in the postwar years had failed because Fascist membership had been obligatory for all civil servants in the prewar period and to sack the whole civil service was seen as being impractical (Ginsborg 1990: 92). At the same time, however, many argued that the consequences of such purges would be further civil conflict. The decision was therefore taken to curtail this policy. The role of the state institutions in Fascist crimes became buried in order to promote the new Italian order (Judt 1994: 2). Talk about the policy of purging the old system, however, gave rise to the first myth of the new Republic: 'In republican Italy ... administrators, policemen, and others who had served the old regime and its foreign paymasters were often left in place, the reality of the continuity they represented overlain by a myth of renewal and revolution' (Judt 1994: 3).

Many civil servants were therefore content to transfer allegiance from the Fascists to the Christian Democrats in the postwar period. This period also saw the continued development of government special agencies controlling many of the major social and economic institutions (railways, etc.), each constituting a separate and autonomous bureaucracy, which resulted in separate enclaves of influence and power within the state (Ginsborg 1990: 147). An example of a parallel bureaucracy was the radio corporation, EIAR. Here, too, the old management had not been purged (Cavazza 1979: 84–5). At the end of the war, the management hierarchy of the renamed RAI (*Radio Audizioni Italia*) broadly supported the Christian Democrats. This is, in part, why the Christian Democrats were able to use RAI so effectively in the 1948 election.

Despite these obvious parallels with its predecessors, the Italian state enjoyed considerable success in the postwar period. Successive governments undertook substantive industrial and agricultural reforms, which resulted in Italy becoming an industrialized country. Often, it was state industries that took the economic initiatives that led to increasing growth, and it was state intervention in the South that secured more jobs and investment for the people of those lands. Finally, the Italian government was at the forefront of negotiations between European partners which culminated in the formation of the EEC in 1957. Economic expansion had immediate and positive spin-offs for social provision. The increase in educational provision, cultural provision, health spending, social housing, etc. ensured that there would be major improvement in the living standards and the quality of life in Italy.

Although private enterprise was strongly encouraged in postwar Italy, the Cold War helped to shape the country's strategic importance to the West. After 1947, Italy received US state aid via the Truman Doctrine and the Marshall Plan – which were intended to turn countries like France and Italy, both with large Communist Parties, away from the Soviet Union and encourage them to embrace liberal democracies. The cultural industries played an important part in this return to order after the war as well as having an important role in creating the moral and political climate in the boom years. With some notable exceptions, newspapers, radio and cinema supported the Christian Democrats after the war. The media was not used as mere instruments of the USA, as portrayed by the left in Italy. Catholic social thought did help shape media policy, but Christian Democrat-led governments were also forward-looking, especially in relation to the modernization of key media after the 1950s, most notably in broadcasting which saw the development of a mass television audience as well as new magazine and mass youth consumer cultures (Forgacs 1990a: 104–6).

Italian society therefore enjoyed many of the benefits accrued in the postwar years. But social unrest remained. In part, such unrest was caused through government failures to deliver long-held promises (across a range of social issues). In the new Republic, groups within society could unite to demand that civil rights be respected and that social provisions be implemented. Even the Communists remained key political operators at a local level and played a positive role in ensuring that governments stuck to the letter of the constitution. However, an upsurge in terrorism in the 1970s, Mafia crimes in the 1990s and political involvement in numerous financial and corruption scandals in the 1980s and 1990s undermined the integrity of the political classes. The downturn in the economic cycle also highlighted the woeful inefficiencies of state administration. Finally, the fall of communism undermined Cold War allegiances in Italy. Italian society then turned on the Italian state and major political parties, with major consequences for all.

The 1948 Italian constitution and media regulation

The decisive break within the postwar anti-Fascist alliance came in March 1947. Alcide De Gasperi, the Christian Democrat prime minister, under intense pressure from both internal and external forces, ditched the Communists and the Socialists from government. Internally, the Catholic hierarchy had warned De Gasperi that the Church could no longer countenance sharing power with the 'atheist' enemy. Externally, the American government, especially after De Gasperi's trip to Washington in early 1947 and the subsequent publication of the Truman Doctrine in March that year, had made plain its belief that De Gasperi should adopt a strict anti-Communist policy. Another factor in the timing of De Gasperi's decision to exclude the left-wing from power in May 1947 was that by that time the work of Constituent Assembly, which had been elected in 1946 to draw up a new constitution, had nearly been completed. De Gasperi could therefore dismiss the opposition without jeopardizing this historical constitutional agreement.

The new Italian constitution took effect in 1948. By highlighting its core elements an overall picture can be drawn of its primary political and social principles. Article 2 contains a declaration of human rights, whether as an individual or association. Article 3 is a declaration of equality for all, 'that all citizens have equal social dignity and are equal before the law, without distinction of sex, of race, of religion, of political opinion, of personal and social condition'. This is a classic liberal statement. The next paragraph of Article 3 goes beyond this towards a more socialist standpoint: 'It is the task of the Republic to remove obstacles of an economic and social nature which, limiting in fact the liberty and equality of citizens prevent the full development of the human personality and the effective participation by all workers in the political, economic and social organization of the country'. Democratic rights were enshrined by the election of a parliament based on proportional represen-tation (PR), the election of Regional Assemblies (not fully enacted until 1970), and provisions granting the use of direct referenda. The Lateran Pacts of 1929, whereby the Catholic Church formally recognized Italy's right of self-determination in return for the recognition of Catholicism as the official state religion, were included in the constitution. The 1948 constitution therefore symbolized a compromise between liberalism, socialism and Catholicism (Sassoon 1986b: 195).

Arguably, constitutional provisions for the mass media were contained in Articles 21, 33, 41 and 43 of the constitution. Article 21 states that 'Everyone shall have the right to express freely his own thoughts in words, writing or any other medium'. Article 33 states that 'Art and science shall be free and their teaching likewise'. Article 41 states that 'Private enterprise shall be permitted in so far as it does nor run counter to the social utility nor constitute a danger to freedom or human dignity ... The law shall determine appropriate programmes and controls to enable public and private economic activities to be run and coordinated for social ends'. Finally, Article 43 states that for purposes of general utility, 'The law may reserve to the state, to the public institutions, or to worker or consumer associations, *ab initio*, or transfer to them by expropriation, subject to identification, certain undertakings or category of undertakings involving essential public services ... important to the community' (Esposito and Grassi 1975a: 44–5). Like other parts of the constitution, these articles have been heavily scrutinized and the subject of a long academic debate and different interpretations. Their importance will become apparent as this book progresses.

In addition to the constitutional provisions for the media, specific legislation for the new RAI had been set out in a government decree, No. 428, of April 1947. The aim of the decree was to ensure the proper democratic management of broadcasting, however, its effect was anything but the democratization desired. Responsibility for overseeing RAI was given to two watchdog authorities: a consultative committee overseeing cultural, artistic and educational policies, and a parliamentary committee, set up to oversee the political independence of broadcasting and the objectivity of news coverage. The parliamentary committee, which was made up of 30 members chosen equally by the two presidents of the two Houses of Parliament, passed on decisions and recommendations to the president of the Council of Ministers (the prime minister) to implement. This made the role of the president of the Council of Ministers, who until 1953 was De Gasperi, crucial in two respects: first, he acted as a filter for all the Commission's decisions; and second, he acted as a buffer between the Commission and RAI (Cavazza 1979: 87). In reality, the decree gave extensive powers to the executive. Measures relating to the Italian press were also contained in Law 47 of February 1948. This law outlined the requirements for formal registration of newspapers and confirmed the editor's legal responsibility relating to content. The law also barred foreign ownership of newspapers and editors, too, were required to be Italian citizens. Other provisions contained in the law related to defamation and publications aimed at children and young adults (Murialdi 2000: 204). It should be noted however that these new provisions did not fully replace Fascist press laws, and journalists continued to be persecuted in the 1940s and 1950s under the fascist Rocco Code (Murialdi 2000: 218).

Political ideology and the struggle between Catholicism and communism

Postwar Italy witnessed a struggle by Catholics and Communists for Italian hearts and minds. The main terrain for the battle was the political sphere: within Parliament and institutions of civil society such as trade unions, employers' federations, etc. But the battle between Catholicism and communism also extended into the cultural, economic, social and religious spheres. And, as already outlined, the battle was also international in that each political party could count on the support of either the USA or the Soviet Union in the era of the Cold War. The Soviet bloc was supportive of the Italian Communists, although relations with the Italian Communist Party became increasingly strained after 1958. The Americans and West European allies backed the Christian Democrats and their allies. The nature of support on both sides was financial, moral and political. And yet, despite the importance of Catholicism and communism in postwar Italy, both political ideologies would gradually lose ground to a third political ideology – consumer capitalism – especially after the 1950s and, in doing so, find common cause.

The hugely influential figure of Alcide De Gaspari dominated the Christian Democrats in the immediate postwar period and was a great unitary figure for the Party. Put simply, he was a political colossus. His resignation in 1953, due to illness which was to prove terminal (he died a year later), coupled with stinging local election losses suffered by the Party in same year, led to major internal problems for the Christian Democrats after 1953. De Gasperi had wanted to construct a modern and dynamic liberal-democratic Party and curb its over-reliance on Catholic associations. He was unable, therefore, to prevent the gradual fragmentation of the Party into *correnti*, or factions. The arguments as to what direction the Party should take came to a head at the Naples Congress in 1954.

The two main groups to emerge from this conference were the right-wing Nationalists led by Mario Scelba and Giuseppe Pella, who supported a strictly Catholic stance, and the moderate Progressives led by Amintore Fanfani, who favoured pursuing a more modern and dynamic agenda. Tensions could be identified on at least three levels: first, at an ideological level, the traditional social theory of the Catholic hierarchy lay uneasily alongside an ever-increasing stance of some factions of the Christian Democrats towards liberal consumerism; second, the interclassist make-up of the Christian Democrats ensured that there were always battles over resources and the direction of state action; third, the death of De Gasperi led to greater fragmentation. This did not mean that the Christian Democrats could not act in concert. The Party was undoubtedly united by a common loathing of the Communists. Also, a majority of the party was in favour of modernization and economic growth. But it did mean that during their 45-year period in government, the Christian Democrats faced internal battles as intense as any external threats. As Paul Ginsborg points out, 'permanence in power did not necessarily equate with unity of purpose' (1990: 54).

It was Amintore Fanfani who emerged from the Naples Congress strengthened. His ideas were to encourage political activism in all social areas, including communication, with the need to educate and meet the aspirations of the people in creating a liberal-democratic Italy. Such activism was promoted with the specific aim of creating a modern Catholic culture (Ginsborg 1990: 167). The long-term effect of Fanfani's policy was to undermine a united Christian Democrat strategy on media issues. From the mid-1950s onwards, there was a small but discernible shift in political thinking which had a major impact on the management of media issues in Italy. This will be discussed in the next chapter in relation to broadcasting.

At this time, the Catholic hierarchy maintained a multi-pronged strategy in its media relations. Yes, it could assert influence in Italian society by virtue of the strong position of the Christian Democrat Party. But like the Christian Democrats, the Church also wanted to create outlets for Catholic opinions in civil society by occupying key positions in the mass media and beyond. For example, in 1948, the papacy set up a Papal Commission to monitor cinema output in Italy. This Commission was often highly critical of the corrupting influence of Hollywood films as well as Italian neorealist cinema. In 1954 the Commission was extended to cover television and radio, having an advisory role and monitoring media output (Monteleone 1980: 215).

In fact, the Church hierarchy was very hostile towards the many sectors of the media. For many in the Church, the mass media were the principal promoters and supporters of consumer capitalism, which was deemed as being inherently atheist and perturbed many clerics (Ginsborg 1990: 241). In this respect, clerics shared the concerns of Communists and key theorists like C. Wright Mills and Theodor Adorno and his Frankfurt colleagues. One example was the perceived corrupting influence of television advertising upon Italian society. Initially, television services were funded by a licence fee. It was soon realized however that the fee was insufficient as the only source of income. The government was reluctant to pump extra funds into a service which could gain a significant income from advertising. But there was stiff resistance to the plan from the Church, which feared the consequences of the American system. Yet, the introduction of limited advertising demonstrated that the Church did not have all its own way in shaping broadcasting policy, and its aims and objectives became increasingly frustrated from the 1960s onwards.

It was the broader economic and social transformation of Italy that most undermined Church authority. In 1958 Pope Pius XII died. He was succeeded by Archbishop Angelo Roncalli, Pope John XXIII. A man of conservative habits in many respects, he was already an old man in 1958, and his papacy was only to last until 1963. His opinions on film and television highlighted his traditional outlook. For example, he disliked television and condemned it for being too feminist! He also sought to tightly control the viewing habits of the clergy (Ginsborg 1990: 259–61). The Papal Commission was turned into a permanent office under his orders. But John XXIII was also a visionary in many respects. He understood, for example, that the tremendous social and economic changes taking place in Italy and elsewhere in the world would eventually necessitate a change of direction on behalf of the Church. The 'economic miracle' was leading to mass migrations and undermining the traditional rural Catholic authority. What John XXIII was hinting at was an accommodation with modern capitalist democracies, thereby declaring an end to almost 200 years of open hostility towards modernity.

As Percy Allum points out, this signalled a return to a plurality of traditions which characterized the Church before the French Revolution. As a result of the latter, the Church was forced to retreat and defend its position, developing 'a new conservatism tied to the magisterium of the Roman hierarchy which translated into forms of apologetic literature against all the new ideologies' (Allum 1990: 79). A second Vatican Council (the first Vatican Council having taken place in 1870) was convened from 1962 to 1965 to debate the future direction of the Catholic Church. The outcome of the Council was a period of turmoil for the Church and the fracturing of ideological and cultural values. This fracturing weakened the ability of the Church to show a united front. More progressive elements of the Church hierarchy welcomed the acceptance of a more tolerant attitude in relation to other creeds and beliefs (including centre-left coalitions), but the traditionalists remained hostile to these trends. Therefore, the effect of the changes on the maintenance of a Catholic hegemony over media policy was not immediate. But the damage caused by the bold step of John XXIII towards greater pluralism in Church relations meant that the boundaries of what was acceptable became ever more blurred.

The Communists: inheritors of the Gramscian spirit?

Despite the internal strife within the Christian Democrats, and the Catholic hierarchy's worries (such as the concerns about conspicuous consumption), it is evident that there was a united approach on one level: a vehement anti-communism. In fact, the Communists, the pariah in so much of the Cold War propaganda, were also defenders of the constitution. For example, in Parliament the Communist Party defended the country against the excesses of the Christian Democrats. When the Christian Democrats attempted in 1953 to change the electoral system –

known as the Swindle Law – they were repelled by the opposition parties, led by the Communists. The Communist Party took part in much of the political horse trading, making agreements on legislation and defending its own interests. It was, however, excluded from influence over state-run media because the Catholics, the Americans and the Christian Democrats vetoed any communist involvement.

At the same time, and unlike their Catholic counterparts, the Communists were slow in acknowledging the potential of audio-visual media and remained somewhat hostile to film and television. This hostility stemmed from seeing film and television as essentially capitalist media, which manipulated audiences and shaped them into capitalist consumers.[2] Therefore, many Communists shared the same suspicions as the Catholics. The Communists' policy was somewhat paradoxical in comparison to the their overall strategy which relied heavily on Gramsci's argument that a proletarian hegemony in civil society was likely to be a necessary precondition for a communist revolution in Western capitalist countries (Lumley 1990: 11–12). This strategy was developed after Gramsci's death by academics who sought to promote a popular culture based on class traditions.

The Communists concentrated on print cultures, which although they helped to sustain working-class solidarity, arguably had less influence on wider society. It was an overtly paternalistic policy to teach the masses 'high culture'. Palmiro Togliatti, the wartime and postwar Communist leader, was a cultural conservative who had little time for electronic media (Gundle 1990: 195). So although the communists had other spheres of influence in civil society, they never showed a major interest in film or state television. It was only when their traditional spheres of influence began to decline in the 1960s that the Communists took stock of the situation and formulated a more positive stance. This decline caused a sharp decrease in the membership of the party itself, which had, incidentally, peaked at 2.2 million in 1954, the year television broadcasting began in Italy (Ginsborg 1990: 195).

Neorealism and the development of film in postwar Italy

The Fascist legacy was felt in some areas of media development, most notably in influencing postwar cinema development in Italy, due in part to Mussolini's belated reorganization of the production and exhibition sectors which took place in the late 1930s. The new coalition government under Alcide De Gasperi could not ignore the influence of cinema over Italians nor its economic pull. The tax imposed on box office receipts was the largest sum the government received from any media or leisure industry. The Italian film industry had by 1945 become protected and unaccustomed to fighting for its market share of box office receipts with Hollywood. So while the end of the war would present new opportunities for Italian cinema, it also brought real and renewed dangers.

These dangers quickly appeared. The government was immediately put under pressure by the USA to re-access a market they had lost eight years previously. In October 1945 the Italian government abolished the prohibitive *ad valorem* tax imposed on American films, which resulted in 300 US films per year being released in Italy until 1954. But Italian producers soon launched a fight back. Soon after the end of hostilities they had formed ANICA – the Association for Cinema and Similar Industries – to negotiate with Italian and American authorities on film-related matters. Their first major success came in October 1945 when the government awarded a subsidy to Italian producers, because of Italy's chronic shortage of foreign exchange, especially US dollars, which resulted in the push to earn export dollars and reduce US imports into the economy. In 1949 a new tax on sound dubbing brought further state funds into domestic film production and made foreign-language films more expensive. Bank loans became easier to obtain for producers and co-production deals with other countries helped. By 1954, fewer than 300 American films were being imported into Italy and domestically-produced films increased their box office take to 39 per cent compared with 53 per cent for US films. Yet Italian film production remained piecemeal with film projects hastily set up to take advantage of Italian subsidies, not a dissimilar picture to other European countries, then and now (Sorlin 1996: 83–5).

Other parts of the film industry fared better. The Christian Democrats kept the Luce Institute running, especially for documentary filmmaking. These films still stressed the societal improvements in town and country through the development of new technologies. The Luce Institute lost its monopoly in other areas, however, including the production of newsreels, which was opened up to competition. Newsreels remained compulsory for cinemas, although an element of competition was introduced so that they were now supplied by different companies in line with international practice in other countries (Sorlin 1996: 85–8). The Communists tried to counter the impact of these films by making their own documentaries, emphasizing the failings of the Christian Democrat-led state. Documentary filmmaking became one front in the Catholic versus Communist battle in the immediate postwar period. And politicians, especially Catholic ones, were quick to criticize film, highlighting, arguably, the medium's unrivalled importance in the early postwar period. Alcide De Gasperi and his under-secretary, Giulio Andreotti, both made speeches about the potential harmful effects of cinema – something that could unite Catholic and communist doctrine. As a result, the Christian Democrats introduced more stringent censorship laws in 1947. The government further strengthened its hold over cinema in 1949 by introducing legislation that ensured extra state help to films of 'artistic' quality. Needless to say, films were judged by a Democrat-led board.

Until 1945, the cinema was primarily a middle-class pastime. Cinemas were situated in mainly urban areas, and only after World War Two (when the Church set up 5,000 parish cinemas, often in rural areas) did it become a truly national means of recreation, asserting finally its independence from music hall and theatre cultures. The postwar cinematic period in Italy is best known for the film movement that would become recognized globally as Italian neorealist cinema. The term 'neorealist' originates from the early twentieth century as a philosophical term denoting objective facts independent of human thoughts. The term was then adopted on a literary basis in the 1920s and 1930s. Its association with Italian film came only after it had been adopted by critics following the cinematic release of Roberto Rossellini's *Rome Open City*. In the 1940s Italian critics tended not to use the term too often and *neo-verismo* was the associated term used.

There are a number of different definitions of neorealism and while there is some consensus over the broad span of films which might be defined as 'neorealist', precise agreement over what individual films should or should not be included in any retrospective analysis of postwar Italian cinema has remained elusive (Landy 2000: 13). Neorealist films were critically acclaimed at home and abroad and some were also financial successes (Sorlin 1996: 91–3). What neorealism never constituted was a party political movement allied to the Communist Party and working to a pre-scripted set of aims or ideas. Its directors – De Santis, De Sica, Germi, Rossellini, Visconti – did not share the same political outlook and came from very different socioeconomic backgrounds. Some were more left-leaning than others, for example, Visconti. Neither did the films have political backing from any one party. Neorealist films were praised by many although they were also criticized by some prominent Christian Democrat politicians because they deemed them too left wing and anti-church. It should not be forgotten that a substantial body of women's fiction was written during the neorealist period (Hallamore Caesar 1996). This could be seen to indicate that the 1940s and 1950s represented a more 'progessive' period for women in some aspects compared with, say, the 1980s and the rise of trash television, striptease and semi-nude models, which many regard as degrading. What is surprising, however, is that the Communists shared concerns that some neorealist films contained too much sex! Although the Communists supported Visconti's *Terra Trema*, they remained very conservative if not hostile in their film tastes.

How might we best characterize neorealism? Firstly, it denoted an aesthetic movement which, although linked to the ideas and policies of the resistance-supporting parties of government from 1943 to 1947, took inspiration from long-held debates and ideas in Italian cinema. Neorealism, to Christopher Wagstaff (1996: 226):

> grew up in a disorganized way, responding to the calls made by many intellectuals before the war for a cinema that would truly be Italian, that would shun escapism, that would exploit cinematography's capacity for representing man in his real environment and that would make known to all Italians the conditions of life experienced by all people in all parts of the nation.

There is little doubt that neorealism constitutes a key example of what we today call *national cinema*. That is, these are films quintessentially

identified with one nation which is clearly identified in narrative strategies. Neorealist films draw extensively on various aspects of Italian
history, geography, culture, language and identity, and provide representations of class, gender, race and sexuality, offering insight into, as Marcia
Landy argues, 'how the "nation" and its "people" are often conflated to
suppress difference and foster the illusion of unity and unanimity' (2000:
20). Whether their insights are illusory or not, neorealist films in many
ways carried the torch for the *Risorgimento* and for the whole Italian
project and, in that sense, were deeply political. In that sense, postwar
Italian cinema, much like television in the 1950s and 1960s and the
postwar education system, constitutes a good example of Italy making
Italians, to paraphrase Massimo D'Azeglio.

Secondly, neorealism constituted a cinematographic movement identified inseparably with certain filmmakers as writers and/or directors. In
Marcia Landy's words, once again (2000: 15):

> Neorealism was a cinema of auteurs, particularly identified with
> works of Vittorio De Sica, Roberto Rossellini, Giuseppe De Santis,
> and Piero Germi, among others. Like the French Wave in their films,
> as well as their writing on film, the 'neorealists' revealed their own
> conception of *le caméra stylo*, a personal, poetic, and therefore
> engaged the sense of the director as 'author' of the filmic text.

A third key characteristic of neorealism, to my mind, is the subversion
of key moral ideas time and time again in successive films (Landy 2000:
15; Sorlin 1996: 105). Notions of good and bad, truth and lies, heroism
and cowardice are rendered more complex and subtle: the 'good' don't
always win and the 'bad' can be rewarded for their misdeeds. The best
neorealist films also combined the sense of loss and despair in the world
with more positive attributes of hope and reconciliation, even if such
references are cursory or fleeting – such as Bruno taking his father's hand
in the final scene of De Sica's *Bicycle Thieves*.

Those responsible for making neorealist films were consummate professionals, which leads me to make a further point. Neorealism has gained
a reputation in the past half century for ground-breaking innovations,
such as being low-cost projects, using 'ordinary people' or amateur actors,
relying on unscripted or semi-scripted plots, making extensive use of
outside location shoots and eschewing conventional genre formats and
tools for manipulating audience emotions (Landy 2000: 14). In other
words, if neorealism meant anything, it was its fidelity to reality and to
the economic, social and political situation in 1940s Italy (Wagstaff 1996:
227). While there is some truth to some of these points, it should not be
forgotten that neorealist films were made by some of Italy's best known
filmmakers, and in fact did not come cheaply when one examines the
general economic climate of the era and recognizes that many of these
films used some of Italy's leading actors and actresses who demanded
appropriate remuneration. Neither was the idea of using ordinary actors
completely original or new to Italian film, as it can be dated to the 1930s.

And many neorealist films did use dramatic conventions and tools to manipulate audience emotions for artistic purposes. As Christopher Wagstaff (1996: 227) cogently argues:

> If we look at the most commercially successful neorealist films – Rossellini's *Roma Città Aperta* (1945), Zampa's *Vivere in Pace* (1947), De Santis's *Riso Amaro* (1948), or Germi's *In nome della legge* (1949) and *Il cammino della speranza* (1950), we see very clearly the depiction of a contemporary social reality contaminated with the machinery of genre and its stereotyped characters: comedy, melodrama, thriller, and, in the case of the last two, the American western.

He adds (p. 227):

> The conclusion to be drawn, for the purposes of the study of Italian cinema, is that no amount of appeal to fidelity will explain the artistic achievement of a neorealist film like De Sica's *Ladri di Biciclette*, which has to be studied with all the formal and technical tools available to the film analyst.

As important as neorealism's critical and, in certain cases, box office success, was the healthy legacy it left for Italian cinema in the following two decades until the early 1970s. Neorealism helped build for Italy an international reputation for art cinema which, arguably, lives on today with numerous film art festivals across the peninsula. Neorealist films were primarily seen as crafted and shaped by their directors and were enjoyed by sophisticated audiences in Italy and art cinema clubs and societies around the world. These audiences provided solid support to the next wave of Italian films in the late 1950s and 1960s by Antonioni, Bertolucci, Fellini, Leone, Pasolini, Rosi and Scola, and again these films were broadly seen as works of art created by their directors.

By the early 1950s, melodramas were the most popular films in Italy, second only to American blockbusters. The 1949 production, *Chains*, was seen by 6 million Italians (Sorlin 1996: 107). Melodramas were closely followed in terms of public popularity by comedies and the most famous actors of the 1950s were the two comedy actors, Macario and Totò. While comedies were appreciated by audiences, they were never treated seriously by critics and won few prizes. These comedians came from the much older tradition of street theatre and puppet shows based on mime and puns, physical agility, verbal slights and bad jokes. They were types of clown. Other important comedy films included the *Don Camillo* and the *Bread, Love and …* series. The *Don Camillo* films revolved round conflicts between a communist mayor and Catholic parish priest. Italian comedies sold well in Italy and abroad and helped account for the rise of a new generation of actors including Vittorio Gassman, Marcello Mastroianni, Alberto Sordi and Ugo Tognazzi. The result was that comedies helped reduce Italian dependence on US films. Italian films accounted for 33 per cent of box office receipts in the 1950s, rising to 65 per cent in the early 1970s. More Italian films were also being made: 114 in 1955, rising to 291 in 1972 (Sorlin 1996: 111–22).

Major structural transformations had brought Italy modernization from the 1950s onwards and Italian cinema, arguably, enjoyed a golden age. The late 1950s and 1960s constituted a decade or more of Italian cinematic accomplishment attained by very few other nations before or since. This period of Italian film does not have a name. The period we call neorealism drew to a close in the early 1950s although its legacy and many of its key players were central to 1960s Italian cinema. As Pierre Sorlin argues, other European countries including France, Germany, Greece and Spain saw the development of new wave cinema in the late 1950s and 1960s, but no one talked about new wave in Italy, perhaps because the leading actors and directors were already well established (Sorlin 1996: 128). The key Italian films in the late 1950s and 1960s included Luchino Visconti's *Rocco and his Brothers*, which followed the story of a woman migrating to Milan from the South. The film acted as an allegory for the social migration taking place from South to North in the late 1950s (Ginsborg 1990: 242). Visconti followed this up by making another film about the South (Sicily in the post-Unification period) based on Lampedusa's novel, *The Leopard*.

For many, though, it was Frederico Fellini's *La Dolce Vita* (1960) that best summed up the positive and negative aspects of the 'economic miracle', the years between 1958 and 1963 when Italy enjoyed an economic boom and major social change. This was a landmark film that showed an Italy far removed from neorealist stereotypes (Landy 2000: 362). The film teamed up Fellini with his favourite male star, Marcello Mastroianni, and portrayed Italy as the leading international centre for hedonistic pleasure and decadence, and in Stephen Gundle's (1996: 309–10) words:

> Is equally as famous for having incorporated in a collage a series of real events and practices (albeit superficially disguised for the purposes of a feature film) and real people, and for having itself given rise to new stars and gestures and a new style. [Anita] Ekberg, a moderately famous actress in the USA, achieved lasting stardom as a result of the film, while the male lead, Marcello Mastroianni, became the new symbol of Italian masculinity abroad ... The film gave a name to unauthorized celebrity photographers who became know the world over as *paparazzi*. Most significantly, the film communicated an idea of Rome as a centre of glamour, hedonism, leisure, cosmopolitanism, and free expression – symbolized by Ekberg's legendary dip in the Trevi Fountain – that continues to fuel the city's tourist and fashion industries.

Italian films regularly won international film prizes and other prestigious awards; but they also won critical audience praise. Some films, for example Fellini's *8½* and *La Dolce Vita*, took a look at cinema and other creative arts writers, directors and intellectuals. Another popular type of

Italian film was the so-called Spaghetti Western from 1964, which was launched by Sergio Leone's *A Fistful of Dollars*, a remake of Akiro Kurosawa's *Yojimbo*, and made Clint Eastwood an international star outside North America. Again, this was a relatively cheap film that would give birth to a mini-film industry (including the two Leone-Eastwood sequels, *For a Few Dollars More* and *The Good, the Bad and the Ugly*). In the following 12 years, 450 of these types of Western were made providing the best example of *filoni*, films that repeated a successful formula time after time (Frayling 1981). Other examples of *filoni* included *Hercules*, made in 1957, which was extremely successful in the South of Italy and which led to 300 'peplum films' – named after the garment (loin cloth) worn by the characters – in the late 1950s and early 1960s (Wagstaff 1996: 224).

Like the films produced in the pre-First World War *Filmopoli* era, Italian films after the Second World War were widely acclaimed for their innovative use of film techniques and for advancing genre formats. Neorealist films, for example those of Roberto Rossellini and Vittorio De Sica, were praised for the use of realistic *mise-en-scene*, and melodramas were commended for their use of montage. Films associated with particular directors, for example Michele Antonioni, were praised for their innovative photographic and lighting techniques (Sorlin 1996: 122–35; Wagstaff 1996: 223). But what is often forgotten or underplayed is that Italians were also responsible for some of the most memorable film scores in postwar world cinema by the likes of Nino Rota and Ennio Morricone.

The 1950s and 1960s also saw the rise of a number of young female actors in Italy – for example, Claudia Cardinale, Sofia Loren and Monica Vitti – who would go on to international success in English and Italian-language films. Italian actresses in the postwar period prior to the 1960s tended to play mothers or *femme fatales*. But a new breed of more autonomous woman began appearing on screen, for example, Cardinale's role in Sergio Leone's *Once Upon a Time in the West*. Generally speaking, this highlighted a broader range of women's representations in the postwar era, unlike what would happen to Italian television in the 1980s and 1990s. The late 1960s also saw the notable influence of Freud and the use of psychoanalysis in Italian films, including those of Bernardo Bertolucci, Luchino Visconti and Pier-Paolo Pasolini (Wagstaff 1996: 223; Sorlin 1996: 122–35).

The 1970s saw the decline of the film industry in Italy. Exhibition remained a more profitable sector than production and some companies ceased trading or moved into distribution and exhibition. Only the advent of co-production deals with European and Latin American companies kept productions going. Faced with the erosion of their audiences, cinemas either closed down or began modifying their operations. In turn, this led to more cinemas relying on erotic films (*luci rosse*). Cinematic attendance did still grow in university towns with the development of film societies, but the rise of television was the main reason for the decline of cinema attendances and the number of films produced declined in the

1980s and 1990s. Attendance figures dropped from 500 million in the 1960s to 100 million in the 1990s. At one point only 800 cinemas were in operation.

Although the Italian film industry continued to produce 100 films annually, it became dominated by American producers and distributors, and big action films (Sorlin, 2000: 147). By the 1990s, a third of Italian films were being financed wholly or in part by television companies, especially RAI, allowing space for famous directors, such as Antonioni or Rosi, or emerging talent like Nichetti or Salvatores. However, films in the 1980s and 1990s did make use of lighter camera equipment to achieve more observational techniques – for example, Nanni Moretti's *Dear Diary*. Otherwise, films directly tackled the growth of television, such as Nichetti's *Icicle Thief*. Some films in the 1980s and 1990s, like *Stolen Children*, contained serious moral messages, while others, such as *Cinema Paradiso*, looked at cinema in a nostalgic light. But the Italian film industry did not collapse as in other countries, thanks to the 1965 law that provided additional state funds and the presence of RAI. Films became different and were far more suited and geared to the television marketplace. Comedy genres returned in the 1990s via the films of Roberto Benigni, Carlo Verdoni, Piero Pieraccioni and the popular series *Vacanze di Natale* ... , starring Christian De Sica – son of Vittorio – and Massimo Boldi (Sorlin 1996: 118–50). The enormous success of Roberto Benigni's *Life is Beautiful* from 1998 would lead to a minor upturn in Italian film fortunes in the twenty-first century (see Chapter 7) and revived, albeit briefly, memories of better times and Italian film glories of the postwar period.

Rebuilding a free press in postwar Italy

The newspaper industry was arguably the main victim of Fascist anti-censorship rules and political repression in the 1920s. Newspapers were subject to Fascist political pressures soon after the regime came to power, and by 1926 the major Italian titles had either been suppressed and forced underground or told to toe the Party line on the major economic, political and social issues of the day. Mussolini was undoubtedly aided by compliant newspaper owners – those of *Corriere della Sera* and *La Stampa* for example – who, in many cases, gave tacit support to the regime, removed 'difficult' editors and then employed editors that would not stir any overt anti-Fascist sentiment. Clearly, the downfall of fascism in 1943 meant that things would change markedly.

But the re-establishment of a free press was a slow process and was heavily conditioned by the ongoing war and material damage to equipment, especially in the South and Rome, which led to newspapers being printed and published in rotation. For those parts of the peninsula liberated by the Allies, the press and radio were wholly dependent on the military government for permission to publish or broadcast. In turn the government was dependent on the PWB – the Psychological Warfare

Branch of Allied Forces Headquarters – which had been created by the Allies to coordinate propaganda and information in newly-liberated areas. The first two-sided news-sheets permitted by the PWB were in Sicily and Calabria (Murialdi 2000: 185). Gradually, newspapers began reopening and they quickly became the key terrain for political ideas and battles among newly re-establishing parties.

At the beginning of 1944, the Allied forces gave the new Italian government limited powers, including authorization for press permits. And in April 1944, following a speech made by Communist leader and minister for home affairs, Togliatti ('*Svolta di Salerno*'), weekly party papers began to emerge. *La Voce* was left wing; *Il Giornale* was liberal and *Il Domani d'Italia* was run by the Christian Democrats. In Rome the main party papers, *L'Unità*, *Avanti!* and *Il Popolo* began reappearing some 20 years after their suppression (Murialdi 2000: 187). These same papers appeared in Milan after liberation on 25 April 1945 (Murialdi 2000: 190). In addition to party-owned newspapers, the Allied forces were keen to encourage a non-partisan, 'independent' press to act as a counterweight to party newspapers, especially in the heavily industrialized cities of the North (Murialdi 2000: 191).

But as I have already outlined, full-scale purges of owners and journalists were ruled out firstly by the Allies and then by the postwar Christian Democrats and so change took place at a slow pace. For example, the early governments delayed the revision of the fascist press laws, allowing them to maintain strict control over press and radio (Murialdi 2000: 188). And journalists themselves, led by the reformed National Federation for Italian Press (FNSI) announced that they were against the abolition of the *Albo dei Giornalisti* (Murialdi 2000: 189). Few newspaper journalists were ever tried for Fascist crimes, and even those newspaper editors tried in 1945–6, including Armando Amicucci from the *Corriere della Sera*, saw their sentences (anything between 12 to 30 years in jail) commuted in the general amnesty announced by Togliatti, before the monarchy referendum on 2 June 1946 (Murialdi 2000: 196). Most journalists went back to their old jobs. This was also facilitated, in part, by the rather 'closed' nature of journalism in Italy and the difficulties that new aspirant journalists faced in entering the profession, either because they did not have the right kinds of industry contacts or the necessary 'cultural capital'. Some still complain today of the difficulties faced by the young in entering what is still a highly regulated profession (Hallin and Mancini 2004).

But while owners were left in place after the war, the Italian press was gradually 'defascistized', with editorial and ideological positions becoming more pluralistic. The postwar period also allowed new groups and organizations to become involved in the newspaper industry. The employers' confederation, Confindustria, took over three financial papers, including *Il Globo*, *Il Sole* and *24 Ore* (the latter two were later merged) and started a local chain of newspapers. Ownership played a direct role in influencing political support for the left and right. But continuing weak sales for Italian newspapers meant that advertisers would play a strong role in influencing political content. Larger advertisers did at times boycott certain left-wing newspapers that were deemed too business 'unfriendly'. Newspapers affected by this became more reliant on smaller advertisers and other marketing possibilities to ensure sales. In the case of *L'Unità*, for example, greater sales could be secured through distributing the paper to workers' clubs around the country and extra income could also be derived from fundraising at cultural festivals which still regularly attract thousands in Italy today and raise millions of Euros for left-wing political causes.

The handover by the military authorities to the new civilian Italian government took place in northern regions on 1 January 1946. The first postwar Italian administrative elections took place in spring that year, closely followed by elections to decide the make-up of the new Constituent Assembly (which would write the new constitution) and a referendum to decide the fate of the Italian monarchy. With full parliamentary elections due as soon as the constitution was agreed, the immediate postwar period from 1946–8 would be crucial in shaping the political direction of the country in the Cold War era. As a key institution of political communication, the Italian mass media, especially news media, would help shape that future. As we shall see, the close relationship between the Christian Democrats and senior executives at RAI meant that radio remained a loyal supporter of government policy. The situation was somewhat different in relation to newspapers.

Firstly, the presence of party-owned newspapers meant that there was a greater plurality of voices and opinions in the Italian press. But the main growth in the Italian press in the immediate postwar period was in non-party owned titles which, as discussed above, were friendlier to advertisers. The *Corriere della Sera* was the leading selling newspaper of this kind and drew its inspiration in the postwar period from leading US and European papers such as the *New York Times*, the London *Times* and *Le Monde*. Non-party owned titles also enjoyed other advantages. In many cases, these newspapers could draw on more news sources from the big American or European news agencies in addition to the Italian ANSA agency. Secondly, the reemergence of major newspaper publishers from the Fascist era brought valuable practical experience. One example was the Italian tradition of allocating space on page 3 of newspapers to high profile journalists, a major competitive tool when one considers the homogeneity of much of the political comment on offer. The result was that the number of newspapers published in Italy grew to 146 by early 1946. Many non-party owned newspapers looked westwards not eastwards for future inspiration and supported the Christian Democrats almost without exception, culminating in the crucial political election of 18 April 1948, which helped cement Italy's place in the Western European and American sphere of influence (Murialdi 2000: 199, 205, 209).

The weekly press, including magazines, also began to reemerge in postwar Italy. The publishing house, Rizzoli, gained permission to publish *Oggi* in July 1945. The main difference between daily newspapers and weekly journals and magazines was size. Whereas most newspapers consisted of two pages, occasionally four, and cost 3 lire, tabloid-sized magazines like *Oggi* consisted of 16 pages and cost 15 lire. In early 1946, the photo-magazine, *Tempo*, appeared, run by socialist-leaning editorial staff. Female titles also reappeared as well as two older titles: *Domenica del Corriere* and *L'Ilustrazione Italiana*. One progressive development in postwar Italian journalism was the development of photo-journalism (Murialdi 2000: 195). Another key development from the 1950s onwards was the success of new weekly magazines focused on culture, current affairs and politics. Again the inspiration for new titles came from the USA (*Life*) and France (*Paris Match*). These magazines included *Epoca* and *Espresso* which began publication 1955. The weekly magazines were far outstripping sales of daily newspapers in that year, and this still holds true today. So while *Corriere della Sera* was selling 300,000 copies by the early 1950s, the *Domenica del Corriere* was selling 600,000–900,000 copies.

Another important development for Italian journalism in the postwar period came via the emergence of an afternoon and evening press which were heavily influenced by French and British titles like *France Soir* and the *Daily Mirror*. These newspapers relied more on soft news rather than politics. Entertainment-led news, interviews, greater use of photography, cartoon strips and crosswords were key features. The main beneficiary was *Corriere d'Informazione* but other new titles included the Milan-based *La Notte* and the Roman afternoon paper, *Paese*.

While some cultural and media industries grew rapidly on the back of the 'economic miracle' of the late 1950s and early 1960s, newspapers in Italy, as elsewhere in the world, began suffering from the increased competition coming from television and a deteriorating economic position. In Italy, by 1960, the number of daily newspapers published had fallen to 93. This would fall to 86 by 1965 (Murialdi 2000: 228). For the Italian press, one positive sign was the start of the new *Il Giorno* newspaper on 1 January 1960, which was jointly funded by IRI and the state petrochemicals company, ENI. The newspaper, unsurprisingly perhaps, favoured greater state intervention in the economy. While remaining pro-establishment, it gave the state important support and acted as a counterweight to commercial press, helping to build a bridge between a rather polarized press in Italy and those allied with private interests or communist/socialist sympathies (Forgacs 1990a: 132).

By the late 1960s, the Italian establishment faced intense political pressure as a result of unrest from the student and working-class movements. The development of the 1960s' radical countercultures in Italy had numerous effects on the media. Firstly, there was the growth in left-wing press such as the *Manifesto* and *Lotta Continua* as well as other newspapers and magazines. The second main change was that journalists became more deeply politicized, seeking greater freedoms from editorial pressures. Journalists wanted greater separation between professional ethics and responsibilities, and ties to political and economic owners. Various demands were made: finances to be made public; opposition of media concentrations; and the development of elected *comitati di redazi-*

one, elected committees of journalist employees (Forgacs 1990a: 139–40). One of the main successes of these committees was at the *Corriere della Sera*. Under Piero Ottone's editorialship in the 1970s, the paper agreed a statement with journalists that its editorial independence would be guaranteed. The paper became more radical, the filmmaker Pier-Paolo Pasolini joined as a contributor and sales went up, peaking at 890,000 in 1973. However, some journalists, including the well known columnist, Indro Montanelli, left, complaining of over-strong union and committee powers (Forgacs 1990a: 140).

Despite the appearance of *Il Giorno* and the success of left-wing newspapers in the 1960s and 1970s, the economic downturn and closure of several Italian newspapers led to consolidation in the industry and the development of (mono-media) concentrations of ownership. One new publishing group led by Attilio Monti took a controlling interest in the group that owned *La Nazione* and *Resto del Carlino*. This group was supported by the Christian Democrats and Moro (Forgacs 1990a: 133). A second newspaper group, led by the chemicals magnate, Nino Rovelli, bought up three Sardinian newspapers. Despite this consolidation, journalist organizations appeared more concerned about newspaper closures and the associated risks of unemployment. While some concerns were raised in Parliament about increasing concentrations of media ownership, the Italian government appeared largely unworried about introducing anti-trust legislation (ownership rules restricting the number of media controlled by any one company in order to promote fair competition), citing Article 21 of the constitution (Murialdi 2000: 233). This resulted in ambivalence in some political quarters in Italy to tackling the thorny issue of media concentration, although limited mono-media anti-trust rules were introduced for newspapers in the 1980s (Law 416, 5 August 1981) and via the Broadcasting Law in 1990. Cross-media ownership rules were also introduced in 1990 and strengthened in 1997.

The next two major events in the Italian newspaper industry occurred in 1974 and 1976. Indro Montanelli, who had recently quit the *Corriere della Sera* in protest over union powers, was already well known as one of Italy's most charismatic and respected journalists. His career had been tarnished by his association and support for fascism in the 1920s, but he later renounced fascism and rebuilt his career in postwar Italy. In 1974, Montanelli set up a new title, *Il Giornale*, with the primary aim of competing with the *Corriere della Sera*. By attracting the financial backing of the petrochemicals company, Montedison, as well as others, including in later years one Silvio Berlusconi, and by attracting senior journalists from his old newspaper, Montanelli sought to target conservative readers. Another feature was that *Il Giornale* sought a national audience as opposed to regional one, although it did launch regional editions in Liguria and Emilia.

The start of *La Repubblica* newspaper in 1976 provided a more serious attempt to construct a national readership in Italy rather than a regional or local one. *La Repubblica*, which was pitched to centre-left, educated readers with average and high incomes, was founded by the former editor of *Espresso*, Eugenio Scalfari, with financial backing from the Mondadori publishing house. The newspaper was published in tabloid format and developed a very strong left of centre agenda which concentrated on analysis and comment, attracting many leading columnists and journalists to its pages. *La Repubblica* later develop regional supplements and by 1979 was selling 145,000 copies each day, thereby breaking even (Murialdi 2000: 254).

The development of these two new titles had an undoubted positive influence in rejuvenating the newspaper industry in Italy which, by 1980, would break the 6 million daily sales figure for the first time in its history (Murialdi 2000: 287). There were other factors however that contributed to a minor upturn in fortunes for Italy's struggling newspaper sector. Firstly, and in common with newspapers internationally, Italian titles were by the 1970s experimenting with new production and distribution technologies. The development of Linotype printing and computer technologies would ultimately help revolutionize the newspaper industry globally, but their impact was already evident in Italy in the mid-1970s. The period of the 'Historical Compromise' saw the Italian Communist Party enter into the Italian government and created more demand for political news. The surge in terrorist acts in the 1970s was another factor which helped the sales of newspapers. One key target for terrorists like the Red Brigades was journalists, including Montanelli. On 16 November 1977, the deputy editor of *La Stampa*, Carlo Casalengo, was shot. He died ten days later from his injuries. Neither was he the last journalist to die during these years. But it was the kidnapping and subsequent assassination of the Christian Democrat leader, Aldo Moro, in 1978, that shocked many in Italy and around the world.

High-profile terrorist acts were also followed by the P2 scandal that involved senior Italian journalists and led to the collapse in sales for Italy's largest newspaper, *Corriere della Sera*. The late 1970s and early 1980s was a very unstable time for Italy. The death of Aldo Moro in 1978 was followed on 2 August 1980 by the Bologna station bomb, which exploded in a packed waiting room, killing 85 people. In 1981, the P2 scandal was uncovered. P2 – standing for Propaganda 2 – was a right-wing subversive Masonic lodge with rather obscure anti-Communist political aims and various criminal activities. Members of P2 came from the high echelons of Italian business and state and many viewed the lodge as a possible conspirator to a coup plot. In addition to the P2 scandal and left- and right-wing terrorism, in 1982 the Mafia assassinated General Carlo Alberto Dalla Chiesa and his wife in Palermo (Ginsborg 1990: 423), reasserting its opposition to the Italian state.

When the P2 list was finally released by the then Italian prime minister, Arnaldo Forlani, in 1981, it contained the names of 28 journalists and four newspapers owners, including Angelo Rizzoli, owner of the *Corriere della Sera*. A total of seven journalists on the list came from the Rizzoli group. The ensuing scandal was devastating for the group, which had to be bailed out financially by leading Italian industrialists, including Fiat and Montedison, in 1985, and for the *Corriere della Sera* which quickly began losing sales. Between 1980 and 1983 the paper lost roughly 100,000 sales each day and key journalists, including Enzo Biagi and Alberto Ronchey, left the newspaper for *La Repubblica* (although Ronchey would return in 1984). This was an extraordinarily opportune moment to reach new readers and Eugenio Scalfari exploited the opportunity to the full. By 1985, *La Repubblica*'s sales had outstripped those of its Milanese rival, selling some 373,000 copies per day. With sales coming equally from different parts of the peninsula, the paper could also declare itself as Italy's first truly national newspaper (Murialdi 2000: 258).

With Italian newspapers selling more than 6 million copies a day from 1980 to 1985, the future looked bright for the country's oldest mass communication medium. These figures were also helped by the rise in demand for specialist newspapers containing financial information and sports news. Italy's major financial newspaper, the Confindustria-owned *Il Sole-24 Ore* saw its daily sales rise from just over 90,000 in 1976 to nearly 171,000 in 1984. Sales of sports newspapers doubled from 1976 to Italy's triumphant World Cup victory in 1982. Italy's best known sports daily, the *Gazzetta dello Sport* saw its sales double and it became the county's best-selling newspaper from 1980 to 1982. By 1984, Italy's second best-selling sports newspaper, the *Corriere dello Sport* was selling close to 439,000 copies daily. The third daily sports newspaper, *Tuttosport*, reached sales of 157,000 by 1984. Sports coverage on television also led to greater demand for specialist newspapers. This was a rather paradoxical situation, as elsewhere the development of television had damaged newspaper sales in Italy and with the development of commercial television in the 1980s, newspaper sales would drop back post-1985.

In the next chapter we begin our discussion of postwar radio and television development in Italy.

5 THE FIRST ITALIAN REPUBLIC: BROADCASTING AND 'MAMMA RAI'

- The development of television in Italy
- RAI and the Bernabei years, 1961–74

The Second World War badly disrupted the operations of all media in Italy and led to the removal or destroying of audio-visual production facilities, printing presses, transmitters, cinemas, etc. Some media fared better than others. Book publication was heavily hit, for example, whereas film production actually went up in the early years of the war, before falling back after the downfall of fascism in 1943 and the subsequent two-year period of civil war and occupation. Other media, like newspapers, were forced underground early in the Fascist period, while the practice of clandestine radio listening only became a significant pastime during the war. While penalties for listening to illegal radio broadcasts could include imprisonment, Italians listened to these broadcasts in their thousands to hear more authoritative news services than those offered by EIAR. The most famous example was the Italian service of the BBC, known as *Radio Londra* or Radio London, which enjoyed a mass audience after 1942. Radio London was trusted more than most other Allied or resistance-organized broadcasts.

After the Allied invasion of Sicily in 1943 and the subsequent Italian armistice, the radio network came under the control of the two fighting armies. In the North, the fascist-led Republic of Salò, helped by the Germans, took control of the radio stations. In the South and newly-liberated areas, radio broadcasting came under the control of the PWB. The main headquarters of the Italian interim government led by Marshall Badoglio in Bari was a key example of where the Allied forces vetted all radio employees and controlled all radio output. Yet despite keeping a close eye on radio content, more radical voices did broadcast. The development of clandestine and anti-fascist radio led, as David Forgacs argues, to ' … the emergence of new uses of radio, a new relationship with the medium on the part of the listeners and broadcasters alike' (1990a: 96).

One of the first decisions made in the liberated parts of Italy was on 26 October 1944, when EIAR changed its name to RAI (*Radio Audizioni Italia*) in an attempt to break with its fascist past. Such a symbolic change did nothing to improve the dire condition of the Italian radio network. One early motive for the rejection of any commercial radio system in Italy was the general disrepair and fragmentation of the communications network. Radio communications in 1945 were dispersed among different anti-Fascist groups. The main priority for the Italian government after the final liberation of northern towns on 25 April 1945 was to reunite the fragmented radio network and reconstruct a national network based on the notion of providing a public service to a national community (Monteleone 1992: 192). Monteleone (1980: 224) quotes the following 'Reithian' definition of public service broadcasting made by Arturo C. Jemolo, the postwar president of RAI and the Parliamentary Commission for Culture:

> in a liberal regime, characterised by the coexistence of different political parties and by the possibility of an alternation of power, the radio cannot be the instrument of government power or of the parties of opposition, but must remain a public service of dispassionate and impartial information, to which all listeners, whatever their beliefs, can draw upon.

This aspiration would be difficult to realize in practice, not least because 'the possibility of an alternation of power', as Jemolo puts it, never materialized, with the Christian Democrats forming part of every coalition government until 1993.[1] One immediate problem was that Italy had two overlapping radio networks: the Blue Network operated in the Centre-North and the Red Network in the Centre-South of the country. This meant that old EIAR stations enjoyed far more autonomy than previously and resisted attempts by the new Italian government in 1945–6 to recentralize the radio system under the control of Rome. Places like Sicily and Naples led resistance to plans abolishing the twin networks. The northern city of Turin, SIP's base in the 1920s and 1930s, and hence having strong ties to the radio industry, also spearheaded resistance. Drawing on past grievances in relation to Turin's film industry (*Filmopoli*), the communist mayor of Turin wired the new Italian prime minister, Ferruccio Parri, in October 1945, arguing:

> Fascism adopted a method of spoiliation against our city removing formerly traditional activities like film production centres and banknote printworks, creating difficulties and great disappointment among the population. If the cultural headquarters of radio should now emigrate it would create new grounds for discontent among our population which has been among the first in the Liberation struggle and which despite difficulties is still today in the front rank of the struggle for reconstruction.
>
> (*Quoted in Forgacs 1990a: 109*)

This kind of lobbying had a certain amount of success, as radio (and television) would only come under full control of Rome in the 1960s.

The task of restoring a unified radio network fell to successive coalition governments comprising all the main anti-Fascist parties. The decisive break between the anti-Fascist alliance came in March 1947. Alcide De Gasperi, the Christian Democrat prime minister, under intense pressure from both internal and external forces, ditched the Communists and the Socialists from the government. As already discussed, internally, the Catholic hierarchy had warned De Gasperi that the Church could no longer countenance any further cooperation with the 'atheist' enemy. Externally, the American government, especially after the publication of the Truman Doctrine in March 1947, had made plain its belief that De Gasperi should adopt a strict anti-Communist policy. Another factor in the timing of De Gasperi's decision to exclude the left-wing from power was that by that time the work of the Constituent Assembly, which had been elected in 1946 to draw up a new constitution, had nearly been completed. De Gasperi could therefore dismiss the opposition without risking this historical constitutional agreement.

These extensive powers were supplemented by the rules governing the appointment of RAI's Administrative Council as defined in RAI's charter. The Council members were appointed by the executive and RAI's parent company IRI, whose own board were political appointees. The Council had the responsibility of managing the day-to-day affairs of the company (Pinto 1980: 87). After 1948, therefore, the Christian Democrats, aided and abetted by the old guard inside RAI and the legislative powers of the executive, were able to occupy and take effective control of broadcasting. The party, under De Gasperi, was a relatively united one and was therefore able to turn RAI into a vehicle of anti-communist propaganda, which was the hallmark of these years (Monteleone 1980: 161). The period 1948–54, before television transmissions began, and when Cold War fervour was at its height, was the time when the Christian Democrats had their greatest hold over RAI (Forgacs 1990a: 114–16).

The development of television in Italy

Television services in Italy started in January 1954 (with RAI's name changing to *Radiotelevisione Italiana*), comparatively late when compared with the country's major European partners. The first regular European television service started in the UK in the last year of John Reith's tenure at the BBC in 1936 and then recommenced in 1947 following its suspension during the war years. Italy's nascent television history can in fact be dated to 1929 when two engineers, Alessandro Banfi and Sergio Bertolotti, undertook the first Italian experiments in transmitting images of a doll at URI's headquarters in Milan. Further experiments were undertaken in 1932 using German technology and these were presented to the public at the 1933 National Radio Exhibition in Milan. In 1939, EIAR constructed a transmitter in Rome and began the first experimental broadcast on 22 July (Sorice 2002: 24). It was not until 1949 that further tests took place, using American technology, followed by the 1951

National Television Congress which discussed various options for starting an Italian television system. On 26 January 1952 the Italian state and RAI signed an exclusive 20-year agreement (until 15 December 1972) to provide Italy's first public television service, despite attempts by Milanese financiers to launch a commercial television service. Experimental broadcasts began in the same year and full television services began on 3 January 1954 with the first announcer being Fulvia Colombo (Sorice 2002: 21; Grasso 2004: 3–16). The first schedule is shown below.

Italy's first television schedule
3 January 1954, 2.30 p.m.

- *Arrivi e partenze,* **presenter Mike Bongiorno**
- *L'orchestra delle Quindici,* **presenter Febo Conti**
- **Pomeriggio sportivo (Sport magazine)**
- **Film:** *Le miserie del signor Travet*
- **L'avventura dell'arte:** *Giovan Battista Tiepolo*
- **Telegiornale (News) (8.45 p.m.)**
- *Teleclub*
- **Theatre:** *L'osteria della posta* **di Carlo Goldoni (live)**
- *Settenote* **(music show)**
- *La Domenica Sportiva (Sport magazine)* **(11.00 p.m.)**

Two days before the start of television in Italy, Pope Pius XII published a key article on television, which would help set the tone for RAI's new service. Under the leadership of Filiberto Guala (1954–6), RAI's Administrative Council helped the Catholics' aim of promoting the policy of self-censorship within RAI, which introduced a strong moral and pedagogic ethic while also preventing any programmes being shown which were considered unsuitable (Sorice 2002: 28). Many on the political left considered that RAI was little more than an arm of *Azione Cattolica*, the main Catholic organization to which Guala belonged (Monteleone 1980: 215). But to portray Guala as merely an instrument of the Catholic hierarchies would be wrong. In fact, he could be described as progressive in two respects. Firstly, he attempted to modernize RAI, instilling more professional ethics, and he believed in providing a recognizable public service. In order to promote such a policy required competent and professional staff throughout the organization. Many young staff and university graduates were drafted into the company, some of whom went on to achieve notable international success in public service broadcasting, journalism and in wider academia. These included Gianfranco Bettetini, Furio Colombo, Umberto Eco, Angelo Guglielmi and Gianni Vattimo.

Secondly, Guala tried, albeit somewhat unsuccessfully, to purge the Turin-based *ancien regime* – radio managers left from the fascist era who were against modernization plans. By pursuing these two policies Guala was clearly following the lead of Amintore Fanfani. This was the wider political project to make Italy a modern democracy which necessitated greater links with the parties and associations of the centre-left, including the Italian Socialist Party. Some Christian Democrats were very suspicious of these broader plans, especially those relating to providing a more inclusive public service broadcaster. The very nature of the television medium, the equation of television = consumer capitalism, which was deemed as being inherently atheist, worried many Catholics (Ginsborg 1990: 241).

One example of early intervention by the papacy concerned television advertising. As previously mentioned, television services in Italy were initially funded by a licence fee, but it soon became obvious that this was insufficient. The obvious answer was revenue from advertising, but this was resisted by the Church. In the end, a compromise, perhaps unique to Italy, was struck. Advertising would only be shown during one half hour show each evening, which was entitled *Carosello*. The show consisted of short cartoons and other short programmes. It was very popular with children as well as adults, and by 1960 was the top-rated Italian television programme. It became an institution which was to last until 1977 (Ginsborg 1990: 240–1; Grasso 1992: 161–3). *Carosello* ensured that RAI received a secure means of funding (licence fee) plus some additional income. The programme raised considerable funds, allowing RAI to expand its public service provisions, and the compromise agreement also allowed the state to divert funds to the ailing newspaper industry (Sassoon 1986b: 154).[2] Yet, the introduction of advertising demonstrated that the Church did not have all its own way in shaping broadcasting policy.

Other important television programmes in the 1950s included the Sanremo Music Festival, which had been running as a radio event since 1951 before moving to television in 1956. The annual event regularly attracted more than 20 million viewers throughout the 1960s, 1970s and 1980s and still forms a key part of RAI's schedules every February. The quiz show *Lascia o Raddoppia* (the Italian version of the American *$64,000 Question*) began in 1955 and would become Italy's most popular show in the early years of television, demonstrating the importance of American culture to Italian public service broadcasting. The show was hosted by the Italian-American, Mike Bongiorno (who presented the first Italian television programme, *Arrivi e Partenze*, in January 1954). The programme's success led to the film *Totò Lascia o Raddoppia*, which also starred Bongiorno. It was an early example of Italian cinema drawing on television for ideas. Although now officially semi-retired, Mike Bongiorno was still making television programmes at the time of writing this book in June 2007.

The children's song contest, *Lo Zecchino d'Oro* was launched in 1959. The programme was turned into an international competition in 1976 and is still produced today from Bologna. Early forms of drama included *Il Mattatore* (1959), starring a young Vittorio Gassman. Many early television dramas drew on Italian theatrical or radio traditions. Radio schedules were left largely unchanged by the start of television, but as time went on more news, sport and children's programmes were introduced to help combat the decline in radio listening. Music programmes, including *Amuri Amuri* and *Il discobolo* remained popular (Sorice 2002: 29–33).

The main threat to RAI's monopoly in the early years did not come from political opposition. Instead, it came from a group within the state apparatus: the judiciary. In July 1960 the Constitutional Court adjudicated on the legal status of the monopoly in relation to the 1948 constitution after a private operator, Tempo TV, owned by the Angiolillo-Lauro group, had been refused a television licence by the authorities. RAI, not surprisingly, was highly critical of any attempt to break its monopoly. But the company was also highly embarrassed by such a court case, because its poor record of impartiality, a key component of its overall public service, would inevitably come under closer scrutiny (Pinto 1980: 13). The Court's decision was that RAI's monopoly was legal, citing Article 43 of the constitution, arguing that 'broadcasting should be considered to be of especial public interest' (Cavazza 1979: 88). Furthermore, the Court argued that a monopoly was also required due to the technical shortage of terrestrial frequencies. At the same time, however, the Court issued a veiled warning to RAI stating that a public service must be both impartial and objective (Cavazza 1979: 88–9). The Court's decision was a turning point for RAI, as we will now discuss.

RAI and the Bernabei years, 1961–74

The main consolidation of television in Italy coincided with the 'economic miracle' of the late 1950s and early 1960s, an era of rapid and dynamic economic growth and massive social transformations that swept across Italy. Between 1959 and 1962, the years that marked the high point of economic expansion, gross national product (GNP) grew by at least 6 per cent annually. In the longer term GNP grew by an average of 5.3 per cent in the 1950s and by 5.7 per cent in the 1960s. Average incomes grew more in two decades than they had in the previous seven put together (Hine 1993: 42). The political and social consequences of this rapid rate of growth were explosive. Mass migration from southern to northern Italy, and from the countryside to the cities, produced overwhelming social demands on housing, health and education. Politically, this rapid expansion led to a gradual shift to the left in voting habits, prompting Amintore Fanfani to formulate a policy which would bring the socialists into government.

The 1960s bought rapid changes in cultural consumption patterns in Italy. Cinema continued its decline, seeing ticket sales fall from 800 million in 1954 to 680 million in 1964, however, record sales were booming and went from 5 million in 1953 to 30 million in 1964. Comics (*fumetti*) were becoming increasingly popular with the *Diabolik* series being introduced in 1962 (Sorice 2002: 52–3). Television too was fast becoming one of the main symbols of the age and was both loved and reviled intensely. Either way, it could not be ignored. Franco Monteleone (1980: 215) calculates that in 1956, two years after television services began, there were 1.5 million domestic viewers and 366,000 televisions in communal use. In 1960, 20 per cent of Italian households owned a television licence; by 1965, the figure had risen to 49 per cent and by 1971 it was 82 per cent. Many more people had access to televisions via bars, clubs and friends. By 1968, the first channel could be seen by 98 per cent of the population; the second channel, which had begun transmissions in 1961, could be seen by 90 per cent (Ginsborg 1990: 432). It was the 1960s, therefore, that saw the true arrival of television.

For RAI, the 1960s were to be no less amazing, seeing massive modernization, expansion and centralization. Ettore Bernabei, former editor of the Christian Democrat newspaper, Il Popolo, was appointed director-general in January 1961. From the very start it was clear that he was going to undertake a thorough shake-up of RAI's internal organization and outside political relations, in line with Fanfani's agenda and the veiled attack by the Constitutional Court. Internally, his aim was to purge the company's old guard who were resistant to any large-scale changes and who had enjoyed a resurgence in influence as a result of Guala's resignation in 1956. Bernabei had a distinct advantage over them in that he had a political patron, whereas they did not (Pinto 1980: 27). Bernabei wanted to loosen the overt political links between the Christian Democrats and RAI, developing a public service in tune with a modern Italy: more professional and autonomous, but still firmly anti-Communist.

Bernabei was able to wield power by virtue of his own position and that of Fanfani's. This did not mean, however, that he was able to overcome all the resistance to change. A pertinent example is the restructuring of the news service, telegiornale. Under the previous regime this had been overtly propagandistic in content. Bernabei argued that such a news service lacked any political credibility and as such was an embarrassment. It was too attached to the Christian Democrats and any attempt to bring the socialists into government would necessitate a change. In 1962, therefore, Bernabei appointed Enzo Biagi to construct a modern and professional 'magazine style' news. The process of change was slow and Biagi himself resigned due to the internal and external resistance to his plans. In time, the change was made with the net result that news programmes contained fewer members of the Christian Democrats and presented a wider spread of opinion (Pinto 1980: 29–31; Monteleone 1992: 102).

Bernabei's achievements were notable. He introduced a second television channel and the quality of programme production rose sharply. There were also innovative developments in both content and language (Sorice 2002: 57). Underlying the expansion of broadcasting was a broader pedagogic strategy. It is worth remembering that in postwar Italy, deep regional disparities in educational and cultural knowledge were still present. Taking literacy rates in 1951, Italy still had a persistent minority of illiterates in many parts of the South and on the islands.[3] For a country embracing industrialization and modernity, such rates were unacceptable. The strategy, called 'pedagogic enlightenment', was facilitated by the favourable economic climate and secure means of funding. This allowed RAI to activate a series of policy initiatives that would strengthen public service provision. In addition to the concerted effort to provide a blanket or universal service, the company was also keen to promote a programming remit that raised cultural knowledge, as Gianfranco Bettetini (1990: 238)[4] argues:

> The project of 'pedagogic enlightenment' informed television production in the 1960s and early 1970s. The role of the broadcaster was to provide 'common-denominator' programming, thereby appealing to all social groups and unifying its viewers. The emphasis was placed on providing a range of programmes pitched at a medium level of understanding. This included targeting groups furthest from this average level and promoting an empyrean culture, regarded as the minimum level required to uphold civil values and societal cohesion.

All programmes in the early years of RAI were therefore aimed at offering education, information and entertainment in line with a strong pedagogic remit: education in the Italian context meant programmes for schools, farming programmes as well as other forms of education such as plays; information, in this context, meant news services, but also social documentaries dealing with controversial subjects such as the South and working women; entertainment meant quiz shows, variety shows and light musical offerings.

Popular television programmes in the 1960s included the quiz show *Campanile Sera*, presented by the evergreen Mike Bongiorno. The programme actually ran from 1959 to 1961 and was based on the radio show, *Campanile d'Oro*. One of the show's main characteristics was that it relied on regional participation. Each week, two teams from the various towns and villages along the peninsula would compete against one another. Other programmes included *Processo alla Tappa*, presented by Sergio Zavoli (who would later become President of RAI in the 1980s), which followed the daily events at the annual *Giro d'Italia* cycle race. Drama included adaptations of Manzoni's novel *I Promessi Sposi* (*The Betrothed*) and, in 1968, of Homer's *Odyssey*. The 1960s also saw Italy's first 'reality' programme, Nanni Loy's *Specchio Segreto*, loosely based on the American *Candid Camera*.

Thus, television took on a strong social role. RAI was a crucial reference point for many Italians during this period, reinforcing its important nickname 'Mamma RAI'. The (upward) social mobility of many Italians, matched also by the numbers migrating, created a society in rapid transition. RAI shaped its programme output according to the perceived needs of a country changing extremely rapidly. By appealing to a broad social and economic social church, by highlighting the changes taking place within society and by identifying itself with those changes, RAI had an undeniable unifying influence. There was also a strong sense of belief on the part of many within the company that one of the best ways of developing the country was by expanding television. This sense of self-belief within RAI was born out of knowledge of the medium itself and the developing relationship between the audience and television (Monteleone 1992: 339, 387).

By 1968, RAI under Bernabei had been built into a formidable political, cultural and economic company. The number of television licences rose from 16.66 per 100 households in 1960 to 62.40 in 1970 (Sorice 2002: 81). The major aims of reorganization, remodernization and the consolidation of a new power regime in line with the aims of Fanfani had largely been achieved (Cavazza 1979: 90). It was 1968, however, that would mark the high point of the Bernabei years. For RAI's hierarchy, the next six years were to be characterized by a succession of bruising encounters. Externally, the post-1968 years saw the relationship between RAI and the main political parties take a nosedive. The main political parties themselves became very unpopular in the face of an explosion of unrest within civil society. The students' movement was joined by sections of the working class acting outside of the traditional trade unions' authority. Lumley (1990: 12) characterizes the first reactions to the student movement as being a moral panic, akin to the reporting of mods and rockers rioting on the seaside beaches in Britain during the 1960s. The students were therefore demonized by large sections of the press and television.

In turn, the students were not particularly well disposed towards the media. They were themselves protesting against the 'atomizing effects' of the 'miracle years' and, for them, much of the blame for this fell at the door of the media (Ginsborg 1990: 242).[5] Established trade unions and political parties were therefore stung into being more proactive proponents of political and social change. This more proactive stance manifested itself in the constitution of an all-party Reform Front group (which was also led by the regions and provinces) which campaigned for a new law on broadcasting. The mobilization of the Reform Front sprang from 'a polemic base of rare strength and breadth, not to mention continuity and determination' (Iseppi 1980: 340).

The second problem for RAI, which was to have extremely damaging consequences for the company in future years, was the gradual partition of the company along political lines. Bernabei, in undertaking the vast expansion and remodernization of RAI, needed to gratify larger and larger numbers of people to maintain his own authority and political requirements. This large number included writers and intellectuals, as well as political appointees from the broad centre-left. By attempting to absorb such a vast plurality of representatives, and buy out potential troublemakers, Bernabei hoped to minimize the criticism aimed at RAI. By and large he was a successful practitioner of this policy, but in the long term, he only succeeded in achieving the opposite, creating a division of RAI into politicized groups which ultimately led to the *lottizzazione* of the company.[6]

The chaos occurring within Italian society was therefore reflected by the internal dissent taking place in RAI. The main aim of the opposition forces, to reform RAI, would only succeed, however, when the time was ripe; that is, when RAI's charter was due to expire in December 1972. When inter-party negotiations did start over the future of RAI they were tortuously slow and RAI's charter was twice extended. In public, the parties had very similar policy objectives. Among the core tenets of agreement were the widespread desire to maintain the monopoly and a wish to strengthen the public service ethic, by allowing wider access among groups and through a more regionalized RAI (Cavazza 1979: 99). But discussions on the future of RAI took place in an increasingly fraught political climate and worsening economic position.[7] The Historical Compromise took four years of continual negotiation before the communists reached agreement with Christian Democrats. Therefore, in negotiations over the reform of RAI, during the early to mid-1970s it was always likely that the socialists and the minor parties were going to gain more than the communists (Cavazza 1979: 106).

6 BROADCASTING AND THE WILD WEST YEARS

- **The economic and political dominance of television in a changing media landscape**

Public service broadcasting in Italy was irrevocably changed by two decisions of the Constitutional Court in 1974 and 1976. In July 1974, the Court was asked (once again) to adjudicate on the legality of RAI's monopoly in response to a case where a foreign television service was broadcasting into Italy, taking valuable advertising revenue from RAI. The Court passed two judgements, Nos 225 and 226. Judgement 225 upheld the legitimacy of the terrestrial monopoly citing Article 43 of the constitution, the public interest article, due to technical scarcity of frequencies. But the Court also launched a broadside against the government. It argued the imperative of a public service monopoly based on objectivity and impartiality. Furthermore, the Court took the unusual step of stating the legal provisions needed to ensure the ideal of a public service. Judgement 226 decided that the monopoly could no longer be justified in respect to cable and foreign-based channels. For the first time, the Court cited Article 21 of the constitution, which states that 'everyone shall have the right to express freely his own thoughts in words, writing or any other medium'. This was a liberal interpretation. With hindsight, therefore, Judgement 226 opened a new historical phase in Italian broadcasting (Ortoleva 1994: 108).[1]

Many of the provisions recommended by the Court in Judgement 225 were included in a new parliamentary bill, which became law in 1975. Responsibility for the overseeing of broadcasting was transferred from the executive to Parliament. These powers included appointing RAI's Administrative Council, therefore allowing parliament a large amount of influence in the running of the company.[2] The Christian Democrats were, however, able to hold onto much of their influence by virtue of being the largest party in Parliament. The remainder of the power fell to the socialists because the Communists had not come to a political accord with the Christian Democrats (Cavazza 1979: 103–5).[3] Therefore, despite the good intentions of the groups demanding reform and the Constitutional Court's broadside, little had actually changed. Instead of the Christian Democrat-centred government deciding broadcasting policy, a Christian Democrat-centred Parliament decided policy.

The 1975 Broadcasting Act formalized the carve-up of RAI by political parties: the system of *lottizzazione*. The Act explicitly states that RAI should be split into two separate network directorates 'responsible for devising and producing radio and television programming' (Esposito and Grassi 1975b: 53). This facilitated the creation of two broad ideological camps: the first network being for a broad Catholic culture and the second for a lay culture. But the undeniably good intentions of the reforms were to last for only a short period, with the result that the broad ideological camps were gradually subjected to political dogma. The partition of the company along party lines ran from the president (Socialist) and the director-general (Christian Democrat) down to the television networks, RAIUNO (Christian Democrat) and RAIDUE (Socialist), the three radio networks (which were given to smaller government parties, the Liberals, Republicans and Social Democrats), and finally to some journalists and administrative staff. Few escaped the political scrutiny. The whole organizational structure of RAI became more geared to a political logic rather than providing a public service. With the system of *lottizzazione*, Italy's premier media institution lost any ideas of political autonomy and impartiality it may have harboured before the reform process began.

Despite these problems, news audiences on the two RAI channels went up with the main Tg1 attracting 17 million (Sorice 2002: 113). But with the separation of the two television networks (this became three when RAITRE started transmission in 1979), and the precise political partition of the whole company, further problems quickly manifested themselves. The first was that each network constructed, in accordance with the 1975 Broadcasting Act, near-identical production and editorial departments and managed its own financial affairs with a large degree of autonomy from the Administrative Council. One effect of having three near-identical networks was that the television-making process was in parts triplicated, and this therefore created unnecessary additional costs (Rizza 1990: 527). The system of allowing network autonomy also led to open internal competition between the three RAI networks; a situation which ultimately led to damaging rifts within the company. This, in turn, led to more time and funds being squandered as RAI embarked on a period of 'navelgazing'. The company was too often preoccupied with internal squabbles rather than sticking to its remit of providing Italy with a comprehensive public service.

More positive measures of the 1975 Broadcasting Act included provisions for greater regional production, which was a key part of wider political and social demands. However, the *lottizzazione* of RAI actually worked against the constitution of a proper autonomous regional network. The two existing networks and political authorities fought a rearguard action against full implementation of the Act's provisions. This was due mainly to a pervasive centralized management culture at RAI and the reluctance of Roman politicians to grant greater devolution. When RAITRE was introduced in 1979, it constituted a marked improvement in RAI's service to the regions but it still provided little more than a regional news service and some minority language programmes. The subsequent cash injection for RAITRE in 1987 was made in order to bolster its national ratings with national programmes, which enjoyed enormous critical acclaim. But RAITRE's provision for regional programmes progressively decreased in the late 1980s and early 1990s (RAI Annual 1993: 40–1). The reforms also helped exacerbate other difficulties, especially the start of colour television services which was delayed until 1977 and was even then very slow to take off. Colour televisions would remain very costly in Italy and only a third of RAI's programmes by 1977 were in colour. Sales of colour televisions would only take off immediately prior to the start of the 1978 World Cup in Argentina (Sorice 2002: 114).

If RAI and the political authorities hoped for a period of relative peace and calm after 1975, they were badly mistaken. In July 1976, the Constitutional Court (Judgement 202) ended RAI's monopoly over local terrestrial broadcasting. The national monopoly was confirmed, however. It was this decision, above all others, that effectively shaped broadcasting development in Italy for the next 20 years. The reason cited by the Court was that technical advances meant that television frequencies were no longer as scarce as they once were and commercial broadcasting could be permitted at a local level. In fact, local television channels in Italy had been growing rapidly in number since the early 1970s. The introduction, by the late 1970s, of hundreds of new and unregulated channels threatened RAI's predominance in every sphere of broadcasting, such as advertising, programming and personnel. Added to this was the lack of a political consensus to regulate the new commercial sector. In the late 1970s and 1980s, apart from a few ad hoc decree laws, the commercial system was allowed to run completely unimpaired by regulations despite over 100 proposals for reform being presented, either in Parliament or by the political parties. Until the passing of the 1990 Broadcasting Act (known as the Mammì Law, after the then minister for post and telecommunications), the Italian system became the 'Wild West' of all broadcasting systems.

The end result of this idiosyncratic system of broadcasting was the emergence by the early 1980s of three quasi-national commercial networks consisting of groups of syndicated channels offering the same programmes. The simultaneous broadcasting of programmes by these channels had been banned by a decision of the Constitutional Court in 1981. At the same time, the Court never banned these commercial channels from broadcasting nationally and they were allowed to continue national broadcasting by using a legal loophole. This was achieved by pre-recording all programmes on video-cassettes and then showing them at slightly staggered times across the country. In this way, and through the use of a legal technicality, commercial channels continued broadcasting. In one respect, however, the commercial sector was disadvantaged in relation to RAI because it was unable to show live programmes.

The lack of regulation allowed one player, by a mixture of entrepreneurial skill and close political ties, to gain a monopoly over the three commercial channels. This man was Silvio Berlusconi, and by 1984 Italy had a television duopoly. RAI controlled three channels and Berlusconi's Fininvest controlled three. The political approval of this duopoly came in the same year, when magistrates in various parts of Italy closed down Berlusconi's channels on the grounds that they broke the broadcasting monopoly. Within three days, the socialist prime minister, Bettino Craxi, a friend of Berlusconi's, introduced an infamous decree reopening the stations. Not surprisingly the decree became known as the 'Berlusconi Decree'. The decree was an overtly political decision and remains one of very few decrees named after the beneficiary, not the subject in hand or the politician responsible for drafting it, as is the usual custom (Menduni 1993: 437).

The programming strategy of the commercial channels did, however, have some positive hallmarks. In the words of one commentator: 'the early years of commercial broadcasting ... rejuvenated the entire broadcasting system' (Sartori 1993: 280). The commencement of commercial television and radio services during times not traditionally covered by RAI (such as the afternoons and late evenings) allowed greater access for groups such as pensioners and housewives, who were not traditionally catered for during the monopoly years, and increased regional and local output. This shift in programme content and styles was defined by Umberto Eco as marking the transition from an old (*paleo*) to a new (*neo*) television system (Eco 1990).

On the whole, however, Fininvest and other commercial operators offered an unapologetic diet of quiz shows, talk shows, television movies, cartoons, tele-novelas and soap operas, bought in an ever-increasing abundance on the international market (European Task Force 1988: 26–7). The constant flow of such programmes was sustained on the twin premise that they were cheap and also because they were popular. The popularity question was obviously important to maximize advertising revenue. In order to monitor audience figures, Auditel, the audience research agency, owned by a consortium made up of RAI and Berlusconi's Fininvest, was set up in 1984. The increasing importance of audience ratings changed the whole relationship between the broadcaster and the public. Broadcasting in Italy was fine-tuned to the wishes and desires of advertisers as never before. Advocates for the new system hailed the new era of the 'sovereign consumer', while detractors decried the arrival of television '*alla spazzatura*': trash television.

Key new programmes at this time included the Sunday afternoon, *Domenica In*, which was six-hours long and split into discrete parts, including interviews, music, quiz shows and sport, all held together by leading presenters such as Corrado or Pippo Baudo. Renzo Arbore's *L'Altra Domenica* encouraged more public participation. Both these RAI-produced programmes sought to be more popular by breaking with programme traditions. New talk shows were also introduced, presented by the likes of Gianfranco Funari and Maurizio Costanzo (Sorice 2002: 123). Both these presenters would eventually leave RAI for commercial television.

The emergence of a new and vibrant commercial broadcasting industry was not restricted to Italy alone. In many Western European countries, including Italy, public service broadcasting continued to be given some degree of shelter from direct competition (primarily via the continuation of the licence fee). But unlike many other public service broadcasters, RAI took a conscious decision to fight its commercial competitor on its (the commercial operator's) own terrain. There were two principal reasons for this: firstly, commercial operators, unhindered by comprehensive regulations, targeted RAI's core audience with popular and cheaper television programmes; secondly, RAI was too divided to coordinate an effective strategic response. Therefore a ratings battle started, inflating programme costs and leading to the mass-importation of fictional programmes and a sharp reduction of home-made drama. The result was that broadcasting policy became geared to audience figures, causing the loss of a comprehensive television service. There was a decisive and discernible shift from viewing the public as citizen to the audience as consumer. RAI took a clear step downmarket in order to match its commercial competitor. No other European public service broadcaster, with the possible exception of the Spanish RTVE, had ever been forced to break so clearly with its old programming formats (Achille and Miège 1994: 34).[4]

The economic and political dominance of television in a changing media landscape

In 1990, RAI and Fininvest together controlled some 90 per cent of the total television market and about 87 per cent of television advertising revenue (Gambaro and Silva 1992: 147). In 1980, RAI (television only) received 148 billion lira (£59 million) in advertising revenue. The entire national commercial sector (before the formation of Fininvest empire) received 77 billion lira (£31 million). Total advertising revenue for television in 1980 was 333 billion lira (£133 million). By 1992, RAI reaped 1,379 billion lira (£552 million) and the commercial sector 3,358 billion lira (£1.343 billion). RAI's total funding by 1992 consisted of 31 per cent through advertising and 50 per cent through the licence fee (RAI Annual 1993–2006: 155). The 1980s saw, therefore, an explosion of advertising revenues for the industry as a whole.

Such figures should, of course, be placed in some form of context. Not all sectors did as well as the television sector. For example, one reason for the high income for broadcasting was the comparative weakness of the newspaper industry in Italy. There had been a lack of government investment in the industry compared to that of television, despite each of the major parties controlling their own newspaper titles. Historically, the regional character of the industry meant that Italy had been slow to develop national titles, hindering the development of a mass readership, and allowing broadcasting to reap national advertising revenues. Italy, therefore, had a situation unlike much of Western Europe, with Italian broadcasting taking a bigger share of advertising revenue than newspapers (Balassone and Guglielmi 1993: 12). The total amount of advertising invested in newspapers and magazines as a percentage of overall investment in the Italian media slowly declined from 1980 through to 1992, from 57.6 per cent to 40.4 per cent. It should be noted that although the press continued to attract a smaller percentage of total revenue, it still enjoyed the fruits of wider expansion in advertising investment in the 1980s, expanding from 717 billion lira (£287 million) in 1980 to 3,896 billion lira (£1.559 billion) in 1992 (RAI Annual 1993–2006: 156–7).

Furthermore, the statistics show that after 1982, Fininvest was able to take a larger proportion of advertising revenue despite enjoying lower audience ratings than RAI. The main reason for this is because RAI operated with an advertising 'ceiling', designed to protect the newspaper industry, which limited the time allowed for advertising and, therefore, income derived (Menduni 1993: 431). To illustrate this point, in 1991 RAI enjoyed a 10 per cent audience advantage over Fininvest during the prime-time slot (8 p.m.–10.30 p.m.). Gambaro and Silva calculate that without the financial ceiling, RAI could have expected to enjoy a 5–7 per cent advantage in total advertising income over its main competitor for this prime-time period. Instead, in the early 1990s, RAI received 29–30 per cent of prime-time advertising revenue. The figure for Fininvest was 57–8 per cent, almost double (Gambaro and Silva 1992: 155).

With the domination of RAI and Fininvest, potential competitors found themselves caught in a vicious circle. Many operators lacked the technical means, especially the lack of Hertzian frequencies, to attract a sufficient national audience, which led to problems in attracting advertising revenues. Without advertising revenue, private operators could not invest in production facilities or buy programmes. Often, those channels that could buy programmes never had nationwide frequencies to attract sufficient advertising. Some national channels therefore provided niche markets not covered by the main two players, typically thematic channels, such as music or shopping. Other private operators became dependent upon the support of RAI and Fininvest through their respective advertising subsidiaries, who provided the know-how to market and sell advertising space. RAI and Fininvest consequently held enormous power over those private operators because those operators lost any effective control over their own programming schedules (Gambaro and Silva 1992: 155). The end result was a consolidated RAI and Fininvest duopoly.

The major advantage in terms of income for RAI and Fininvest was the sheer quantity of channels, therefore allowing a mazimization of total television hours. However, the sheer size of the duopoly was also its major weakness. While income was maximized, making the Italian system comparatively rich, the resources available *per hour of television* were relatively low. In this respect, Italy came bottom of the table in comparison with other Western European countries and the USA (Balassone and Guglielmi 1993: 25–6). The sums of money given over to fund programmes were relatively small, creating a greater dependence on cheaper genres of programming, such as imported programmes from America, Latin American countries and Japan. For Fininvest, such provision was allowed because of the lack of statutory rules regarding programme content. From the very beginning it sought to provide popular, inexpensive programming, boosting audiences and maximizing advertising revenues. A report by the European Task Force in 1988 calculated that 75 per cent of Fininvest schedules were made up of films, variety shows and quiz shows. It is also not surprising therefore that Fininvest captured 60 per cent of advertising revenue between 1980 and 1988 (European Task Force 1988: 28–9).

RAI could not simply follow the example of Fininvest because of the obligations to provide a diversity of programming output, under the aegis of its public service commitments. For example, Fininvest was not under any obligation until 1991 to provide a news service, stemming from the fact that Fininvest was banned from providing any simultaneous or live national broadcasts in the pre-1990 period (see the decision of the Constitutional Court 1981). Fininvest did not have to provide regional services or educational and cultural provisions either, but these were expensive investments that RAI was obliged to make. RAI was therefore caught in a hopeless situation: either to maintain its recognized service with the risk of becoming increasingly less popular with audiences and advertisers; or to follow Fininvest's strategy. RAI's strategic planning veered towards the latter option and so began a number of fierce battles to acquire the genres of programming deemed to make the system commercially viable: that is, cheap and popular material. Consequently, domestic drama production for the two RAI networks dropped between 1975 and 1985 by 50 per cent and 77 per cent respectively (European Task Force 1988: 78). RAI embarked on an increased importation of fictional programming (soap operas, tele-novelas and serials), intensifying the battle between the two main competitors and resulting in a bidding war. Italy became a major market for television and film producers worldwide as a result – with the two major broadcasting players giving no quarter in a war of attrition, prices were artificially inflated.

There was also a strong revival in the Italian media-star system (Gundle 1996). RAI found itself waging a battle to keep its main presenters from taking lucrative offers from Fininvest. Provision of entertainment-based programming fronted by long-established personalities was a major strategic ploy for Fininvest. Mike Bongiorno was the first of many household names to leave RAI for Fininvest. RAI's hand was forced therefore, and it came under intense pressure to keep other stars from literally 'going over to the enemy'. The contracts for such presenters also increased, adding to overall costs. With such inducements, however, some leading personalities who crossed over to Fininvest later rejoined RAI. Likewise, the 1980s and 1990s saw the rise of *soubrettes*, partially-clothed young women who would take part in many quiz and variety shows assisting (male) presenters. Although very popular, many criticized the overtly sexist trends in Italian broadcasting under the duopoly system.

The system grew due to an explosive mixture of a new and dynamic political and economic climate coupled with sheer opportunism on the part of the private sector. The system, to quote one source, was 'expansion as the result of a Czarist-style military campaign' (Balassone and Guglielmi 1993: 26). Instead of adopting some form of deregulation, as in other European countries, or re-regulation, Italy found itself operating two parallel systems: a regulated public service and an unregulated commercial sector (Ortoleva 1994: 88). Both systems relied heavily on political patronage for their survival, but at the cost to RAI of its independence. It is the inability of a regulated public service to function properly in the face of an unregulated commercial sector that helps explain why RAI went downmarket in the 1980s.

But to characterize the Italian broadcasting system during these years, as many have done, as the 'Wild West' of world broadcasting would be somewhat misleading. To start with, the system was never completely lawless, and the term equates too closely to the purest form of laissez-faire development. Political decisions may have been running behind the speed of events, *but they were made*. To say the system was completely ungovernable is wrong. The duopoly was a classic result of trasformism, an old method of linking political decisions to a consensus of social and economic elites stretching back to the dawn of Italy. Governing elites were intimately linked at every stage of development in the Italian system, both in RAI and the private sector. The fact that over 100 legislative proposals were formulated by political and social groups from 1976 until a law was finally passed in 1990 should not be accepted as evidence that politicians were properly able to regulate the system. Certainly a consensus was unattainable, at least as far as a comprehensive legislative package was concerned, and instead the system was governed by *leggine* – small, piecemeal laws, which could command sufficient consensus. This constitutes a key example of how the Italian political system of bargained pluralism shaped broadcasting policy but not, it should be added, with any notable success.

The rapid growth of the duopoly in the late 1980s caused one commentator to declare that RAI and Fininvest had created, whether intentionally or not, a form of codependence (Giacalone 1992: 23–5). It is argued that Fininvest needed RAI to justify having three channels. In other words, if you take one channel from Fininvest you must also take one from RAI. RAI, so the argument goes, could justify, in return, its expansion and shift to popular programming in terms of pointing to Fininvest and claiming it was acting in self-defence. But the idea of codependence, although partly valid, was also misleading. RAI was of inestimable value to Fininvest in two ways: firstly, Fininvest was allowed to expand and control three channels, simply because RAI controlled three channels; and secondly, Fininvest was able to exploit the unpopularity of RAI's monopoly within Italy. But in return, commercial television gave RAI relatively little. Yes, commercial broadcasting did create extra services during the day and the night, and yes, it was forced to adopt a less 'paternalistic' outlook. But a stronger, predatory commercial opponent, unfettered by law, was always likely to make the running, with the sluggish public competitor struggling desperately to keep afloat. It is no coincidence that between 1985 and 1989 the ratio of RAI's assets to its total debt provision fell from 37.3 per cent to 7 per cent (Gambaro and Silva 1992: 88). In short, Fininvest made its profits, but RAI sacrificed much of its public service and became heavily indebted.

The political problems besetting RAI also had their origins in the confused and overlapping responsibilities regarding the control and management of RAI, and in the heterogeneous nature of the internal organization in the post-1976 period. The main culprits were the political parties, who sought control not only over RAI, but also over day-to-day management and operational decisions. Often, therefore, narrow party, or even factional, needs took precedence over the broader interests of the company, subverting the democratic intentions of the 1975 Broadcasting Act which passed supervisory control over RAI from governmental control to parliamentary control, and left in place a system widely criticized even by the parties themselves.

The main example of RAI's subjugation to the needs of the governing parties came about in the development of the system of *lottizzazione*. The full story of the process of *lottizzazione* is long, complicated, and involves questions of internal organization, which extend beyond RAI to any major organization. Under the terms of the 1975 Broadcasting Act (Law 103), overall responsibility for directing and overseeing RAI was given to a parliamentary commission with extensive powers, which included: 1) an annual decision fixing the level of RAI's licence fee and total advertising revenue; 2) appointment of the members of the Administrative Council, which had day-to-day control of the company; 3) providing the overall aims and objectives upon which the public service should be premised; and, 4) outlining the principles by which the company should be structured and organized.

These powers therefore allowed Parliament via the commission certain controls that bore directly upon the operations of the company, giving rise to an overlapping of responsibilities. The net result was that in the following years the distinction between the powers of the two bodies became increasingly vague, with the principal problem being the difficulties in defining the differences between responsibility for directing policy matters and responsibility for operational, day-to-day decisions within the company. The commission and the board of directors at RAI were both responsible for policy decisions. This brought about a need for both parties to discuss and to cross-refer decisions, making the decision-making process slow and confused.

The problem of operational responsibilities was slightly different, but equally complex. The reforms reduced the powers of the director-general, which had expanded as a direct consequence of the Bernabei years. The consensus was that the office of director-general had become something akin to the dictatorship of national cultural output. Law 103 attempted to spread the load of responsibility over operations and management from the director-general to the whole Administrative Council. Added to this power-sharing agreement was, of course, the involvement of the Parliamentary commission. What were the exact powers taken away from the director-general? This has been the source of some conjecture and disagreement, with different commentators unable to decide who precisely had the final say, the director-general or the Administrative Council. What is clear, however, is that the overlapping of responsibilities was one reason for the mini-reform of RAI in 1985, which reinstated the powers of the director-general to assume clear operational responsibility for the company, over and above that of the Council or commission. It also allowed the Christian Democrats, by virtue of their control over the office of director general, to reassert their grip over the company. For De Vescovi, it was at this point that the 1975 Broadcasting Act was fully betrayed (1986: 45).

The positions of the Administrative Council and the director-general were the highest level at which the system of *lottizzazione* operated, and date from a decision made by the governing parties at the time of the reforms in 1975. The president of the Administrative Council was an appointee of the socialists, and the director-general was an appointee of the Christian Democrats. The whole Administrative Council was compromised by its political associations. Political influence also filtered down through the organization because the appointment of all deputy directors-general, directors of news programmes and other senior management was decided at board level. This therefore facilitated the carve-up of the networks into strict political spheres and produced a system where journalists sometimes had little choice but to classify their political allegiances in order to find work. The whole bureaucratic apparatus was subjected to the requirements of the parties. So when, for example, the communists were brought fully into the political mainstream in the aftermath of the formation of the national government in 1976, senior positions were made available within the company for the Party. The process of absorbing different functions under party control became the norm.

The system of *lottizzazione* existed at an institutional or macro-structural level, but it also operated at a more personal or micro level, especially in the politically sensitive area of news and current affairs. One good example was the system of '*Editore di Riferimento*' (Ortoleva 1994: 89–90): the special relationship between individual journalists or senior management and particular politicians. The historical precedents for this type of relationship do exist, the most famous being the agreement between Bernabei and Fanfani. The greatest exponent of this system, and the person to whom it owes its name, was Bruno Vespa, director of Tg1 (RAIUNO news) between 1989 and 1992. Vespa was appointed in the aftermath of the wider political upheaval in 1989 which saw the political agreement reached between the socialists and the centre-right factions of the Christian Democrats. The new alliance became known as the 'CAF', which stands for the initials of the three architects of the deal, the socialist Craxi, and two Christian Democrats, Andreotti and Forlani. Within RAI, the director-general, Biagio Agnes, was replaced by Gianni Pasquarelli, who was deemed more sympathetic to the new political leaders. Bruno

Vespa was promoted to the directorship of the main television news as part of the wider political deal and remains today RAI's leading political journalist and presenter of the popular current affairs programme *Porta a Porta*. During his period as director, Vespa never made any particular secret of the fact that he had an '*Editore di Riferimento*', namely the new secretary of the Christian Democrats, Arnaldo Forlani. In October 1992, the journalists and staff under Vespa passed a vote of no confidence in him, citing as a reason his continual interference in editorial policy and his preference for always having the Party's spokespersons interviewed.

Bruno Vespa was, however, neither the first nor last director to have a vote of no confidence passed against him. RAI had always had a close identification with ruling elites, news content had always been a coveted area of political protection, senior appointments may have always been made according to the relative strength of each Christian Democrat faction, and other political groups may have been accommodated into the system, but the difference now was that the company was formally split as a bureaucracy according to political allegiances. The system of *lottizzazione* therefore was not only the political occupation per se of RAI; it was, instead, the precise bureaucratization of the company based on political allegiance (Ortoleva 1994: 92). Questions of internal organization – the division of complex tasks to senior and junior management, the precise nature of the functions and structure of various departments – often required the involvement of the politicians or party functionaries. Organized groups within RAI, such as senior management and trade union representatives, required the help of the different parties to find solutions to the everyday questions affecting a major organization, and which were normally outside the remit of overt political interference, as Peppino Ortoleva (1994: 92) argues:

> The fact that all production and managerial responsibilities were subdivided, especially after 1975, on the basis of political affiliation did not derive exclusively, as is often thought, from the wishes of the political parties to occupy key positions in the television system; it also derived from the needs of the company to regulate the management structure and the division of tasks amongst middle and senior ranking management that, in an organisation as large and complex as RAI, threaten the everyday functioning of the company.

The idea of RAI as a company politically bureaucratized should not conceal another aspect to the concept of *lottizzazione*: that the policy was a one-sided relationship or a relationship of master and servants. The flip-side of the process of political occupation was a creeping awareness that political involvement brought with it certain liabilities. The disadvantage of adopting the explicit policy of interference was that the political parties were held accountable and responsible for RAI and its networks to a far greater extent than if these companies had maintained a large degree of autonomy (as foreseen in law). It is true that unlike the state bureaucracy, organizations like RAI could exploit these political links in order to promote corporate aims and policies, and this is what happened.

The first effect of this was that the political parties found themselves open to the demands, however capricious, of RAI's companies. In other words, the parties were being lobbied by the para-state they sought to control. Often, such lobbying involved requests for some form of mediation in connection with bureaucratic functions. But mediation also extended to providing financial assistance when required. During the late 1980s especially, RAI as a whole would regularly depend on extra financial handouts from the politicians as a result of exceeding budgetary limits. The system of *lottizzazione* did not only involve the process of 'political partition', but also the process of 'political obligation': this denotes the active involvement of political parties in order to resolve the day-to-day problems of keeping a large organization functioning properly (Ortoleva 1994: 92).

It is in this context that the relationship between the three RAI networks (RAIUNO, RAIDUE and RAITRE) developed in the post-1975 period. The provisions under the 1975 reforms for the emergence of separate television and radio networks and news services, and the formation of separate identities, allowed a greater degree of internal and external pluralism in the broadcasting system which, at that time, was still operating under a strict monopoly. The formation of different networks within one company would allow wider access to political and social groups that had campaigned for greater representation in state broadcasting in the late 1960s and early 1970s. The new system did have certain advantages. Firstly, the division into networks introduced a new competitive edge into RAI. The increased access and differentiation of the programming resulted in an upturn in audience figures. To counter the creation of RAIUNO and RAIDUE, the reforms made provisions that stated that the networks, while enjoying a large degree of autonomy, would also remain coordinated with respect to scheduling and production facilities.

A degree of coordination was provided mainly through the auspices of the office of the vice-director-general, which received the programme schedules from RAIUNO and RAIDUE. There was, however, a major flaw in the operations of this department. As Nora Rizza (1989: 26) argues, 'The moment that budgetary controls were given to the networks, each one automatically devised its own schedules'. The effect of this lack of strategic cohesion between the networks became increasingly detrimental to the overall operations. In addition to its own internal bureaucracy – which controlled a whole range of strategic and policy issues – each network enjoyed the powerful backing of national politicians. As a result, each began operating to suit its own needs and the two networks became increasingly estranged from each other. In turn, this estrangement did RAI incalculable damage. Faced with an increasingly bullish private sector (which subsequently became monopolized by Fininvest in the post-1984 period), RAI was too preoccupied fighting internal battles.

In addition to the political and organizational shortcomings of the 1975 reforms, there was also a failure to bring about a decentralized media system. Many reformers argued that decentralization would further strengthen participation of the regions in the decision-making and production processes, as well as generating a greater degree of access for social groups to the media. And yet, the planned decentralization of RAI never materialized in the ways hoped. From 1979 until 1987 RAITRE had only a very marginal impact upon the wider television system, broadcasting regional news and also cultural and educational programmes. In 1987, the restructuring of the third network completely reinvigorated not only the network, but also the whole Italian broadcasting system (Gundle 1996: 213). Its effect was something akin to the impact of Channel 4 in Britain. An injection of cash and new innovative programming formulae brought the viewing figures for the third channel up from 3.6 per cent in 1987 to 8.4 per cent in 1989 (Monteleone 1992: 475).

The inability to construct a regionally-based television network in Italy also stems from the lack of strong commercial television operators at a local or regional level. The decision of the Constitutional Court in 1976 to end RAI's local broadcasting monopoly held out the promise of providing a regional service RAI had failed to deliver. The post-1976 period did indeed see a huge expansion in the local television and radio market. The evident enthusiasm displayed by hundreds of operators to set up local radio and television channels should not conceal the reality, however, that Italy had (and still has) a very weak and uncoordinated local commercial broadcasting system (Barca 2007). The licensing of commercial frequencies in the late 1970s, by the Ministry of Post and Telecommunications, on a non-discriminatory basis of *farsi spazio da se* (first come, first served) simply created too many operators. The low-quality signals covered too small an area to attract sufficient advertising and commercial viability. The result was an uncoordinated and inefficient system spawning an active secondary market. Operators were encouraged to lease or sell their frequencies to advertising agencies that in turn created quasi-national channels to encourage and attract advertisers. The most successful exponent of this policy was Berlusconi. With the aid of his advertising company, Publitalia, his organization was able to acquire long-term leases at low cost. The next move was the emergence of a brand name for the leased frequencies, and the introduction of near simultaneous broadcasts throughout large parts of the country. This allowed operators to maximize national and local advertising revenues. The first such channel of this type was Canale 5, owned by Fininvest, and a national commercial system was born instead of the local system as envisaged by the Constitutional Court (Gambaro and Silva 1992: 78, 148).

One reason for the continuance and maintenance of a centralized Italian state rather than a federalized structure has been the perception that it helped to knit together disparate regions, each with its own cultural and social customs, economic disparities and linguistic differences. In broadcasting also, a regionally organized RAI would be the antithesis of what its traditional role in the postwar period had been: to encourage and promote cohesion in a united Italy. The formal centralized nature of political rule has always been at odds with the disparate economic and social make-up of the real Italy. So although fine speeches were made by politicians in the postwar period to achieve greater regional involvement in all areas of life, the task of carrying out this instruction has always been given to political agents whose natural instinct has been one of distrust for the regions. The 1948 constitution, for example, contained a specific pledge to a system of regional government. Such a system was only fully set up in 1970. The problem of regionalizing the broadcasting system was part of a far wider difficulty. Asking Rome, therefore, to devolve its powers to regional production centres would need a strong political will to follow through the plans to full fruition.

There was also one more factor that militated against the development of a regional media system in Italy: there was little historical precedent of decentralized media development. The historical organization of media in Italy has been more of a polycentric rather than decentralized nature in the three areas of production, content and networks (distribution). The media system since the 1960s has seen a progressive move away from a polycentric system to a more polarized one, whereby today the vast majority of media companies and organizations in Italy are based in two cities: Milan in the North and Rome (Centre-South).

The polycentric system was characterized by the predominance of particular media in different Italian cities and regions and by an implicit division of labour between the primary localities of the peninsula: a system that, probably, contributed significantly towards the cultural unity of the country (Ortoleva 1995: 222). This process can be highlighted by giving the following examples: the historical link between the telephone (STET) and electricity (SIP) networks, the radio company (the pre-war EIAR, and, from 1945, RAI) and Turin; the enduring importance of Naples in representing a national popular culture; Roman dominance over the film industry from the 1930s, best highlighted by the opening of Cinecittà in 1937; and, finally, the concentration of the publishing industry in Milan. The first cracks in the polycentric system came in the late 1950s. The increasing dominance of national media in the postwar period, partially as a direct result of the policy of the day to unify cultural output, created tensions in the way these media were organized.

One such example is television, where the battle between executives based in Turin (the traditional base of RAI) and Rome raged on during the 1950s and early 1960s, until Bernabei centralized RAI's operations in the capital. Even media traditionally controlled in the regions were affected by centralizing pressures. As already discussed, the newspaper industry remained (and in many cases still remains), until the 1970s, regionally based. With the inception of new production and distribution technologies (exemplified by the birth of *La Repubblica* in 1976), some newspapers built a small but notable 'national' audience (even though that particular newspaper has regional supplements in major cities including Milan, Turin, Florence, Bologna, Rome and Naples). One response of successive governments in the 1970s, as a direct result of this process, was to look for ways to increase access to and use of the media for minority groups, whether social, cultural or regional.

Ortoleva (1996: 186) argues that the spatial organization of media production, content and networks in Italy has played an important and successful role in promoting shared discourses, especially as the country was relatively late to unite and, as we have seen, was forged by a political and cultural elite. In his words:

> The importance of the media in the definition of national identity lies not simply in their *content*, in how they perpetuate or modify representations and stereotypes, 'mental maps', and shared values, but also, and perhaps above all, in their *structure*.

Ortoleva argues that in the past 30 years, primarily due to the overwhelming dominance of public and commercial televison, the centralization of the media in to two cities, Rome and Milan, has created a number of tensions affecting national identity. The process of centralization has firstly provoked a backlash of localism: small towns and cities have revived or reasserted local forms of expression and culture. Secondly, the relationship between Rome and Milan has changed from one where each had distinct but separate roles in Italy's media ecology, to a situation where the two cities are now preeminent and all powerful, but where they also compete directly for economic and political patronage, losing in the process their distinctive roles (Ortoleva 1996: 196). It is no coincidence that the development of a bipolar media system has coincided with the upsurge in local and regional political parties demanding greater autonomy or, in some cases, independence.

By April 1993, the political eruptions in Italy had overtaken all other events. The referendum on 18 April to amend the electoral laws was widely seen as marking the definitive end of the First Republic (Braun 1995: 11). By then, leading politicians had already been tainted or discredited by the political corruption scandals. Also, the governing parties had seen their vote collapse after defeat in the 1992 elections, defined as 'the Waterloo of the First Republic' (Braun 1995: 13). A bandwagon for reform started to roll and within six months the new government under the former governor of the Bank of Italy had initiated the reform process.

7 THE SECOND ITALIAN REPUBLIC: CINEMA AND THE PRESS SINCE 1992

- **The Italian film industry: from decline to *Life is Beautiful***
- **The newspaper industry and the rise of the internet**

The collapse of the old political regime and the resulting winds of change blowing across the Italian peninsula from 1992 were both unforeseen and dramatic. The downfall of the Christian Democrats in Italy after almost 45 years of continuous political leadership made it the first European government Party to resign, dissolve completely and then reform under a new name. In the post-1989 period, this was a practice associated with fallen Communist regimes, but not Western European governments. There was no one cause for the collapse of the Christian Democrats and their allies. Instead, there were a number of interlocking reasons: some are more historical in nature and include the continued absence of a viable or alternative opposition which could take over political control. This was also a major problem in previous Italian regimes whereby opposition was continually absorbed into the governing elite (transformism or *trasformismo*). Yet, this alone does not explain the nature or timing of the crisis. Nor was the crisis inevitable in the way some commentators argue (Ginsborg 1996: 19–20). A complex set of events took place which, together offer a somewhat subtler explanation.

The end of the Cold War was a direct causal factor in the downfall of the five government parties in Italy. The Christian Democrats, buoyed up by the defeat of their great enemy (the Italian Communists having changed the name of the Party months before the collapse of the system in the Eastern bloc), continued to rule the five-party coalition. But under the surface the problems suppressed for so long began to grow, including a deepening of resentment felt in the North against the central government in Rome. For example, taxes raised from the industrially rich North paid for projects in the poorer South or for state-controlled industries dominated from Rome. By the late 1980s, federalist and separatist parties had sprung up, demanding economic independence from Roman interference. Oft-repeated claims included allegations that taxes were being squandered by the Christian Democrats for their own political reasons and that money was being paid into Mafia-controlled regions in the South. People were no longer constrained to vote Christian Democrat purely to keep the Communists out of power, especially in the North, and were better able to protest against the Roman political hegemony. In short, the electorate responded with a new-found freedom.

Even politicians and other leading state officials openly expressed contempt for a democratic system in urgent need of reform. Firstly, there was the system of PR used in Italy which constantly resulted in weak and fractious governments and was responsible for much of the political clientelism. In an attempt to change this system, a leading Christian Democrat politician, Mario Segni, set up a referendum campaign to abolish the multiple-choice preference vote. Segni, who had fallen out with many fellow Christian Democrats and also with the Socialists, led a lone battle against the established parties and much of the mass media. It was therefore a triumph for Segni, when in a referendum held in June 1991, Italians voted to change the system. This was the first sign of public discontent and the start of a series of events which would eventually bring down many of the country's ruling elite.

The vote in June 1991 was, of course, a sign of wider displeasure. It did not only represent discontent about the mechanics of the electoral system, but discontent with the workings of the state in general. The state institutions had become hardly more than a series of fiefdoms governed by political appointees. In many sectors, jobs were only given to those holding the party card with the result that state power was essentially dispersed to the parties and the state enjoyed little effective autonomy or independence. It became a despoiler of citizenship instead of promoting it. The bestowal of state patronage created wider disparities in the quality and level of state services throughout the country. Also, such disparities extended beyond state services to include the question of state income. Politically orchestrated tax avoidance was seen by many as another example of a corrupt state. For many Italians, left with a highly complicated and unequal tax system, an expensive but ineffective state healthcare system, unfinished public projects and crumbling buildings, confidence in the whole political process was seriously eroded.

Yet, there were other reasons for the discontent, including a deepening economic crisis. Italy's economic performance in the period after the oil crisis of the mid-1970s had been good. Performance indicators show that throughout the 1980s the Italian economy continued to grow at a healthy rate. For example, between 1979 and 1990, gross domestic product (GDP) rose by 50 per cent, well above the average for the rest of the European Community (EC) (Ginsborg 1996: 21). But there were negative consequences of the economic boom. To begin with, much of it had been financed by loans, resulting in an explosion of public debt. The main culprit here was the Italian government. In the 1980s, public debt rose as the government produced a budget deficit year on year. This situation may not have become so serious, however, if it had not been for international pressure. The negotiations leading to the Maastricht Treaty in 1992 outlined the framework for European monetary union, including stringent convergence criteria for aspiring entrants. The two economic requirements of the Treaty for monetary union were that public debt should be no more than 60 per cent of GDP, and that the budget deficit should be no more than 3 per cent of GDP. If we consider the position of Italy in 1992 when the Treaty was signed, her precarious economic plight can be understood: public debt stood at 103 per cent of GDP, and the budget deficit stood at 9.9 per cent. In addition, the inflation rate was at 6.9 per cent, well above other leading EC members (Ginsborg 1996: 22). The result was increasing international pressure on the government to rectify the errors of the late 1970s and 1980s in allowing public debt to spiral. This pressure resulted in the start of a prolonged crisis of confidence which culminated in Italy's withdrawal from the exchange rate mechanism (ERM) in September 1992.

The period of greatest political turmoil came between 1992 and 1993. The first trigger point was the news of the investigations conducted from Milan into political corruption and from Palermo into links between the Mafia and the political establishment. Both investigations heavily implicated the Christian Democrats and their allies. The elections that followed shortly afterwards in April 1992 signalled the beginning of the end for the five-party government coalition. Deprived of their overall majority, a period of political instability followed. Within a year of the vote, Craxi, Forlani and Andreotti would all become victims of the corruption and Mafia investigations. May 1992 saw a rise in civil discontent sparked by a Mafia atrocity, but symptomatic of wider concerns. On this occasion, the protest was part of a wider Italian and international outcry at the savage murder of Judge Giovanni Falcone as he travelled into Palermo from the airport. A little over a month later, another anti-Mafia judge, Paolo Borsellino, was blown up in the centre of Palermo. A palpable sense of shock and grief led to a wave of civic protest, especially in the South and the atrocities spurred on the wider Mafia and corruption investigations. When the Amato government tried to curtail the corruption investigation, public opinion remained hostile to any form of amnesty for corrupt officials. The fall of the Amato government brought to power a government consisting of 'technocrats', under the leadership of the governor of the Bank of Italy, Carlo Azeglio Ciampi. The Ciampi government marked the end of 45 years of continued Christian Democrat dominance and the task of this new government mirrored that of other 'crisis management' governments in Italian history. It aimed to introduce new institutional reforms that would help restore public confidence in the political process, and to decide the best set of economic and social policies to repair the damaged fabric of Italian society. As in the postwar period, the role of the media would assume particular responsibilities in achieving these aims.

The Italian film industry: from decline to *Life is Beautiful*

The general state of many Italian media companies in 1993 was poor. Television and radio companies were in crisis. RAI was threatened with bankruptcy and Berlusconi's Fininvest was saddled with debts. Newspaper sales in Italy peaked in 1992 and began to fall away thereafter. And things were no better for the Italian film industry. From selling 500 million tickets a year in the mid-1960s, cinema attendance had declined to 100 million by the mid-1990s. Several thousand cinemas had closed in the intervening 30 years and indigenous film production was down to an average of 100 films per year, still high when compared to many European countries but low by historical postwar levels. The television and video industries were providing very tough competition for Italian cinema, showing up to 100 films per week, and Italian film distributors and exhibitors often favoured deals with American studios meaning that those Italian films that were made did not always get a distribution deal (Sorlin 1996: 147).

Gian Piero Brunetta (1995b: 425–31) puts forward the following reasons which help explain the decline in Italian cinema in the 1980s and 1990s. The first point is that Italian films were no longer being exhibited as they once were on the international cinema circuit. This applied to commercial cinema houses and international film festivals. The reason for this, Brunetta argues, was that international audiences no longer identified with Italian films in sufficient numbers post-De Sica, Fellini, Visconti, etc. Part of the blame also lay closer to home in that the Italian authorities were not promoting modern Italian cinema sufficiently enough abroad. This deficiently was in part rectified by the formation in 1998 of Italia Cinema, an organization with the explicit remit to coordinate with key cinematic institutions in Italy – ANICA, Cinecittà, etc. – to promote Italian films abroad. The international marketplace is key, Brunetta argues, because Italian cinema has traditionally been well supported internationally and this support has often fed back in to the Italian collective conscious and, crucially, provided support for Italian producers with home audiences. In short, foreign markets have demonstrated a passion for postwar Italian cinema that cannot be underestimated.

In a similar vein, Brunetta also argues that the rise of the multiplex cinema in the past two decades has also hurt the Italian film industry. While the development of multiplexes has led to a rise in the total number of cinemas, these cinemas have either been developed by the big American exhibitors, for example Warner Village, or are tied to American distribution deals. The argument here is that smaller Italian cinemas, which have traditionally been more likely to show home-grown films, have been forced to close down.

Brunetta's third explanation is that audiences have turned to other media to watch films and dramas. To back up his arguments here, he points out that Italian television companies RAI and Mediaset doubled their output of Italian-made TV drama between 1998 and 2001, rising from 357 to 750 hours (see Buonanno 2006 for the most recent discussion on the revival of Italian drama). While television has been a clear causal factor in the decline of cinema attendances in Italy – more and more people watch films on their televisions or watch videos/DVDs – linking this argument to home-grown TV drama has its flaws. For example, the argument ignores RAI's strong tradition for television drama in the 1960s and 1970s, a time when cinema-going was still relatively buoyant. Also, and as we saw in the last chapter, the decline in cinema audiences in the 1980s and 1990s actually coincided with the near collapse of Italian-made TV drama in favour of cheaper foreign (US) imports (Richeri 1990: 262–5). Although RAI attempted to boost domestic TV fiction and film production in the late 1980s by placing fiction on an industrial footing (via better training of scriptwriters, directors, producers, etc.), and encouraging greater sales potential to America and European countries, these initiatives met with very limited success. Some high quality drama and films came from such initiatives, such as *Cinema Paradiso* and *Il Postino*, and television dramas such as *La Piovra*, all of which won high critical acclaim in Italy and abroad. But the quantity of film and fiction production remained very low. The problem was, as Giuseppe Richeri argued, that: 'Instead of reducing the pressure on typically commercial programmes, and dedicating itself more to its institutional functions, the RAI continues to be convinced that its main sphere of activity is one that puts it in direct competition with the private sector' (1990: 265). In a later work, Richeri would conclude that: 'RAI is therefore making less fiction than previously and less than what is necessary' (1993: 8). There is little doubt however that the increase in TV-made drama in recent years has led to Italian filmmakers migrating to television to get their projects made. Noted filmmakers such as the Taviani brothers have done television projects in recent years and, in the case of Giordana's *La meglio gioventù*, enjoyed a limited and successful cinematic release after being entered for the Cannes Film Festival.

The next point made by Brunetta relates to the historical legacy of postwar Italian cinema. Neorealism's legacy to Italian film was massive and influenced a successive generation of filmmakers and cinema-goers in many countries. But some Italian writers, like Adriano Aprà, argue that the undoubted merits of postwar Italian filmmakers matter less to younger filmmakers in Italy. In other words, young and aspiring filmmakers need a new generation of filmmaker heroes in order to reassert cinema's historical role as a social and cultural mediator. Brunetta's final explanation for the decline in Italian cinema relates to the capacity of film critics to talk down home-grown films. The result, he argues, was that many Italians turned away from the cinema because it failed to touch hearts and minds and relate to their multiple ontological realities. Many Italians simply saw cinema as increasingly irrelevant to their lives and developed other cultural pastimes.

But when many were beginning to despair of the Italian film industry's fortunes, the early years of the twenty-first century signalled a modest upturn in cinema attendances and film production levels. There are a number of possible reasons for this. The Italian centre-left government introduced fiscal measures in 1998 which have had a modest positive effect on production figures. In March 1999, the Italian film industry relived past glories when Roberto Benigni's *Life is Beautiful* won three Hollywood Oscars. The fact that Benigni tackles the twin subjects of life under fascism and the Holocaust with comedy was not wholly new: Fellini and Rossellini both employed comedy in their films about fascism, *Amarcord* and *La Macchina* (Landy 2000: 118–19). Benigni's masterful comic performance and direction combined with the sensitive handling of the tragic events under examination won international plaudits for originality and for heralding a return, albeit temporarily, to the golden age of Italian cinema. On the back of this success, the Italian film industry has enjoyed notable gains in the past six years. Presenting data from ANICA, the number of Italian films (including co-productions) rose from 98 in 2005 to 116 in 2006, with total film investment rising by some 27 per cent between 2001 and 2006. The total box office share for Italian films went up from 19.28 per cent in 2001 to 24.76 per cent in 2006, although Hollywood films marginally increased their box office share from 59.91 per cent to 61.94 per cent over the same time period. And while cinema attendances remain below 100 million, there are hopes that modest gains in recent years will continue on the back of recent economic growth after years of Italian economic stagnation (ANICA 2007).

The newspaper industry and the rise of the internet

One keenly contested battle in the 1980s was between the *Corriere della Sera* and *La Repubblica* for the title of Italy's most popular-selling newspaper. Both newspapers introduced new weekly colour magazines in 1987: *Corriere*'s *Sette* and *La Repubblica*'s *Il Venerdì*. Other supplements followed like *La Repubblica*'s popular Monday finance supplement, *Affari e Finanza*. The *Corriere* then introduced the lottery game 'Replay' in January 1989 and for some weeks afterwards saw its sales top 1 million, enough to make it Italy's most popular newspaper once again (Murialdi 2003: 239). *La Repubblica* responded by introducing its own version of lottery game and reached 800,000 sales.

The late 1980s also signalled an intensification of takeover battles in the newspaper and magazine sectors as various media groups sought control of Italy's most prestigious titles. This was part of a wider international trend towards commercialization, consolidation and privatization, but Italy's situation was complicated by various political manoeuvres and the presence of other major media groups, led by Silvio Berlusconi, RCS and Mondadori. In 1987, the Ferruzzi Group of Ravenna, a financial and industrial conglomerate led by Raul Gardini (who would commit suicide in 1994 after financial scandals led to the group being declared bankrupt), entered the media market by acquiring Montedison, which owned the Rome-based *Messaggero* newspaper and also a 22 per cent stake in RCS. Gardini began a series of purchases, primarily of struggling newspaper titles and television channels, including *Italia Oggi*, and Telemontecarlo (which was long seen as being a possible contender to RAI and Mediaset's stranglehold over the Italian television market).

The period from 1987 to 1991 was also highlighted by a bitter fight for one of Italy's major publishing groups: Mondadori. The key player in this story was Carlo De Benedetti, chief of Olivetti Computers. In 1988, De Benedetti took over one of Europe's major finance houses, Société Générale de Belgique, and began looking for media companies to purchase. Top of his list was Mondadori which owned half of the *La Repubblica* group (including *Espresso* and local newspapers), as well as other prestigious magazine titles such as *Panorama* and *Epoca*. Together with the RCS publishing group, RAI and Fininvest, Mondadori dominated the Italian media scene. Silvio Berlusconi was also a minor shareholder in Mondadori. In addition to his television interests, Berlusconi also controlled *Il Giornale* and the leading weekly television listings magazine *Sorrisi e Canzoni*, which was also Italy's biggest selling magazine (Murialdi 2000: 291).

The battle for Mondadori was long, drawn out and complex and involved successive legal and political interventions. But the essential dates and events are these. De Benedetti made his first approach to take a stake in Mondadori in 1986, but these overtures were rejected as premature. The death of the Mondadori's president, Mario Formenton, in 1987, led to his inheritors splitting into two camps: one led by Luca Formenton and De Benedetti; and a second group led by Mimmo and Leonardo Mondadori who were allied to Silvio Berlusconi. De Benedetti then bought the non-Mondadori controlling shares in the *La Repubblica* group and announced with Luca Formenton the formation of the 'Grande Mondadori' group, uniting the *La Repubblica-Espresso* group to Mondadori. Battle then commenced for the company, as other shareholders united around Berlusconi. Then, in December 1989, Luca Formenton changed sides after striking a better deal with Berlusconi, which involved promised 300 billion lira in cash and shares (Murialdi 2003: 244, especially footnote 15).

This u-turn by the Formenton-led bloc of shareholders resulted in legal cases between warring groups and political controversy as government parties began siding with various shareholders. Craxi and the Socialist Party backed Berlusconi, whereas their coalition partners in the Christian Democrats were split over the issue and the former Communists backed De Benedetti. A final compromise deal over Mondadori would only come in 1991, when Berlusconi and De Benedetti agreed to split Mondadori, with Fininvest taking 89.75 per cent of the new shares in the company. Berlusconi took control of the Mondadori name and prime magazines from the stable, including *Panorama* and *Epoca*. De Benedetti took Mondadori's 50 per cent share in the *La Repubblica*, *Espresso* and local newspaper titles. They split the advertising arm of Mondadori – Manzoni (Murialdi 2003: 252).

The downfall of the First Italian Republic had a major impact on the Italian newspaper industry. Newspaper sales in Italy peaked in 1992 at 6.809 million and thereafter began to fall. One of the immediate reasons was increased competition from television after 1991, when Berlusconi began nightly news programmes on each of his three channels. Another reason for the decline was the political crisis in 1992 and 1993 which saw the dissolution of the Italian Socialist Party and the fracturing of the

Christian Democrats into three smaller parties. One immediate consequence was the closure of party newspapers which were wholly dependent on their political masters. *Avanti!* and *La Voce Repubblicana* were the main casualties. The main Christian Democrat paper, *Il Popolo*, did survive. Outside of these closures, however, the scandals enveloping the entire Italian political class provided great copy for newspapers as well as other media, and investigations into corruption and bribery scandals were followed on a daily basis. With the downfall of many leading politicians in 1993, newspapers devoted much space to exploring the prospects for the so-called 'Second' Italian Republic, and to the new generation of political leaders and parties emerging from the various scandals. Even if the corruption scandals had not been uncovered by newspapers – The *Tangentopoli* or 'Bribesville' investigations were due to the efforts of investigating magistrates based in Milan and elsewhere – the Italian press played an important role updating Italians bewildered by the economic and political turmoil and provided essential food for thought for those looking for debate and discussion about the country's future (Murialdi 2000: 296).

The economic climate for the newspaper industry in Italy was becoming ever more difficult, however, due to the decline in sales after 1992 and the ever-increasing competition coming from television for advertising revenues. Newspapers were forced to think up new and imaginative ways of selling copies. Perhaps the most imaginative idea, which was immediately copied by other titles, came in January 1994 from the initiative of then editor of *L'Unità*, Walter Veltroni (currently mayor of Rome), who struck on the novel idea of offering a weekly video-cassette (now DVDs) of an Italian, US or international film with the newspaper for a modest surcharge on its cover price. This resulted in the newspaper's sales rising from 118,000 in 1993 to 137,000 in 1994, but competitors quickly followed suit and *L'Unità*, the official newspaper of the renamed Party of the Democratic Left – PDS, found itself in major financial problems. The decline in the Party base post-Cold War, and a sharp fall in sales to just 50,000 copies by 2000, led the PDS to suspend publication. The newspaper was restructured and began publishing again on 28 March 2001. Paradoxically, the paper endured these problems at the very time when the PDS was the main coalition partner of the centre-left government.

By the turn of the century, Italian newspapers enjoyed daily sales of 5.936 million copies. This was 0.8 per cent higher than 1998 sales, but lower than the 1992 peak figure. As a result, Italy became the third lowest in Europe for press readership with 102 newspapers being sold per 1,000 inhabitants. Italy's leading daily newspaper in 1999 was the *Corriere della Sera* (sales of 685.635), followed by *La Repubblica* (611,663), *Gazzetta dello Sport* (432,992), *Il Sole-24Ore* (391,067) and *La Stampa* (390,184). Sales for weekly magazines also went in to gradual decline (2.5 per cent) compared with 1998 figures, although sales of monthly magazines rose by 2.75 per cent in 1999. Total advertising income for mass media topped 14 billion lira in 1999, of which television took the lion's share (55.3 per cent) and newspapers 35.6 per cent (Murialdi 2000: 303–5).

From 1999 onwards, the Italian newspaper industry also faced further challenges in the form of the internet and the appearance of free newspapers in the main Italian cities. Let's examine the internet first. In 1999, 27 per cent of Italian households had an internet connection and it was calculated that 5 million Italians regularly used the net. Again, this was a lower figure than for many European countries although, paradoxically, Italy enjoyed one of the fastest growth rates in another area of digital take-up: mobile phone sales. For newspapers, the main worry was the declining figure for newspaper sales among 16–24-year-olds. One study, again from 1999, showed that only 19 per cent of this age group read a newspaper on a daily basis. To compound this decline, the newspaper industry internationally was going through its biggest shake up in a generation with the advent of the digital era that included internet and online journalism and digital television, plus 24-hour news channels.

Newspapers reacted in a number of ways to arrest the decline in sales and advertising. First, they took a leaf out of commercial television's book by adapting content to be more inclusive and including more tittle-tattle, showbusiness news, sports news, crime, etc. In other words, newspapers published more populist stories that might help attract new, younger readers. More sections and supplements were added which targeted different socioeconomic groups. Also, a number of newspapers such as the *Corriere della Sera*, underwent other major changes shifting from broadsheet-size to become a smaller 'Berliner-style' newspaper (Murialdi 2000: 306–9, 2003: 300–3).

Drawing on developments in the USA and elsewhere, Italian newspapers began producing online editions. While the first Italian online newspaper dates from 1994, the main push to get online came in two spurts in 1997 and 2000. Today, all major Italian newspapers have online editions: *Corriere, Repubblica, Sole-24 Ore, Stampa*, as well as the main political weeklies, *Espresso* and *Panorama*. In the beginning, newspaper online editions closely mirrored print versions, but over time online newspapers have become more distinct entities. They are financed through advertising, can be updated 24 hours a day, and allow far more interactivity than traditional newspapers. Online blogging and greater reader participation is a key feature, expanding the definition and boundaries of journalism in a global internet age. Some Italian newspapers, primarily financial newspapers which attract business and political elites, have been able to develop subscriber-based income streams. Many newspapers, though, have struggled to make profits from their online editions due to international competition coming from other newspapers, especially English-language editions and internet portals such as MSN, Yahoo! and Google, which all offer online news in local languages (Murialdi 2000: 306–9, 2003: 300–3). In late 2006, 18 million Italians had broadband connections to the internet.

From 1998 onwards, major international and Italian newspaper publishers began to set up new free newspapers for distribution in major towns and cities at bus, rail and underground stations as well as other prominent public places. Making use of cheaper production and distribution technologies, and available content from journalists and news agencies, these newspapers present news in small bite-size chunks and articles are rarely more than 200 words long. They rely heavily on colour photography, and present less hard or political news and more infotainment or soft news. The fact that such newspapers are free is because they are entirely funded by advertising, which can take up as much as half of the total newspaper space. The target audiences for these newspapers have typically been those who do not normally buy any newspaper (hence, new readers) but who have 10–30 minutes on their way to and from work or during work breaks to read such newspapers. This has led to morning and afternoon free newspapers appearing, hitting the streets before rush-hour begins. The main players in this market have been the Swedish Metro group, which publishes *Metro* in various European cities, RCS, which publishes *City* and the Il Messaggero Group, which publishes *Leggo* in major Italian cities (Murialdi 2000: 306–9, 2003: 300–3). The new free newspapers have had a detrimental impact on newspaper sales for the main Italian titles, with the exception of sports newspapers like the *Gazzetta dello Sport*, sales of which have risen slightly in recent years.

The number of daily local, regional and national newspaper titles published in Italy in 2002 was slightly over 200. The ten largest newspapers account for slightly more than 60 per cent of total national circulation. Total daily newspaper circulation in Italy remains relatively low, hovering at slightly less than 6 million copies in 2006. Daily newspaper share of advertising revenues was slightly over 23 per cent in 2004, when it was just over 50 per cent for the television sector. It should also be noted that Mediaset owns an extensive publishing portfolio and that members of the Berlusconi family (but not Silvio Berlusconi himself) own two newspapers. Given the continued dominance of television over the Italian media scene, I will now turn my attention to examining broadcasting in the Second Italian Republic.

8 SILVIO BERLUSCONI

- **The first Berlusconi government, 1994**
- **Constitutional Court decision, December 1994**
- **The 1997 Broadcasting Act (Law 249)**
- **Berlusconi and conflicts of interest**
- **Why does media ownership matter?**
- **The second Berlusconi government, 2001–6**
- **Conflicts of interest: analysis of the Gasparri and Frattini Laws**
- **The Frattini Law**
- **The Freedom House report 2006**

Despite the continuous process of legislative proposals in the late 1970s and 1980s, the duopoly system was only officially sanctioned in law in August 1990 (Law No. 223, 6 August 1990). The torturous parliamentary passage of the Act and the constant list of amendments produced not surprisingly, perhaps, an Act described by its author as: 'the best that was possible at the time' (quoted from Giacalone 1992: xiii). The best was rather little. There were few legal obligations for commercial channels to provide a public service, except for a national news service. While there were provisions to safeguard standards of taste and decency, there were no quality thresholds or standards for programming. The crucial Article 15 states that no group should control more than 25 per cent of the national channels. The law did not specify the number of national channels, but no one was in doubt that 12 licences would be allotted, allowing RAI and Fininvest to retain three channels a piece. The licences were not announced until August 1992, formally entrenching the duopoly in statute. The law allowed Berlusconi to maintain his media empire with the exemption of his newspaper, *Il Giornale*, which he transferred to his brother's control due to cross-media regulations.

By 1992, RAI was deeply involved in a number of the crises.[1] The first was the crisis of the *partitocrazia* (rule of parties), which had taken an extremely tight hold on RAI (*lottizzazione*), more than on any other public institution.[2] The dissolution of the two main political parties controlling RAI, the Christian Democrats and the Socialists, left a power vacuum at the heart of the company. Also, without party support, RAI faced financial bankruptcy. The second crisis was RAI's official position as state broadcaster (Bull and Rhodes 1997: 4–5). The financial scandals threatened the stability of the Italian nation-state. As the most visible of all state institutions, RAI faced a period of immense unpopularity. Such a situation could further deteriorate if large bribery scandals were unearthed inside RAI as in other state institutions. In 1993, the Italian government led by the former governor of the Bank of Italy, Carlo Azeglio Ciampi, announced an overhaul of RAI and public service broadcasting. From the outset, there were two interlinked strands to the reform process that can be summarized thus:

1   A desire on behalf of the government and the new Administrative Council to maximize the financial, production and organizational resources available to RAI, and to promote the efficient usage of these resources while retaining a high degree of effectiveness in its various broadcasting operations. This objective was motivated by the dire state of RAI's finances.
2   The reappraisal of RAI's service to the public. The mandate given to the new Administrative Council was to dismantle the *lottizzazione* system and provide a public service, which was more independent, accessible and relevant, and was related to the complexities of modern Italian society.[3]

The first objective was to resolve the dire financial situation in which RAI found itself. In the last 15 years RAI has undergone major structural and organizational changes. As a result, the company has enjoyed a sharp revival in its financial fortunes. This can be demonstrated by presenting some headline figures. From a financial loss of 479 billion lira in 1993 (£192 million),[4] the company had gone back into profit. Such an improvement in economic fortunes was achieved by cutting back on expenditure and attracting additional income. Expenditure cuts occurred across the board, including programme budget cuts in the mid-1990s.

Additional income came primarily via the abolition of RAI's financial ceiling restricting advertising income, increasing its total annual advertising revenue by between 6 and 10 per cent in the mid- to late 1990s before the advertising market went in to decline.[5] In addition, the company undertook a campaign to curb persistent non-payment of the licence fee. In 1991, 72.53 per cent of Italian households owned a television licence. By 2004 the figure had risen to over 85 per cent (RAI Annual 1993–2006). Finally, RAI was granted additional government aid in the form of loans, especially when the company was on the verge of bankruptcy in late 1993.

The company also attempted to cut costs via the introduction of new structures that coordinated some of the commissioning and scheduling functions formerly controlled by the three networks. In effect, it was this reform that ended the tripartite system of network control.[6] This new restructuring policy was therefore based on ensuring more effective use of internal resources, unlike under the political imperatives that had determined so much of RAI's previous organizational strategy. There was also intense opposition to many of the changes. Much of this opposition had originated within the networks themselves and stressed the positive aspects of the old structure of organizing television services (Guglielmi

and Balassone 1995: 125). The networks, therefore, still retained important commissioning and production decisions, and were closely involved
in the changes undertaken.

One feature of public service broadcasting in Italy which has remained
more intractable, however, is the problem associated with devolving
broadcasting services to the regions. The reform process undertaken since
1993 has failed to change this situation, although there have been
numerous proposals. The main idea was for the reform of RAITRE based
on the German ARD model (Demattè 1993: 19–39). It was rejected after
an intense internal campaign by RAITRE executives and the resignation
of an Administrative Council member, Elvira Sellerio, in June 1994. The
official reason why it was finally rejected was the lack of financial
resources. The final cost was estimated at 1,000 billion lira (£400 million)
(Jacobelli 1996: 64). For a company undergoing radical pruning, the costs
were seen as being too prohibitive and contrary to the overriding project
of lowering RAI's burgeoning debt. In other words, the regional reform
came too soon into RAI's financial recovery.

In June 1993 a mini-reform of RAI was passed by Parliament altering
the power structure within the company with a view to dismantling the
lottizzazione system. The main aim of Law 206 was to reform the
much-criticized appointment system. Members of the Council were no
longer chosen by a parliamentary commission and the state-owned IRI
(RAI's parent company), but were instead chosen jointly by the two
presidents of the Parliament. Since 1976, the Commission had been little
more than a puppet for the party hierarchies and enjoyed minimal
effective autonomy. By giving the power over appointees to senior
institutional figures (in Italy, the two presidents are the second and third
most senior figures, following the president himself) the system for
controlling RAI became the responsibility of institutional guarantors, and
therefore theoretically above party politics. But theoretical independence
has traditionally counted for little in Italy. The proof of the pudding
would be in the eating.

The wider political clear-out, the process of *delottizzazione*, was
impossible to achieve. In a country where public appointments have
traditionally been the spoils of political victors, such appointees have
inevitably been recognized or 'tagged' by their alleged political affiliations.
Such a system had at least two possible functions for political elites. On
one level it was a highly symbolic gesture that indicated who were the
current 'movers and shakers'. Secondly, and much more seriously, the
appointment of a politically-friendly Administrative Council allowed
political elites to influence subsequent appointments to politically sensitive
posts inside the company, especially the news services. During the reform
process, the process of political tagging occurred irrespective of whether
there was hard evidence to support it. Hence, the professors in 1993 were
appointed by a government led by Carlo Azeglio Ciampi. This government was made up of non-party 'technocrats', but was backed in
Parliament by a centre-left majority, including the ex-Communists. By
implication, therefore, RAI was defined in many quarters as being in the

pockets of the centre-left. This was despite the fact that the primary purpose of the Ciampi government was to make institutional changes (a new voting law) before fresh elections were called. It was a transitional government.

The fear was that after elections in April 1994, the success of any new political coalition would inevitably lead to the conservation and reaffirmation of old political habits – that is, some form of *relottizzazione*. When the right-wing Berlusconi government came to power in May 1994 those fears were confirmed. The forced resignation of Claudio Demattè's Administrative Council in June 1994 was an act of pure political expediency. The actions of the Berlusconi government undermined the fundamental tenets of public service broadcasting, and, as Enzo Biagi observed, struck at the very heart of good democratic governance (1994: 48–51). The unpalatable truth was that a culture of party interference was too deeply ingrained. Yet this new form of political interference was different to the system preceding it. Firstly, the tripartite-controlled RAI had vanished. The dissolution of the Christian Democrats into smaller parties and the complete disappearance of Craxi's Socialist Party necessitated this. So even if the three-network system had survived, the balance of power within the company was nevertheless irreversibly altered. Few doubted this.

The first Berlusconi government, 1994

The whole political climate was turned on its head when on 26 January 1994, Silvio Berlusconi, head of Fininvest, announced that he would be entering the political fray for the forthcoming elections, utilizing Forza Italia clubs (grass-root AC Milan supporters' organizations) as the campaign base. Within two months of announcing his official candidature, Berlusconi had led a disparate coalition of sorts to a triumphant election victory. Accusations that Berlusconi's involvement in national politics created a potential conflict of interest were made shortly after his announcement that he would enter politics. Few doubted that he could mobilize the full weight of his economic wealth and media outlets behind his drive for political power. And, indeed, the media did play a very important role in Berlusconi's election victory in 1994. But it became clear early on that his television channels would be used *selectively* to promote his political aims. While political and social commentators were mobilized to work across the three channels delivering Berlusconi's message, there were distinct differences when it came to news programmes. The University of Pavia was one of a number of universities undertaking research into the 1994 electoral campaign news coverage. In its analysis, the university found that RAIUNO and RAIDUE gave the most balanced coverage of the electoral campaign (in terms of time devoted to each party in line with their parliamentary strength), closely followed by RAITRE and Berlusconi's Canale 5. By far the most partial coverage of the elections came from Berlusconi's Italia Uno and Retequattro channels.

While these two channels target broad audiences, they tend to attract younger and older people respectively. Both channels favoured Forza Italia. On Retequattro, Berlusconi's party gained 68.4 per cent of all news coverage while on Italia Uno the figure was 52.8 per cent. The ex-Communist PDS gained just 9.3 and 11.6 per cent of news coverage, despite being the largest parliamentary party (Ricolfi 1997; Rositi 2004).

The Retequattro case study is particularly interesting. Its news director, the former RAI journalist Emilio Fede, had never hidden his devotion to his political master and presented, according to some, the most partial and biased news programme in Italy. Berlusconi's opponents maintain that Fede's role was crucial because Retequattro attracts large elderly audiences with relatively low educational attainment. The implication for some critics was that this social group tends to be more susceptible to Fede's strident pro-Berlusconi views. It is also interesting to note that Berlusconi has never, to date, really mobilized his main Canale 5 news service. Its director until 2005, Enrico Mentana, is a highly regarded journalist in Italy and maintained a broadly balanced news service. Again, Berlusconi's opponents have often argued that better educated social groups tend to watch Canale 5 and were, therefore, less likely to be susceptible to pro-Berlusconi propaganda. It is interesting to note that Berlusconi and his team used well-honed advertising techniques to identify and target potential swing voters and revolutionized Italian political communication during the 1994 campaign.

Berlusconi was elected head of a coalition centre-right government in April 1994 and he was not shy in asserting his government's dominance over RAI. RAI's reforming Administrative Council (nominated by the Ciampi government in June 1993 and led by the late Claudio Dematté), was introducing major reforms to the public service broadcaster, including dismantling the *lottizzazione* system. But buoyed by the outcome of the European parliamentary elections in June 1994, Berlusconi's government lost no time in stamping its authority over RAI. On 24 June 1994, the then minister for parliamentary relations, Giuliano Ferrara, announced that the government had blocked the Administrative Council's reconstruction plan (RAI, like Fininvest in the early 1990s, was saddled by enormous debts). The Administrative Council resigned within a week and procedures were set in motion to select a new board. Within months, one member of the new Administrative Council, Alfio Marchini, resigned in protest at appointments to the news services, declaring that there was too much political interference in company decisions and that the Administrative Council had been placed under excessive political pressure when debating the new appointments. Berlusconi's government effectively reasserted political domination over an RAI that had sought to try and depoliticize the company in the aftermath of the political turmoil.

The strength of opposition to the alleged *relottizzazione* of the company, and to the announcement of the senior appointments in particular, began to build up a head of steam, attracting a large anti-government consensus. The concern expressed, both by Parliament and within the country at large, brought a response from Scalfaro, the president of the Republic, in the form of an open letter read in Parliament on 11 November 1994. The contents of the letter included an appeal for adherence to the key concepts of pluralism and impartiality, restating the central importance of the mass media to the democratic process and the concept of *Par Condicio* (equal treatment):

> On at least two occasions recently, I have been obliged to bring to your attention a matter which I consider vital for a democracy, that is, of *Par Condicio*, that must be accorded to all political groups. The principle of *Par Condicio* should allow all political and cultural groups the right to be heard across the broad spectrum of the mass media. (La Repubblica, 15 November 1994.)

What Scalfaro was reconfirming was the need to abide by constitutional provisions covering the media and the provisions set out by successive statutes of broadcasting law. There was nothing original or novel in his argument. As the guardian of the constitution, he was merely appealing to the parties to abide by these provisions. The importance of the letter was that it was an unmistakable attack on the Berlusconi government and this led to further political arguments. In the wider journalistic world, too, which was so accustomed to working under the system of political patronage, the response was one of shock. One of Italy's most senior and respected journalists, Enzo Biagi, supported by many senior colleagues and academics, launched the following appeal via the *Europeo* magazine in November 2004 to the president of Italy: 'The attack against the public service of RAI, conducted from outside and within the company, now denotes a situation of serious danger to the freedom of information and communication: for democracy in Italy'.

The climax of this fevered debate was a vote of no confidence passed by the Italian Senate on 2 November against the Administrative Council. The country was being polarized by the argument surrounding the control of the state broadcasting company. In the sphere of public debate, the broadcasting issue was only equalled by the political wrangle taking place over social spending for the forthcoming public spending round. With mass public demonstrations across the country, both for and against the government, and students occupying the universities and schools, as in 1968, social unrest reflected and propelled the rising political tension. As well as political and social discord, the institutions of the state themselves were hopelessly divided. The increasing bitterness in the battle of words between President Scalfaro and elements of the government over the principle of the *Par Condicio* was self-evident.

The Berlusconi government resigned on 22 December 1994 following the withdrawal of Bossi's Northern League from the coalition. The ironic feature of the first Berlusconi government was, of course, that its tough and assertive control over the media, especially public service broadcasting, did not prevent it (the coalition) from imploding after just nine months. Although Berlusconi controlled three commercial television channels and numerous magazines, and his wife and brother owned two national newspapers, and despite the fact that there was overt political interference in RAI, this did not save his first government from ignominious collapse.

Constitutional Court decision, December 1994

In those final December days of the first Berlusconi government, the Constitutional Court entered the television debate once again. The Court was asked to consider the legal argument of the minor national commercial channels, Telemontecarlo, Rete A and TeleElefant, regarding the claim that the position of Fininvest constituted an oligopoly and a dominant market position, and therefore breached the constitution. The main decision of the Court concerned Article 15 of the Mammì Law which lays out the provisions limiting the number of channels owned by any one concessionary to 25 per cent of the total number of channels. The Court argued that the ownership of three channels as guaranteed by Article 15 constituted an advantage in terms of the utilization of resources and advertising income. This advantage not only distorted the rules of competition in the broadcasting industry, but constituted a potential risk to fundamental values of free speech, thought, etc. In the Court's opinion it was the duty of legislators to stop the formation of a monopoly and instead create a system which allowed the greatest possible access. The Court therefore decided that Article 15 was 'incoherent, unreasonable and unsuitable', adding that national television needed new regulations that should:

> respect the constitutional requirement to safeguard the freedom of speech. Therefore, whatever the legal provisions adopted, it should not be possible that the final result allows one quarter of all national channels (or a third of all commercial channels) to be concentrated in the hands of one company ...

In short, therefore, the Court was saying that Fininvest had to lose one channel. The Court also argued that the system was unlawful if smaller commercial operators were not granted the necessary frequencies to enjoy national coverage. The Court granted a period of transition so that new legislation could be introduced, rather than pass a definitive judgement. The ball was instead passed back to the politicians to decide on the legislation required. The decision of the Court, although technically against Fininvest only, effectively condemned the duopoly as being unconstitutional.

The Court was not only backing the president in his call for a *Par Condicio*, but was also explicitly stating that a *Par Condicio* was not possible under present conditions. Perhaps it is not purely by chance that, on the same day the Court announced its findings, Fininvest were fined for repeated violations of the rules governing the coverage of elections. After the collapse of the first Berlusconi government, Berlusconi immediately demanded fresh elections to end the political stalemate. He argued that the breakdown of the government constituted a betrayal of the voters and, therefore, no other political group had a mandate to govern. This claim brought fresh conflict with the president of Italy who argued that the government was mistaken for two reasons: first, Italy was a parliamentary democracy, and therefore it was a matter for Parliament to decide who had the political mandate to govern; second, and more relevant to the media, that no new elections could be called until the broadcasting issue had been resolved and *Par Condicio* had been achieved.

In January 1995, the Constitutional Court weighed into the broadcasting debate once again, deciding on the legal validity of a series of proposed referenda, sponsored by the leader of the Radical Party, Marco Pannella, including further amendments to the voting system and three referenda on the future of the broadcasting system. The Court gave the go-ahead to the referenda on broadcasting (for June 1995). Each referendum would take the form of a question put to the electorate. The broadcasting referenda proposed were: a referendum on the proposal to privatize or part-privatize RAI (subsequently carried); a referendum proposing changes to the regulations regarding advertising (failed); and finally a referendum on the proposed reduction of the number of commercial channels held by any one operator (failed). In fact, the rejection of last referendum put the Italian people at odds with the Constitutional Court decision.

The whole situation became highly volatile. The new 'technocratic' government of Lamberto Dini stressed that one of its main tasks would be to sort out the broadcasting question, but doubt remained that the government would have the parliamentary strength to pass a comprehensive package of reforms. And this turned out to be so. Elections were finally called for May 1996 resulting in a narrow victory for the Romano Prodi-led Ulivo (Olive Tree) alliance. The next shot at putting Italy's unruly media system in order would fall to the centre-left.

The 1997 Broadcasting Act (Law 249)

The new broadcasting legislation – the so-called Mecannico Law – proposed a reduction in the number of Mediaset's terrestrial channels from three to two, with Retequattro being withdrawn to become a satellite channel (Fininvest's television interests were floated on the Italian Stock Exchange in 1995 under the name Mediaset; Silvio Berlusconi still holds a controlling share of the company). The Law also proposed the reduction in the number of RAI channels allowed television spot advertising from three to two (Article 3, Law 249, 1997), meaning that RAITRE would become wholly reliant on the licence fee. The Mecannico Law was in line with Constitutional Court rulings of 1994 and went against the referenda held in June 1995 (although these were not legally binding). Crucially, however, the Law specified no date for the reforms to be made and passed this decision to the new 'super-regulator' for the Italian media, AGCOM – Autorità per le Garanzie nelle Comunicazioni, brought into being by the 1997 Act.

AGCOM had broad responsibilities for Italy's audio-visual and telecommunications industries and its main tasks included: encouraging competition in the audio-visual and telecommunications markets and supporting inward investment; supervising and enforcing compliance with Italian and European legislation in these areas; advising the Italian governments on audio-visual and telecommunications policies; providing conflict resolution or an arbitration service to players in the above-mentioned industries; and encouraging the adoption of industry-wide guidelines on standards and quality of service (AGCOM 1999). One of AGCOM's first tasks was to examine all aspects of planning for the development of a new digital terrestrial broadcasting system in Italy (including drawing up a new 'Frequency Spectrum Distribution Plan'). Another aim of AGCOM was to reduce the 'high risk' of investing in digital television in Italy for broadcasting and other commercial companies, and to encourage their participation in a new broadcasting system (1999: 97).

AGCOM was (and still is) aided in its efforts by a number of regional bodies (Regional Committees for Communications) as well as a National Council of Users which advises it on consumer issues. It should be noted however that AGCOM's powers have been hampered by insufficient sanctions available at its disposal, by various loopholes contained in the 1997 legislation, and by political interference in the appointment of its commissioners. For example, AGCOM was unable to enforce the 1997 Act provisions relating to Retequattro and RAITRE, arguing that the growth of these two channels was covered separately in the 1997 Act (Law 249/1997, Article 2, Clause 9, quoted in Andreano and Iapadre 2005: 102). European quotas (i.e. the Television without Frontiers Directive, 89/52/EEC) were not fully enforced as there were no sanctions for AGCOM to apply to companies that fail to comply. And the fact that AGCOM commissioners were voted into office by the Italian Parliament led many to question the political independence of the institution from centre-left and centre-right political blocs.[7]

Another key feature of the 1997 Broadcasting Act required RAI to restructure itself into separate internal divisions, with a publicly-owned holding company (RAI) governing five separate divisions (Article 31, Law 249, 1997), paving the way, it was hoped, for the partial privatization of one or more of these five divisions which, in turn, would comply with the result of the 1995 referendum. It is interesting to note that the centre-left government under Prodi, and then the successive D'Alema and Amato governments, chose to confirm the referendum result relating to RAI but ignored the Mediaset-related referenda results.

The Italian government was looking for ways to privatize some of RAI's operations. Leading candidates for privatization included RAISAT (which controlled RAI's satellite channels) and RAIWAY (RAI's transmission sites). RAI wanted to bring private capital into these and other parts of the company. But it became increasingly clear that these plans also extended to the company's core public services, RAIUNO and RAIDUE (Fontanarosa 2000): up to 49 per cent of each channel would have been sold off and listed on the Italian Stock Exchange. In return for a stock market listing, both channels would renounce their share of the licence fee, which would then be shared among RAI's other core public service activities. The major beneficiary would be RAITRE.[8]

There are a number of reasons why a centre-left government might have wished to privatize parts of its services, including RAIUNO and RAIDUE. Firstly, the sale of assets would raise considerable sums for the company and the government, which could then be diverted to the public service mission. Secondly, any privatization would comply with the result of the 1995 referendum. The third reason for introducing private capital was that it would also introduce new players into a market that had the unenviable record of being among the most concentrated broadcasting sectors in the world. The final reason was that there were examples of commercial broadcasters that still managed to provide public service programming. The Italian state would still be the majority shareholder, and RAIUNO and RAIDUE would still have some public service obligations. In other words, a public service broadcaster need not necessarily be a wholly public company.

However, there were notable disadvantages of privatizing RAI's operations, especially its core public services. Briefly, any privatization of RAIUNO and RAIDUE might undermine key tenets of public service broadcasting. Commercial companies tend to under-supply 'merit goods', which lead to long-term benefits and it is difficult to see how newly-privatized RAI channels could provide the public service remit they were then supplying (see Note 1, p. 154). There were, however, other reasons not to privatize RAI's core services. Firstly, there were many political parties and senior RAI executives implacably opposed to the idea. In addition to left-wing parties (Greens and Communists) and elements of the Democrats of the Left, some parties on the centre-right were also opposed to the idea. The second reason was that any privatization would be resisted by parts of the Italian commercial sector, causing further instability for the television market. Commercial broadcasters feared a newly-privatized RAI as it could threaten their main source of funding – advertising revenues. This explained, perhaps, the strange sight of RAI's great adversary, Silvio Berlusconi, opposing the centre-left's ideas to privatize RAI in this manner, although we will discuss his plans for RAI after 2001 later in the chapter. The third reason not to privatize RAIUNO and RAIDUE was that it might lead to the development of an Italian public service all'americana. With these two channels moving to the commercial sector, RAITRE would be left in an exposed position. Even if RAITRE inherited the licence fee from the other two channels, and poured this money into programmes and other necessary reforms, the channel's isolated position in the marketplace might undermine its chances of long-term growth and development.

Such changes, had they been fully implemented, would have represented a radical shift in the structure and organization of the Italian broadcasting system. The reforms could have undermined the RAI and Mediaset duopoly. But having introduced what was, arguably, a radical piece of media legislation that would have helped transform the face of Italian broadcasting, the centre-left then failed to have these provisions implemented before losing power to Berlusconi's centre-right alliance in 2001. This is despite having the legal support of the Constitutional Court. It is worth asking why the centre-left failed in its attempt to curb the power of the RAI/Mediaset duopoly. There are two broad lines of thinking. On the one hand, the three centre-left governments from 1996 to 2001 were arguably *unable* to push through implementation of the 1997 Law due to political weaknesses and problems with the legislation. Law 249 was the product of laborious negotiations and trade-offs between various factions of the centre-left and centre-right alliances, and, arguably, the final piece of legislation suffered as a result. For example, key responsibilities were given to the new media regulator, AGCOM. Although defined as an independent authority accountable to Parliament, AGCOM commissioners were appointed by the Italian Parliament and their independent status was often questioned. Asking a politicized regulatory authority to implement a highly contentious piece of legislation was always likely to be problematic, especially when RAI and Mediaset were lobbying vigorously behind the scenes against implementation. AGCOM was able to justify its failure to implement aspects of the Meccanico Law by citing Article 2 of Law 249 which stated that 'concentration standards are not binding if the violation stems from "the spontaneous development of the company which does not produce a dominant position or eliminate or compromise pluralism and competition" ' (Andreano and Iapadre 2005: 102).

On the other hand, commentators argue that some on the Italian centre-left were also *unwilling* to see provisions of Law 249 fully implemented. The former member of RAI's Administrative Council between 1998 and 2002, Vittorio Emiliani, argues that the major reform of Italy's media lacked sufficient political will because politicians from both sides of the political divide secretly favoured the status quo position. They either favoured a public service broadcaster that was politically compromised and subservient to factional interests and/or they did not want to see Berlusconi's company significantly weakened or broken up (Emiliani 2002: 58).

Silvio Berlusconi and the so-called conflicts of interest

Berlusconi's reelection to power in 2001 at the head of a centre-right coalition led to regular political arguments over his so-called conflicts of interest. These arguments centre on opposition claims that:

- Berlusconi introduced 'favourable' legislation for Mediaset, helping to boost the company's profits; and

• he wielded a high degree of political influence over both the country's main television broadcasters, Mediaset and the public service broadcasting company, RAI, which together attracted 85 per cent of television audiences and advertising revenues (*The Economist* 2001; Hibberd 2004a, 2004b, 2007).

Political opponents argued that Berlusconi had accrued substantial economic and political benefits, while compromising media pluralism in Italy. A recent Council of Europe-funded report (Venice Commission 2005) heavily criticized the Berlusconi government (2001–6), arguing that two pieces of legislation (the Gasparri Law, which relaxes media ownership rules, and the Frattini Law, which sets out rules relating to conflicts of interest in public life) do little to resolve issues relating to Berlusconi's dominance of Italy's broadcasting media. This follows other international parliamentary debates and reports that have been equally condemnatory of the Italian media system (Freedom House 2006). Although Berlusconi was swept from power in April 2006, he remains leader of the opposition and could reassume power in some future election. Furthermore, the legislation passed by his government is unlikely to be reversed by the new centre-left government in Italy, given its slim majority in the Senate.

The increasing importance of media ownership

The mass media play an increasingly important role in advanced, post-industrial societies. The media, for example, act as a central institution of political life and also constitute a key commercial sector in the early twenty-first century. Questions relating to who owns media companies and corporations are also becoming more important as the role of the media increases. My University of Glasgow colleague, Gillian Doyle, has recently argued that '[media ownership] matters to society because a number of potential harms may result from concentrated media ownership, including the abuse of political power by media owners or the under-representation of some viewpoints' (2002: 171). Indeed, one of the main reasons for media regulation across the globe is to ensure that such abuses do not take place and that essential rights prevail, such as freedom of expression. Freedom of expression is enshrined in Article 10 of the European Convention on Human Rights, which states that:

1   Everyone has the right to freedom of expression. This right shall include freedom to hold opinions and to receive and impart information and ideas without interference by public authority and regardless of frontiers. This article shall not prevent states from requiring the licensing of broadcasting, television or cinema enterprises.

2   The exercise of these freedoms, since it carries with it duties and responsibilities, may be subject to such formalities, conditions, restrictions or penalties as are prescribed by law and are necessary in a democratic society, in the interests of national security, territorial

integrity or public safety, for the prevention of disorder or crime, for the protection of health or morals, for the protection of the reputation or rights of others, for preventing the disclosure of information received in confidence, or for maintaining the authority and impartiality of the judiciary.

(Venice Commission 2005: 10)

Pluralism of the media is considered by most experts as one vital aspect of freedom of expression. Citing Doyle, once again, 'pluralism is generally associated with diversity in the media; the presence of a number of different and independent voices, and ... differing political opinions and representations of culture within the media' (2002: 11). There are two types of pluralism: external or structural and internal. External pluralism relates to the diversity of ownership within a specific market. It is achieved when there is a plurality of broadcasters and outlets in a sector. Internal pluralism refers to the diversity of output. It is achieved when extensive coverage and diversity of programming are provided by media outlets. While restrictions on media ownership can help preserve diversity of ownership, they are not sufficient to guarantee diversity of output, reflecting different political and social views, and other policy instruments should be used to encourage greater internal pluralism (i.e. strong and independent media regulators) (Doyle 2002: 12; Venice Commission 2005: 11).

While the policy of *lottizzazione* caused many problems for RAI (it was highly bureaucratic and costly, created bitter internal disputes between the three networks that, arguably, affected programme quality, and undermined RAI's pretence to be impartial), this system guaranteed a certain degree of internal and external media pluralism. As Daniel Hallin and Paolo Mancini (2004: 108) have argued:

> The system was actually a complex mixture of external pluralism – in the sense that the different political forces had their 'own' channels – and internal pluralism, both in the sense that RAI was governed by a common body and in the sense that each channel still had personnel from a variety of different parties. News programmes on each channel reflected the full spectrum of Italian politics ...

The second Berlusconi government, 2001–6

Not surprisingly, the second Berlusconi's government was a little more cautious and circumspect in its relations with RAI in the early months of its life. The prospect of a Berlusconi victory in 2001 preoccupied the media inside and outside Italy. The UK-based *The Economist*, in its now infamous editorial of April 2001, launched a blistering attack on Berlusconi and his democratic credentials:

> In any event, in any normal country the voters – and probably the law – would not have given Mr Berlusconi his chance at the polls

without first obliging him to divest himself of many of his wide-reaching assets. The conflict of interest between his business and affairs of state would be gargantuan. Worth perhaps $14 billion, he is intricately involved in vast areas of Italian finance, commerce and broadcasting with ramifications into almost every aspect of business and public life; his empire includes banks, insurance, property, publishing, advertising, the media and football. Even during his ill-fated earlier stint as prime minister, in 1994, he issued an array of decrees that impinged heavily on his commercial activities. If he wins again on May 13th, he will control a good 90% of all national television broadcasting. He has made not the slightest effort to resolve this clear conflict.

This editorial began a bitter war of words between Berlusconi and *The Economist* in the last two weeks of the election campaign. Arguably, the intervention of an English-language magazine had little effect on domestic Italian public opinion, but the editorial heralded a new phase in the bitter wrangling between the Berlusconi government and the foreign press corps.[9]

As previously mentioned, the ironic feature of the first Berlusconi government was that its tough and assertive control over RAI and public service broadcasting did not prevent it (the coalition) from implosion. That Berlusconi controlled three private television channels, other magazines and newspapers and denied the state channels due impartiality and independence did not save his first government from ignominious collapse after only nine months. And while media policy did not constitute the straw that broke the coalition's back, the reappointment of RAI's Administrative Council and directors of the three news services and channels in July and September 1994, did create major tensions within the Berlusconi coalition, especially with the Northern League.

One would expect, therefore, that this time around, the Berlusconi government would take a more cautious approach to RAI, if only to encourage harmonious relations within the coalition. Instead the company has seen protracted and bitter internal arguments (stoked by external political forces) and an ongoing series of pernicious political attacks, which have struck at the very heart of its public remit. These arguments and attacks have centred around the appointment of two Administrative Councils since 2001, each accused of being politically partial, and accusations made by Berlusconi himself against two of RAI's senior journalists, both of whom were subsequently suspended by the company. Italian journalists as well as foreign commentators and the centre-left opposition therefore accused the second Berlusconi government of compromising RAI's impartiality and independence. Let us look at these allegations in more detail.

In relation to RAI, the appointment of its new pro-Berlusconi five-person Administrative Council came only in February 2002, at the end of the scheduled mandate of the centre-left appointed Council; but it nevertheless led to the promotion of senior managers and journalists favoured by centre-right coalition parties. Berlusconi himself argued that 'new appointments would ensure that RAI provided objective information and abandoned the factionalism that characterised its "military occupation by the left" ' (Willan 2002).

Behind the scenes, the parties engaged in negotiations via the two presidents of the Italian parliament ('institutional' figures who had been given the task of nominating RAI's Administrative Council in the 1993 reform law – No. 206, 25 June) detailing the final outline of RAI's new five-person Administrative Council and dividing the spoils between three government-friendly appointees and two opposition-friendly ones. Berlusconi's treatment of RAI followed a similar pattern to that of other Italian governments in promoting supportive managers and journalists to key positions. The centre-left had done this in 1996 and the opposition centre-right had, with some justification, argued that RAI was dominated by centre-left appointees. In 2002, an Administrative Council dominated by the centre-left was replaced with a Council dominated by the centre-right. The Council then appointed a government-friendly director-general and other key senior positions, leaving some spaces of influence for the political opposition (i.e. RAITRE) and allowing RAI to maintain a modicum of internal pluralism.

But Berlusconi then went beyond usual political protocol when, in May 2002, he singled out veteran RAI journalists and political commentators, Enzo Biagi and Michele Santoro, and the comedian-satirist Daniele Luttazzi, criticizing them for making 'criminal use' of RAI at the licence-payers expense (Willan 2002). In his now infamous Sofia Declaration (his comments were made on a visit to Bulgaria), Berlusconi added that he had nothing against their continued appearance, 'but since they don't change ... ' (quoted in Willan 2002). The fact that Berlusconi had singled out these three did not surprise too many commentators. Luttazzi and Biagi were criticized by the centre-right in the run up to the 2001 election, the latter for his interview with Oscar-winning actor and director, Roberto Benigni.[10] Santoro had also been accused of bias against Berlusconi.

The fact that a politician criticized a public service broadcaster and its journalists and presenters is nothing new. But what made this case more serious was that all those named by Berlusconi were subsequently removed from RAI's television schedules in autumn 2002. This is despite the fact that Santoro and Biagi were long-standing and senior RAI journalists fronting popular commentary programmes. In January 2005, a Rome court condemned RAI for removing Michele Santoro and he eventually reappeared on television screens in September 2006. Apart from guest appearances, Biagi never returned to television and has since gone in to semi-retirement (Biagi and Mazzetti 2005). While the then president of RAI, Antonio Baldassarre, argued that Biagi and Santoro had been dropped due to scheduling considerations, many commentators and politicians (including those in Berlusconi's coalition) remained sceptical. Certainly, programming considerations did form part of the negotiations between RAI and Biagi, but it is hard to avoid the conclusion that RAI's top brass were simply following political orders (Biagi and Mazzetti 2005).[11]

Arguably, Berlusconi sought revenge against those he perceived to be critical of him during the 2001 election campaign. This episode, more than any other, clearly demonstrated that RAI's autonomy existed only on paper in statutes and agreements. Historical precedents aplenty mean that no one should be surprised at this situation. And it is not a condition that afflicts Italy only. But the Sofia Declaration did set a dangerous precedent and, arguably, internal pluralism in RAI was compromised. The banishment of the 'Sofia Three' constituted a reduction in the diversity of voices and opinions. Top (Mediaset) talk-show host, Maurizio Costanzo, even quipped that Mediaset was more open to dissenting voices than RAI.

The strength of national and international opposition to the series of events outlined above created a large anti-government consensus by June 2002. Many commentators feared that Berlusconi's full frontal attack on RAI, coupled with new legislation granting senior institutional figures, including himself, immunity from prosecution while in office, undermined vital freedoms in Italy.

The Administrative Council, led by Antonio Baldassarre, was thereafter split by irreconcilable political differences, with two Council members sympathetic to the opposition resigning in autumn 2002 and a third member, broadly sympathetic to the government, following shortly afterwards. The Council was eventually changed in February 2003 when, after an aborted attempt to bring in former editor of the *Corriere della Sera*, Paolo Mieli, the senior RAI journalist, Lucia Annunziata, was elected as the new president of RAI. When she resigned in 2004, citing unacceptable political pressures, a centre-left politician, Claudio Petruccioli, was appointed president. The old *lottizzazione* system had resurfaced, but one that better fit the new 'majoritarian' system of two political blocs: the 'three plus two' Administrative Council system with the director-general being a government appointee. This shift was strengthened by the 2004 Gasparri Law that handed back responsibility for appointing RAI's Administrative Council to Parliament and the executive, ending a ten-year period where the two presidents of the Italian Parliament – institutional figures – made such appointments (Maltese 2005; Hibberd 2007).

Conflicts of interest: analysis of the Gasparri and Frattini Laws

As we have seen, the key pieces of legislation in Italy over the past 15 years or so have been the Broadcasting Acts of 1990 and 1997. Berlusconi voted against parts of the 1997 Act and fought the implementation of both, especially those articles relating to Mediaset and Retequattro. It is not surprising therefore that the incoming second Berlusconi government would revise or reverse parts of the 1997 Act. At the same time, however, the new government had to act before 31 December to accommodate the Constitutional Court's decision of 2001, which had set a new deadline for action to be taken.

In November 2003, the Italian Parliament passed a new media law and sent it to the president of the Republic's office for presidential assent. What normally constitutes a procedural formality was turned on its head when, in December 2003, President Ciampi refused to sign Law 249, the Gasparri Law declaring that parts (primarily Article 15) contravened Constitutional Court decisions on external pluralism (see *Corriere della Sera*, 16 December 2003). The Law was sent back to the Italian Parliament for further consideration. In order to beat the Constitutional Court's imposed deadline of 31 December, the government launched the 'Save Retequattro' decree, which allowed Retequattro to broadcast beyond the end-of-year deadline. Berlusconi's supporters hailed the decree as support for the parliamentary law. Opposition politicians argued that the decree ran contrary to constitutional provisions. After some alterations the Gasparri Law was passed in May 2004, this time gaining presidential assent.

Regulation and support of audio-visual industries contained in the new Gasparri Law encompassed an enormous scope and included a wide range of measures which, to a greater or lesser extent, impinged on both economic and cultural objectives. It is beyond the scope of this chapter to evaluate all such measures but my aim, instead, is to consider some of the most important ones. The all-important Article 15 of Law 249 focuses on ownership and cross-media ownership rules. The Gasparri Law proposes two major changes affecting (external) pluralism with 1) the introduction of a maximum threshold of 20 per cent of national channels that a broadcaster is allowed to operate and 2) the introduction of an integrated communications system (*sistema integrato delle comunicazioni* – SIC). This new definition has greatly expanded ownership thresholds not previously covered by media rules, including:

- national and local broadcasting, including pay-per-view, advertising, licence fees, sponsorship and tele-shopping revenue streams;
- publishing (newspapers, magazines, books, electronic publishing);
- cinema, television and music production and distribution;
- advertising (including hoarding advertising) as well as revenues from the internet.

(Venice Commission 2005: 17)

The key point to stress about Article 15 is that it allowed Mediaset to retain Retequattro on terrestrial television, while RAITRE would no longer be forced to give up advertising, as both companies fell safely within the 20 per cent SIC threshold. This overturned provisions contained in the 1997 Act and ran contrary to the 1994 and 2001 Constitutional Court rulings. The Law was, however, consistent with the 1995 referenda results. Evidence suggests that Article 15 allowed Mediaset to expand at a faster rate than its competitors, affecting public service broadcasting, pay-per-view and newspaper markets in Italy. Growth in media markets around the world was driven by spot and sponsor advertising and pay-per-view subscriptions, not licence fees. Relaxation of media and cross-media ownership rules inevitably benefitted above all those companies that derived their income primarily from advertising and subscription payments – Mediaset and SKY Italia. For RAI, which still derived more than half its income from an index-linked licence fee, the risk of falling behind its competitors was a very real one. This provided more ammunition to Berlusconi's detractors who believed the new Law put his commercial interests first and those of the industry and public service broadcasting second.

At the same time, the new law helped RAI. Minister Gasparri was correct in stating that without his law, RAI would have suffered further financial difficulties (*La Repubblica*, 4 August 2003). The law saved RAITRE having to give up advertising, totalling 150 million euros per annum (£100 million). The Law also highlighted the co-dependence or *quid pro quo* nature of the Italian broadcasting market. While the idea of co-dependence outlined earlier is a useful one, there is little doubt that Mediaset stood to gain more from the legislation. The law did not make adequate financial provisions for RAI in meeting the costs of moving to digital.

Although the Venice Commission (2005: 19) saw some positive signs of external pluralism in the expansion of digital television and radio services, its authors add:

> Many of these channels are likely to have very small audience shares, but with similar amounts of output. The Commission finds therefore that the threshold protecting media pluralism, as measured by 20 percent of channels, is not a clear indicator of market share. Neither is this threshold an unambiguous indicator of balance and pluralism in the television and radio market as a whole. Larger companies will enjoy greater purchasing power in a wide range of activities such as programme acquisitions, and will enjoy significant advantages over other national content providers. They can also enjoy an unlimited share of the audience if this scheme is put in place. An individual company could enjoy extremely high degrees of revenue shares in individual markets, whilst at the same time remaining below the 20 percent threshold for the whole sector.

In conclusion, the Commission considered Article 15 largely ineffective as an indicator of diversity. Its report highlights concern regarding the concentration of political, commercial and media power in the hands of Silvio Berlusconi, arguing that the Italian government has a duty to protect, safeguard and promote external media pluralism. The report further states that, in Italy, 'the status quo has been preserved even though legal provisions affecting media pluralism have twice been declared anti-constitutional and the competent authorities have established the dominant positions of RAI and the three television channels of Mediaset (2005: 5).

The Gasparri Law also outlined plans to part-privatize RAI, stipulating that no company or individual could control more than 1 per cent of shares or form voting blocs with more than 2 per cent of shares. These rules were designed to prevent a takeover of the company by a group of small shareholders. One criticism of this form of privatization was that if the company were sold off piecemeal it would leave the Italian Treasury (which took over ownership of RAI after the dissolution of the Italian state holding group, IRI) owning a controlling share of the company. However, this would not have stopped political interference in the company's day-to-day affairs; neither would it have done much to undermine Mediaset's dominance, an argument put by some on the centre-left. The date for the RAI privatization was 2007, but this date had already become delayed prior to Berlusconi's defeat in April 2006, and is now indefinitely postponed pending the new government's proposals for the company.

As already stated, plans to privatize RAI first surfaced under the centre-left government in 1997 and involved privatizing RAI's transmission sites (RAIWAY) and also the two most popular public services channels, RAIUNO and RAIDUE (Fontanarosa 2000). Under such plans, up to 49 per cent of each channel would have been sold off and listed on the Milan Stock Exchange. Both channels would have renounced their share of the licence fee, which would have then been shared among RAI's other core public service activities, especially RAITRE. This type of privatization would have presented Mediaset with more direct problems because without licence fee monies, the two channels would have become more commercial, directly threatening Mediaset's dominant share of advertising revenues. Some critics argued that this was a deliberate attempt by the centre-left to undermine Berlusconi and Mediaset and sell part of RAI to a multi-media company with centre-left connections.

Dealing with the conflicts of interest issue

Neither the first Berlusconi government nor the subsequent governments of the left-wing coalition enacted legislation relating to the conflicts of interest question. In 2001, Berlusconi committed himself to solving the issue. Rules for the resolution of conflicts of interest were finally adopted on 13 July 2004. The new Frattini Law defined conflict of interest thus:

> Conflict of interest arises from a situation in which the public official has a private interest which is such as to influence, or appear to influence, the impartial and objective performance of his or her official duties ... The public official's private interest includes any advantage to himself or herself, to his or her family, close relatives, friends and persons or organisations with whom he or she has or

has had business or political relations. It includes also any liability, whether financial or civil, relating thereto.

(Venice Commission 2005: 26)

However, one notable category of person was excluded from the new rules. Paragraph 4 of Article 1 states that the provisions of the Law do not apply to publicly-elected representatives, members of government and holders of judicial office. Likewise, the Law only declares incompatibility between the management of a company and public office, *not* between ownership and public office, and so sanctions are envisaged not for *owners*, but only for *company managers*. Even officials who find themselves in a situation of a conflict of interest must inform the competent authorities, but are then under no other obligation to remove such conflict of interest. As the Commission (2005: 32) concludes:

> In all, the situations of conflict of interest defined in the law and to which the law attempts at finding a remedy do not appear relevant to the specific issue of the political control of RAI by the owner of Mediaset, for example ... In the light of the above, the Commission is of the opinion that the Frattini law is unlikely to have any meaningful impact on the present situation in Italy.

This Council of Europe-funded research was not the only international report concerning the Italian media system. Another report that has attracted media headlines in the past three years is the annual Freedom House Report 2006 (Hibberd, 2007).

The Freedom House report 2006

Freedom House is a leading US-based non-governmental organization specializing in media issues. It was founded more than 60 years ago by Eleanor Roosevelt. Each year it analyses the state of press freedom worldwide. In 2003, Italy joined Turkey as the only countries in Europe to be rated as 'partly free', which was the first time since 1988 that media of an EU member state had been rated so poorly (Freedom House 2006). In its 2006 report, 23 European countries (92 per cent) were rated 'free' and two (8 per cent), Italy and Turkey again, were rated 'partly free'. The report makes for very pessimistic reading. The organization's main finding was that media freedom in Italy remained constrained by the dominant influence of Silvio Berlusconi. As the report argues:

> In 2004, Mediaset received 58 percent of all advertisement revenues, while RAI received 28 percent. The other commercial nationwide networks receive less than 2 percent of revenues, and the hundreds of local/regional television stations combined receive only 9 percent. In late 2003, the government enacted a temporary waiver ('Save Retequattro' Decree) that removed a previous restriction on one person owning more than two national broadcasting stations, allow-

ing Retequattro, one of three television stations owned by the Berlusconi-dominated Mediaset group, to continue terrestrial broadcasting.

It continues:

Although freedom of speech and press are constitutionally guaranteed, media freedom remained constrained in 2005 by the continued concentration of media power in the hands of Prime Minister Silvio Berlusconi. The Gasparri Law on Broadcasting has been heavily criticized for not providing effective de-monopolization measures and thus doing very little to break up the 'duopoly' of RAI and Mediaset in broadcasting media. The Frattini Law prevents the prime minister from running his own businesses; it does not prevent him from choosing his own proxy, including a family member.

(*Freedom House 2006*)

The Freedom House report (along with the Venice Commission's report) present a damning verdict on the current state of the Italian media system. Berlusconi is widely vilified by these international organizations and the solution to Italy's ills is to resolve the conflicts of interest issue.

9 MOVING TOWARDS DIGITAL: ITALIAN MEDIA IN THE NEW MILLENNIUM

- **Programming and scheduling in a digital era**
- **Audiences**
- **The advertising market in Italy**
- **Digital switchover**

The exploitation of digital technologies for primarily *economic* growth represents a central plank of government policy across the industrialized and developing world. By exploring ways of introducing digital television and telephony services, the Italian government has followed broader trends that have seen the expansion of service industries in order to promote economic regeneration in a post-industrial age. The precise historical motives for adopting digital television have been widely discussed, but it is worth recapping these briefly:

- The use of digital technologies should mean a dramatic increase in the quantity of television and radio channels (compression).
- Digital technologies also offer a better quality images and sound.
- Digital technologies offer the possibility of new 'interactive' services such as internet, email, home banking and shopping.
- Digital technologies are also bringing about a gradual convergence of previously distinct markets and industries.
- The introduction of digital services requires the development of new hardware appliances and software applications such as set-top boxes or decoders built into television sets. This should help stimulate national industrial production in these products and associated goods and services. This should, in turn, also enhance national competitiveness in the international marketplace (Cornford and Robins 1999: 109; AGCOM 2000: 11).

The Italian television system has remained stable for the past 20 years, or more precisely from the time of the public-private consolidation creating the RAI-Fininvest (Mediaset) duopoly in 1984. Although there are 11 national television channels in Italy, the leading channels are the three RAI networks and the three Mediaset networks.[1] These six channels attract some 90 per cent of the viewing audience and around 85 per cent of television advertising. Canale 5 is the principal Mediaset channel and currently Italy's second most popular channel behind RAIUNO. The seventh national television channel, La7 (formerly Telemontecarlo), is owned by Telecom Italia (Italy's main telecommunications company) and enjoyed a 2 per cent share of daytime viewers in 2004 (for the first time in its history). Of daytime viewers, 7 per cent tune into local TV channels. At the local level, there are some 650 local television channels, most of them run primarily by small companies and organizations. The only change of any significance in recent years has been the expansion of satellite television in the form of Sky Italia, owned by Rupert Murdoch's News Corporation group. In 2004, Sky Italia exceeded 3 million subscribers, carving out a 4 per cent share of daytime viewers (Sorrentino and Hibberd 2007).

Plans for digital terrestrial television (DTT) were set out in legislation passed by the outgoing centre-left government in 2001 and DTT was introduced in 2004. The sudden rise in DTT was due in part to a statutory subsidy lowering the price of set-top boxes (box sales reached 1.5 million units by April 2005). In 2006, 30 per cent of Italian families currently had multi-channel TV and access to an ever-expanding array of television channels and programmes. Despite this expansion, it should be noted that RAI and Mediaset hold three of the five digital multiplexes. Digital terrestrial development has been particularly exploited by Mediaset and La7 due to the introduction of prepaid cards allowing pay-per-view services. The broadcasting and telecommunications regulator has recently raised the question of whether set-top box subsidies gave the development of DTT an unfair competitive advantage in relation to other media platforms. The Prodi government is likely to reduce or remove such subsidies. There was no major cable television supplier in Italy until Telecom Italia introduced Alice Home TV in 2005 (TV on ADSL) (Sorrentino and Hibberd 2007).

It is not too difficult to see how digital plans affect RAI and its public service remit. Faced with potential new channels and services, and with the long-term decline of its traditional source of income, the licence fee, RAI, in line with other public service broadcasters, has adopted new profit-orientated and public service strategies to raise finance and to prepare for the challenges digital television will bring.[2] The first strategy has been to introduce new digital satellite and terrestrial channels. The expansion of niche channels is a deliberate attempt by the company to target different social groups with disposable incomes. While some new services are tied to the company's public service remit, the majority of these new operations have been driven by commercial imperatives. New public service channels include: the 24-hour news channel RAINEWS; the sports channel RAISPORT Sat; and the education channel RAI Educational. These services are funded by the licence fee. In addition, new thematic subscription channels were launched on satellite in 1999: Art, Album, Cinema, Gambero Rosso, Ragazzi and Show.

The second strategy employed by the company has seen the general development of its commercial businesses, including new mobile phone and internet companies. The main aim here was for RAI to develop its news services, weather reports, traffic news and train schedule services for the third generation of mobile phones (UMTS). RAI's other commercial operations include RAISAT, which developed the company's move into pay-per-view, RAI CLICK, which owns its internet services and RAIWAY, which manages RAI's transmission sites. The third strategy has seen an increase in the number of RAI's business partners in order to explore possible synergies. With the onset of digital, traditional broadcasters and new media companies are forming alliances to control content and its distribution. It should also be noted that many of these companies are information technology (IT), telecommunications or internet companies.

Programming and scheduling in a digital era

The relatively closed structure of Italian television has led the main competitors, RAI and Mediaset, to construct similar television schedules. For example, Canale 5 offers programming which mirrors that of its main competitor RAIUNO and each transmits two programmes offering a mix of public affairs and 'soft' news in the morning and afternoon. These programmes are then interrupted at lunchtime to make way for the most popular Italian and American soap operas. Currently airing are two soap operas named *Vivere* and *Centovetrine* and the ever-popular (American), *Beautiful*. The two lunchtime news programmes then follow. RAIUNO then airs various television drama series (almost always imported and often reruns), such as an American and a German series currently being broadcast. The only substantial difference, heightened in recent years, is the ever-increasing presence on Canale 5 of reality shows, which RAI airs predominantly on RAIDUE. During evening prime time, the main television channels feature films which are alternated with Italian-produced drama programmes and home-produced quiz shows and variety shows, as well as other entertainment formats.

The second Mediaset channel, Italia 1, has traditionally targeted younger viewers. Early morning TV starts off with cartoons, which children may watch before going to school. Sports programmes follow later in the morning in order to pick up the various groups returning from school. In the afternoon there are more cartoons and other programmes, which are for the most part imported, especially from Japan, all aimed at children, adolescents and young adults. Programming is targeted to these audiences in the early evening and prime time.

In recent years, an effort has been made to experiment with languages and new formats, or even to adapt typically imported programme formats, such as the sitcom, with the aim of creating a following among younger audiences who are increasingly attracted to other cultural alternatives such as the internet. Such experimentation has produced successful programmes and new formats, which have gone on to be shown on the main commercial network Canale 5 once they have caught on with the mass youth public. RAI has imitated these programmes as well, and thus new characters and television presenters have been successfully introduced.

Such programmes have tried to halt the fragmentation of youth audiences, so as to create schedules which start with attracting small children and then adolescents or young adults. Hybrid programmes are created which bridge the youth markets, favouring awareness among pre-adolescents to the themes, problems and lifestyles of their older siblings. This also contributes to viewer loyalty, which originates in infancy and is maintained over the course of time.

As with other advanced capitalist countries, attracting audiences for news programmes in Italy presents an ever-increasing challenge. While the 1990 legislation obliges all television channels to broadcast daily news programmes, Italia 1, in particular, has met the greatest difficulty in developing news programmes that will successfully interest their young audiences. For several years now some channels have opted for 'tabloid' daily news programmes, in which the major political and economic stories can be sidelined in favour of 'soft' news, mainly from the world of music and entertainment. Bridging the gap between hard and soft news are more experimental formats – i.e. satire – which have been somewhat controversial (Sorrentino and Hibberd 2007).

Mediaset's third channel, Rete 4, attracts a predominantly elderly and female audience. Rete 4 airs television series and reality shows such as the successful *Forum*, in which a (retired) judge uses a studio 'court' to resolve civil cases. Rete 4 has endeavoured to put into place a popular early evening news, composed of current events and soft news concerning entertainment figures or sports. A substantial dose of personal interest is lent to events by the main presenter, Emilio Fede, who dominates proceedings. Silvio Berlusconi's entry into politics has also helped transform the programme, as Fede has never hidden his personal or political support for Berlusconi. While still maintaining popular appeal based on a mix of news stories including human interest items, and driven by the appeal of the main 'star' of the programme, Rete 4 has wholeheartedly interpreted events in such a way as to complement Berlusconi's political efforts (Sorrentino and Hibberd 2007).

RAI's public service commitments do not always emerge strongly from an examination of the amount of time given to daily news coverage, though the company has increased this amount in comparison to Mediaset. Where the distance between public and private operators becomes more apparent is in other forms of current affairs programming. Once confined to hard news only, current affairs programming has progressively expanded to encompass various forms of talk shows, which have contributed to the process known as the 'tabloidization' of television. The expansion of these formats explains the growth in current affairs programming on the part of RAI to the detriment of arts programmes (Sorrentino and Hibberd 2007).

Private television has a higher percentage of serials and films. This explains the lower percentage of home-made productions for Mediaset. Over the years both RAI and Mediaset have tended to offer more and more Italian-produced series, and these programmes enjoy a great deal of success (Buonanno 1999, 2006). This is due in part to the European

Commission's Television Without Frontiers directives, which specify minimum limits on home, European and independently-produced television and radio programmes (Sorrentino and Hibberd 2007).

Entertainment programmes also have a large presence on the main commercial channels, although changes have taken place in recent years. The greatest victim has been the perennial variety show – featuring a presenter or host, dance troupes and singers, once a staple diet of Saturday evening – which has been slowly replaced by reality shows. RAI has consistently produced about 75 per cent of its programmes, while Mediaset often struggles to make 50 per cent. This has meant that commercial channels have faced difficulties in meeting European programme quotas outlined in the Television Without Frontiers directive (Andreano and Iapadre 2005). RAI buys 10–12 per cent of programmes from other Italian producers while the other European countries have increased their supply of programmes to the Italian market (Sorrentino and Hibberd 2007).

Audiences

RAIUNO and Canale 5 are the two leading television channels in Italy. Both take special care in their choice of programming, particularly during prime-time evening schedules, so as to involve the 'general' audience, often families. Over the last decade, Mediaset's second channel, Italia 1, has enjoyed a steady increase in its ratings, targeting younger audiences, which has now forced RAIDUE into third place in the audience rankings. Rete 4, Mediaset's third channel, has maintained its position in sixth place, targeting older, female audiences from lower middle-class backgrounds (Sorrentino and Hibberd 2007). RAITRE caters for regional audiences through the provision of daily news services and often produces minority programmes or cutting-edge productions.

The main difference between the three major public and private networks lies in their main target audiences. As previously stated, Canale 5 is a general interest network, Italia 1 targets younger audiences and Rete 4 predominantly targets women. The three RAI networks, however, do not position themselves like this, in part due to the very close ties to the political system, as outlined in previous chapters.

The Italian radio broadcasting system is highly fragmented. Despite new laws (No. 66, 2001 and No. 112, 2004) attempting to reduce the number of radio stations, around 1,500 of these still remain. They can be divided into five categories:

1   RAI radio stations, Radiouno, Radiodue, Radiotre, Notturno italiano and Isoradio.
2   National private radio.
3   Syndications – regional chains of local networks that transmit part of their daily programming together sharing advertising revenues.

4   Local radio, considered to be those stations which serve a territory with no more than 1.5 million inhabitants.
5   National and local non-profit 'community' radio stations focusing on a common theme, whether it be of a cultural, political or religious nature (Sorrentino and Hibberd 2007).

Such fragmentation also affects consumption patterns and the market for many radio stations is quite small and threatens to weaken even further. Elemedia, a company owning three national radio stations (and a member of the publishing group *La Repubblica-Espresso*, one of Italy's most prominent publishers) and RAI are Italy's two main radio broadcasters, controlling 36 per cent of advertising revenues. The top five radio broadcasters take 55 per cent of advertising revenues. Smaller radio stations comprise over 32 per cent of total advertising revenues, confirming activity in a sector marked by individual and strategically-offered diversified content, whether it be all-music radio, news radio, or even themed programming covering topics ranging from cultural content to religious affairs (Sorrentino and Hibberd 2007).

Strong activity has led to a growth in the overall number of radio listeners as well as in total profits generated. Some 36.56 million people listened to the radio daily in 2004, with a strong increase in consumption taking place in cars. Profits have also grown, reaching 400 million euros in 2004, an increase of 21 per cent over the previous year's figures. The evolution of the Italian radio broadcasting system has allowed Radio Deejay (of the Elemedia group) to stake its claim among the top radio players, overtaking RAI's Radiouno as Italy's most popular station. The top five radio broadcasting stations remain stable (Sorrentino and Hibberd 2007) and their audience shares are shown in Table 9.1.

Table 9.1 The top five Italian radio stations in 2004

Station	Audience share (%)/bold
Radio Deejay	10.9
RAI Radiouno	10.5
RDS	7.9
Radio 105	6.3
RTL	6.0

Source: Audiradio

The advertising market in Italy

The presence of RAI and Mediaset, each with three general interest networks, dominates the Italian advertising market, thanks to a particularly advantageous policy towards television advertisers. The result is that advertising investment has increasingly been directed to television, which currently absorbs half the total resources, to the detriment of print media (see Table 9.2).

Table 9.2 Market share of advertising in Italy (%), 1990 and 2004

	1990	2004
Newspapers	24.6	23.4
Magazines	17.9	15.9
Print media total	42.5	39.3
Television total	49.0	50.3
Radio total	3.3	5.4
Cinema	0.2	1.2
Other	4.9	3.8

Source: RAI Annual

Television's dominance in the Italian advertising market can also be attributed to the historical weakness of the print media in Italy. As previously stated, the advent of commercial television initially had a positive effect on the whole advertising market, which saw significant growth and, as a consequence, brought beneficial results to the other media, including newspapers and periodicals. But the recession of the 1990s caused widespread economic difficulties. In 1993, for the first time in 20 years, there was a drop in total advertising revenues. In recent years television advertising revenues have enjoyed a period of growth, about 9 per cent or more in the past two years, while newspapers and periodicals have seen a decrease. Due to this trend, television's share of the advertising market has returned to over 50 per cent of the overall advertising market. Radio's constant growth in recent years has resulted in a corresponding increase in radio advertising, though it still remains a peripheral player: starting from a 3.3 per cent share of the total in 1990 and expanding to a 5.4 per cent share in 2004.

The increasing importance of advertising revenues has accentuated the competition between the two main television groups. Advertising represents almost the only means of financing for Mediaset, and around half of the income of public television. For RAI, the total amount of income derived from the licence fee has fallen by 10 per cent in the last ten years, declining from 58 to 48 per cent (see Table 9.3).

Advertising revenues in 2004 amounted to 58.1 per cent of the total earnings for the Italian television market (6,374 million euros). This marked a decrease from the 61.9 per cent share it held in 2000, though profits for the main television players rose by 18 per cent in the same period. The reason for this was the substantial increase in revenue from pay-for-view television, which went from 652 million euros in 2000 to 160 million euros in 2004, almost entirely derived from Sky Italia.

Table 9.3 Sources of revenue (%) for RAI and Mediaset 2000 and 2004

	2000	2004
RAI		
Advertising	38.7	37.5
Programme sales	2.1	3.6
Licence fee	58.1	48.7
Other	1.2	10.2
Mediaset		
Advertising	93.6	95.9
Programme sales	5.2	2.0
Other	1.2	2.1

Source: RAI Annual

Largely due to this, the Italian television market grew by 18.2 per cent between 2000 and 2004. It should be noted that Italy's total advertising market remains small compared to its major European competitors and current legislative proposals, introduced by the minister for communications, Paolo Gentiloni, aim to open up the market to new players and impose more stringent anti-trust rules (Sorrentino and Hibberd 2007).

Digital switchover

Although the original timetable for the switchover from analogue to digital television provided in the Gasparri Law for 2006 has not been met, the digital revolution will modify the entire structure of the Italian media system. The current new date for switchover is 2012. Consumption patterns will inevitably change as a result of the additional media platforms and content available. This will change further the social importance of the media. By March 2005 there were 24 national digital terrestrial channels, plus two pay-per-view channels, four radio channels and three channels allowing for local radio coverage. The digital transformation will inevitably spark competition between satellite, digital terrestrial and even wideband platforms, producing greater convergence between television, internet and telephony (both fixed and mobile networks). It seems unlikely that Sky Italia's satellite monopoly will be threatened in the near future. Sky Italia now exceeds 3 million subscribers and it broadened its services by offering the 2006 World Cup, four new channels which started in autumn 2006, and high definition (HD) television, targeting the 5 per cent of Italian families who already possess HD television sets. Out of the four companies currently in the digital terrestrial market – RAI, the Holland Coordinator & Service Company,

Mediaset and Telecom Italia Media – only the latter two, with four and six channels each respectively, offer specific sports and entertainment subscription services (Sorrentino and Hibberd 2007).

Local television stations have also been attracted by the digital opportunities afforded by digital terrestrial, but have thus far been unable to identify forms and strategies to allow them to take advantage of such innovations (Barca 2007). The transition to digital terrestrial will argu-ably serve to encourage greater consolidation in the local television sector, with more mergers of local operators and possible buy-outs by major national broadcasting networks (Barca 2007; Sorrentino and Hibberd 2007).

The digital marketplace will also see more services supplied by telecom companies using ADSL broadband. Two companies are already present in this market, Fastweb and Telecom Italia, and other companies such as Wind, Tele2, Tiscali and HG3 will most likely also enter the market. There is likely to be greater separation between content and network providers. Due to the Gasparri Law allowing greater cross-media owner-ship, many of the principal publishing groups are examining how they can enter the digital marketplace. Digital television, radio and broadband markets are still emerging in Italy although strong pressures exist support-ing the current duopoly. In his recent work on digital television, Alessan-dro D'Arma (2007: 1) has argued that:

> My analysis broadly corroborates what has been argued examining digital transition policies in a number of other countries, most notably the importance of domestic agendas in explaining govern-ments' motives behind the formulation and implementation of such policies. At the heart of the initiatives on digital switchover in Italy is the issue of competition in the terrestrial television market, historically characterised by the duopoly of Berlusconi's Mediaset and state broadcaster, RAI. Depending on the political orientation of the government in office, digital transition in Italy has primarily been about either breaking the RAI-Mediaset analogue-based duopoly or extending it into the digital future.

In relation to the 2001–6 Berlusconi government, he also notes (2007: 19):

> In particular, the case of DTT policies from 2001 to 2006 illustrates how a government determined to promote the interests of the domestic industry – the centre-right one rallying behind the business interests of its leader Silvio Berlusconi – has successfully promoted its controversial agenda, despite considerable internal as well as external resistance. The Berlusconi government has conveniently seized the opportunity of introducing a new communication technol-ogy – DTT – as a means to preserve the dominant market position of the incumbent private broadcaster. It has made policy choices which have allegedly contravened EU law and have clearly been

detrimental to the interests of Sky Italia, the satellite-based digital platform owned by Murdoch's News Corporation. In short, it has enjoyed considerable autonomy to shape the digital transition in consonance with its policy agenda.

As regards radio, Italy had already chosen the DAB-T standard before its adoption by the European Telecommunication Standards Institute. The transition to DAB-T will provoke changes in the Italian radio market and will allow transmission of text, images and data as well as audio. Digital radio can receive programme titles, song lyrics, electronic newspapers, geographical maps, meteorological information and traffic news. Again, however, strong pressures exist supporting current radio operators (Sorrentino and Hibberd 2007).

10 CONCLUSION

Each nation-state has developed media systems in line with its own internal political and social conditions, market imperatives and institutional practices (Corner *et al.* 1997: 5). This is clearly illustrated by the development of the media in Italy where political elites have played a major role in steering media development and where a unique market has developed since Unification in 1861. This book has focused on the key events and processes in the development of Italy's media – press, cinema, radio and television – and has explained media development within broad economic, political and sociocultural parameters.

Chapter 1 traced the history of Italy and its media to the Unification of the country in 1861 and looked at the difficulties of uniting a politically and economically divided country. It also discussed the problems faced by post-Unification governments in reconciling the new Italian state to its people and the role of the media in that process. The chapter finished with an examination of the Fascist period and drew attention to the regime's close control of certain mass media, especially the press industry, and its rather halting stance to domestic cinematographic production and growth of the nascent radio industry.

One aim of this book has been to examine the importance of the Italian nation-state to the development of its mass media. The durability of the modern nation-state can be accounted for by the fact that it is a social and cultural entity as well as political construction. Anthony D. Smith identifies the 'benefits of membership' a nation brings which help explain why the nation-state has remained so pervasive in the era of (high) modernity and globalizing pressures. These benefits include: an answer to the problem of personal oblivion and the promise of a glorious future; the provision of personal regeneration and dignity as part of a 'super-family'; and, most importantly, the prominence it gives to realizing the ideal of fraternity through rituals and symbols (1991: 162). Smith argues that this latter point is the most decisive reason for the success and durability of the nation-state as a collective identity. He concludes that (1991: 163):

> transcending oblivion through posterity; the restoration of collective dignity through an appeal to a golden age; the realisation of fraternity through symbols, rites and ceremonies ... those are the underlying functions of national identity and nationalism in the modern world, and the basic reason why the latter has proved so durable, protean and resilient through all vicissitudes.

There is little doubt that modern mass media play a key role in the realization of fraternity or *sensus communis* through symbols, rites and ceremonies as well as in promoting cultural values and beliefs essential to the maintenance of the nation-state. You could even argue that the modern media is 'old fashioned' in that newspapers and broadcasters will often claim a strong social function in providing comfort and support to those sections of society who often feel most isolated or withdrawn from economic and political life: the pensioner; the poor; the working classes; social and ethnic groups living on the margins of societies. The media can rightly argue that they do more than most companies and institutions in tempering the sense of alienation that modern social conditions can promote.

At the same time, however, the modern mass media is the product of industrial capitalism and (post) modernity. Their development is explicitly linked and tied to the development of cities and urbanization, industrialization, nation-states, democracy and, latterly, global economic, political and social relations. We might even argue that the modern mass media often provide the loudest and most committed cheerleaders for the process of globalization and the economic opportunities it affords some but not others. Therein hides a paradox at the heart of modern mass media. They are both a product of, and a reaction against, (post) modernity: on the one hand they are the product of global capitalism; on the other hand, they often provide content or services that help people cope with the sense of alienation that modern social conditions can promote. This Janus-like characteristic means that media can simultaneously be accused of promoting hate, social unrest and even, in some worst case scenarios, genocide and ethnic cleansing on the one hand, but at the same time be held up as paragons of civic and political virtue by raising monies for charities or uncovering social or political scandals that help improve society.

This book has argued that the Italian media have developed over time within the historical parameters of the nation-state. The fortunes of the mass media have been firmly tied to the mast of the Italian nation-state, which has resulted, at times, in benign and enlightened political rule and economic growth that has allowed the media to develop accordingly. Other historical periods have been characterized by state-led repression and acts of political violence committed against key institutions of civil society, including the mass media. Focusing on the contemporary period, the postwar European settlement brought its own challenges for Italy with Cold War tensions, etc. but it also resulted, arguably, in a period of relative peace and unprecedented economic prosperity for the Italian people. Without doubt, the media played their part in promoting discourses supporting a democratic and united Italy, helping it through a period of unprecedented social development and economic growth, especially through the provision of content – newspapers, films, websites, television and radio programmes – that sought to entertain, inform and educate the Italian public. One only needs to cite Italian film from the 1940s to the 1970s or the development of RAI to highlight this point. The Italian media have encouraged collective viewing and listening habits, allowing citizens to talk to each other as well as providing information and acting as a forum for public debate. At the same time, much of Italian cultural consumption in the twentieth century was of foreign-made media content that was either dubbed or translated into Italian. Evidence would suggest that consumption of non-Italian-made products, especially American film and television, has had an important impact on the construction and negotiation of Italian national identity. So attention is drawn here to the ways in which domestic audiences relate foreign media products to their own social lives.

This book has also argued that the Italian media have played an important role in encouraging Italian social unity in other ways apart from the provision of media content. In Chapter 5, we discussed the importance of Italy's polycentric media organization, which saw different media develop in various Italian cities and regions, creating a division of labour between the primary localities of the peninsula. This arguably contributed towards the cultural unity of Italy. I also argued that this system has been progressively eroded in the past 40 years and the structure of Italy's media system is today characterized by the rise of Rome and Milan as the two dominant, but competing, media centres in Italy. This has caused political antagonism between the two main cities and resentment from other parts of Italy which has manifested itself in other areas of Italian political and social life. As we have seen, distrust of the Italian nation-state has grown, with demands from some regions for greater autonomy from Rome, especially relating to taxation and fiscal policy. Again, Italy is not alone in experiencing these autonomous pressures in Europe.

The nation-state has also become threatened by the jump to a postmodern condition which, as we have discussed, has occurred through the rapid expansion of global capital accumulation, aided by instant telecommunications, global mass media and a supply of cheap, international labour. This has created conditions in which new social orders – multinational conglomerates, non-governmental organizations (NGOs) – and cultural identities have emerged, as we consume more commercial and international media content. The spread of the internet is often seen as a key development in this area, allowing people to consume media that belongs to a different culture and language (normally English), territory and time zone. This, so it has been argued, loosens cultural and social ties between citizens. And yet, the nation-state retains its position as the key social, economic and political unit through which human beings organize themselves and their media systems. Even in an era of global television, film finance and production, international editions of newspapers and the development of programme formats, including multiple 'reality' strands, national audiences still constitute the key target group for government, policy-makers, media companies, programme-makers and advertisers. The generic terms 'general public', 'citizen', 'consumer', etc., refer, more often than not, to members of nation-states. National audiences still tend to consume national media.

While the Italian media have been a major force for good in the postwar period, they have also actively engaged in systematic political and social exclusion, especially in the Cold War period. The deliberate policy of political exclusion was at the behest of governing parties, the Catholic Church and foreign governments. Political subservience also undermined claims that the media enjoy substantial independence or autonomy from political elites. Broadcasting has been particularly susceptible to these pressures: one only has to think about the 1948 general election campaign and its aftermath, when the Communists were systematically excluded from radio broadcasts, or when, in the 1960s, RAI opened its doors to elements of the Italian left without embracing a fully inclusive political culture. Finally, we should consider the appearance of the tripartite RAI. Italy, though, is not alone in facing these accusations. Cases of overt and covert political interference have become a permanent feature of media in Western Europe. For example, the development of *Proporz*-style appointment committees in Austrian, German and Swiss broadcasting, whereby key posts were shared among political parties, or the vetting of senior broadcasting executives at the BBC by the secret services (Humphreys 1994: 321; Smith 1995: 79).

The politicization of the media has been a constant feature of postwar Italian life. Political parties have owned newspapers and have kept close control of public service broadcasting. Even commercial media have been strongly politicized, relying on strong clientelistic ties with political parties in order to gain state funding or political help. This model of media development is very typical of Mediterranean countries, but the form it takes varies from country to country. The advantage of the Italian system is that, for all its faults, it has encouraged a degree of internal and external pluralism over the years. Disadvantages of this system include the media enjoying little real autonomy from political elites and the low esteem in which key professional groups, such as journalists, are held (Hallin and Mancini 2004: 109).

One feature that emerges from analysing media in Italy is that there are strong lines of continuity. For example, political control over RAI continues unabated, although it now takes a different form. The precise system of *lottizzazione* is no longer practised as it formerly was under the Christian Democrat, Socialist and Communist triumvirate. But the appointment of Administrative Councils and all senior managerial positions in RAI is still subject to detailed negotiations between political parties. Strong clientelistic relationships remain between the media and parties on both sides of the political divide.

But there are also clear differences between today's Italian media system and its relationship with political elites and the situation in the Berlusconi years. As I argued elsewhere in this book, advanced capitalist societies now have more market-driven media industries as a result of a response to economic and technological change (Doyle and Hibberd 2003). One of the key features of this shift is the high degree of cross-media ownership present in many countries. In that sense, Italy is not unique in experiencing the following trends: moves away from mono-media ownership to cross-media ownership; the development of media companies with substantial non-media interests; and the gradual convergence of 'old' and 'new' media industries under the control of single multinational corporations. The development of media moguls, as we know, is not confined to Italy.

But while most media moguls wield political influence indirectly by lobbying political elites for favourable legislative changes and/or by influencing the court of public opinion via their media outlets, Berlusconi has chosen to lead from the front. There are numerous reasons for this, all mentioned in the various biographies of the man. These might include: the only viable option to save himself and his friends from prying magistrates; a gap in the marketplace for a centre-right party; the lack of leaders available to lead such a party in 1994; Mediaset's negative economic plight that required urgent action; Berlusconi's sense of patriotism to a country suffering hard times; his sense of moral and political purpose to save Italy from 'communist' influences (Lane 2004; Ginsborg 2003). The Berlusconi phenomenon is therefore the product of international media and business trends and domestic Italian political culture.

There is little doubt that Berlusconi has used his parliamentary majority to reverse 'unfavourable' legislative and judicial judgements to his commercial and political advantage. Protectionism and self-interest are strong features of Berlusconi's media policy. He has turned from being a client of the First Republic's political class, receiving favours from his patron, Bettino Craxi, to becoming a patron and client of the Second Italian Republic. As prime minister, he bestowed patronage on Mediaset, Italy's foremost media empire, owned by the media magnate, Silvio Berlusconi, and managed by his family and close business associates. In return, Mediaset granted Berlusconi a disproportionate amount of positive news coverage and publicity.

The concentration of political and media power in the hands of Silvio Berlusconi has, at times, hindered the *development* of media pluralism in Italy. Witness his interference at RAI. Whether Berlusconi's actions have reduced the overall *amount* of media pluralism in Italy is harder to ascertain. Certainly, high concentration of ownership means fewer suppliers of media good and products, which in turn implies less pluralism (Doyle 2002: 13). But little empirical work has been done on the precise sociocultural and political impact of Berlusconi's domination of the media. The little evidence that does exist would point to some political impact at election time (Rositi 1994; Ricolfi 1997). But media pluralism is also measured by the range of media output available to the public and surely the arrival of the internet and other satellite and terrestrial digital services in the past decade has increased the number and range of media outlets and products?

While this book remains very critical of the current situation, it recognizes that future developments might help change things. One recent development has been the expansion of satellite television in the form of Sky Italia, owned by Murdoch's News Corporation group. In 2004, Sky Italia exceeded 3 million subscribers, carving out a 4 per cent share of daytime viewers. The arrival of News Corporation to the digital satellite market provides hope that the Italian media market is not as closed as some would like to think. The development of DTT might also lead to more media players. Despite this expansion, it should be noted that RAI and Mediaset hold three of the five digital multiplexes. Digital television, radio and broadband markets are still emerging in Italy and future predictions are difficult to make due to uncertain consumer demand for new services. The situation in radio broadcasting is similar. But at the same time, the multiplication of television channels may not effectively guarantee greater pluralism. The Gasparri and Frattini Laws allowed Berlusconi and Mediaset to maintain a dominant hold in the broadcasting sector without reaching the antitrust limit. Pressures to retain the status quo remain strong (Venice Commission 2005).

In conclusion, a key argument of this book has been that the democratic nation-state has maintained and entrenched citizenship in the postwar period. And however imperfect its political system may be in practice, Italy provides a clear illustration of this argument. In the postwar years, the Italian nation-state rebuilt the country's political and social fabric after years of fascism, occupation and civil war. Successive postwar governments decided that political and social renewal was best achieved through the entrenchment of political power in Rome. A strong Italy became an essential element of the West's plans to fight the Soviet bloc with the onset of the Cold War. Italians may still distrust their political system and politicians on the back of corruption and financial scandals, but their sense of shared belonging through common culture and language has been reinforced by the mass media since Unification. In that sense Italy demonstrates strengths and weaknesses as it progresses in the early years of the twenty-first century.

TIMELINE OF POLITICAL EVENTS IN ITALY, 1861–2007

1861

As the result of Giuseppe Garibaldi's military conquests in Sicily and the southern part of Italy, and Count Camillo Benso di Cavour's diplomacy, the Italian nation-state is founded, marking the end of centuries of foreign rule in large parts of the peninsula. Italy forms a constitutional monarchy under King Victor Emmanuel II. The first capital of Italy is Turin where Cavour forms the government. Cavour dies a few months later from complications brought about by a malaria-type illness.

1860s

The Brigand Wars result in the loss of more life than during the Unification of Italy. Disaffected groups rebel against the new state as economic and social conditions worsen in many parts of the South. Some parts of the North enjoy an economic revival under the new Italian state. This North/South economic divide still influences Italian political and social policy today.

1865

Italy's capital moves to Florence.

1866

Venice is liberated from Austrian rule and becomes part of Italy.

1870

On the pretext of protecting the Pope after French withdrawal, the Italian military occupies Rome. The capital of Italy moves to Rome in 1871.

1876

Agostino Depretis forms his first government and perfects the art of *trasformismo* or transformism; that is, forming alliances between individuals and groups into coalition government. Francesco Crispi and Giovanni Giolitti are also key users of this political method.

1893

The Banca Romana scandal breaks, implicating leading Italian politicians, including Giovanni Giolitti, and journalists.

1896
Italy's imperialist hopes are dashed at the Battle of Adowa in March.

1898
Complaining about increasing bread prices, about 100 demonstrators are killed by the military under General Fiorenzo Bava-Beccaris in Milan. The incident becomes known as the Bava-Beccaris Massacre.

1900
King Umberto I of Italy is assassinated by anarchist Gaetano Bresci in Monza (he survived two earlier attempts in 1878 and 1897).

1903
Giovanni Giolitti heads a government that seeks a historical alliance between Socialists and Catholics (*Connubio*). Giolitti would govern Italy three times in the period up to 1914 (1903–5, 1906–9, 1911–14).

1911–12
Italy colonizes what is modern-day Libya.

1915
Italy enters the First World War against Germany and Austria.

1917
The Italian military suffers humiliating defeat and mutiny at the Battle of Caporetto.

1919
The *Partito Popolare Italiano* (PPI) is formed by Catholics led by Luigi Sturzo. The Fascist Party is founded by Benito Mussolini. Italy gains Trentino, South Tyrol and Trieste under the postwar peace treaties, but Italian protestors march against the so-called 'mutilated peace' (*vittoria mutilata*), Italy's failure to receive all the land promised by the Allies. National elections leave the Socialists (PSI) as the biggest party in Parliament followed by the PPI.

1921
The Italian Communist Party (PCI) is founded.

1922
The 'March on Rome' brings Mussolini's Fascists to power.

1924

Socialist parliamentarian, Giacomo Matteotti, is murdered by Fascists. Opposition parties withdraw from Parliament.

1926

Opposition parties declared illegal and prominent opposition members are arrested.

1929

The Catholic Church and Italian state sign the Lateran Pacts, a series of accords and treaties which bring formal recognition of the Italian state by the Church and of a sovereign Vatican state by Italy. Pacts include financial settlement for loss of Papal Territories.

1935–6

War in Abyssinia (modern-day Ethiopia) leads to the declaration of an Italian empire in East Africa. Italy forms Axis with Nazi Germany.

1937

Leading Italian communist and political thinker, Antonio Gramsci, dies after more than a decade in Fascist prisons.

1938

Fascists introduce anti-Semite laws which would eventually see Jews excluded from professions and eventually deported to concentration camps during the Second World War.

1939

Italy annexes Albania.

1940

Italy enters the Second World War with Germany and Austria and occupies British Somaliland in East Africa.

1941

Italy declares war on the Soviet Union.

1943

Allied armies under the command of the American General Dwight Eisenhower and the British General Sir Harold Alexander land in Sicily and then proceed to land on the Italian mainland. Mussolini is subsequently forced from power, and is replaced by Marshal Badoglio. Italy signs an armistice with the Allied powers, declaring war on Germany. The Italian government and monarchy withdraw from Rome to Brindisi. In response, German forces overrun large parts of northern and central Italy, rescuing Mussolini from prison and placing him at the head of a puppet northern Italian government (Republic of Salò). Italy is effectively split in two.

1944

Italian Communist leader, Palmiro Togliatti, returns from exile in Moscow and announces alliance with anti-Fascist parties ('*Svolta di Salerno*').

1945

Last parts of northern Italy are liberated from German rule on 24 April (subsequently celebrated as Liberation Day). Mussolini is assassinated by partisans three days later and his corpse is paraded in Milan. The leader of the renamed *Democrazia Cattolica* (DC), Alcide De Gasperi, forms a new government in late 1945. De Gasperi will remain Italy's prime minister until 1953 and will play a central role in shaping postwar Italian democratic life.

1946

Winston Churchill gives his famous 'Iron Curtain' speech in Fulton Missouri, USA, in March. National elections are held in Italy on 2 June for the Constituent Assembly which will draft Italy's new constitution. A referendum is held on the same day which votes to form an Italian Republic, thereby abolishing the Italian monarchy (54 to 46 per cent). Thereafter, 2 June becomes celebrated as Republican Day.

1947

Alcide De Gasperi travels to the USA to gain American political support and financial aid from President Harry Truman and Secretary of State George Marshall. He is advised by the Americans to drop the Communists and Socialists from his government (Truman would make his famous Doctrine speech on 12 March and initiate the Marshall Plan to grant economic and technical assistance to European countries). Once the new constitutional arrangements have been agreed by the Constituent Assembly, the Communists and Socialists are thrown out of the national government. Italy cedes land and territories under a postwar peace treaty.

1948

The new Italian constitution comes in to force. Key national elections for the new Italian parliament see a bitter struggle between the PCI and DC. The DC and De Gasperi win the largest number of seats. The PCI and PSI are defeated. Hopes of political stability are threatened when an assassination attempt on the Communist leader Palmiro Togliatti leads to mass protests and civil unrest.

1949

The Italian Parliament agrees to join the Northern Atlantic Treaty Organization (NATO), sealing Italy's support for the USA and her allies against the Communist Soviet bloc.

1950

Civil disturbances in the South of Italy.

1951

Italy joins the European Coal and Steel Community, forerunner to the European Economic Community (EEC).

1953

National elections see victory for the DC, although their vote declines. The results lead the Party splitting into *correnti* or factions, especially after De Gasperi's death in 1954.

1954

The DC's reform of the electoral law is rejected in Parliament. The law was designed to boost the majority of the largest party in Parliament and quickly earns the nickname the 'Swindle Law' or *legge truffa*.

1955

Italy becomes full member of the United Nations (UN).

1956

The PCI supports Soviet intervention in Hungary and criticizes the uprising. Communist leaders, including the current Italian president, Giorgio Napolitano, would in later years regret this support. The PSI distance themselves from the Communists by criticizing Soviet actions.

1957

Italy becomes one of the founding member states of the EEC. The document giving life to the EEC is signed in Rome.

1958

National elections see the DC increase their share of the vote in what is viewed as a triumph for DC moderate leader, Amintore Fanfani. Amintore would dominate Italian politics in the late 1950s and 1960s. Angelo Roncalli (John XXIII), becomes Pope.

1960

The DC government led by Fernando Tambroni resigns after he attempts to bring the neo-Fascist MSI party in to his government coalition.

1962
Second Vatican Council opens in Rome and initiates major reforms of the Church including the end of the Latin mass in favour of the vernacular.

1963
National elections see the DC lose votes, opening the way for the Socialists to join the DC-led government of Aldo Moro. Pope John XXIII dies.

1964
The Communist leader, Palmiro Togliatti, dies. More than a million people line the funeral route.

1967
Student protests mark the start of three years of political and social unrest in Italy, culminating in the Piazza Fontana bomb in Milan and the so-called *Autunno Caldo*, the 'Hot Autumn' strikes of 1969. Divorce is legalized in Italy heralding the start of major social reforms many of which run against official Catholic doctrine.

1970
Further civil unrest and protests occur in southern Italy.

1971
Contraceptives are legalized.

1973
Communist leader Enrico Berlinguer first proposes the Historic Compromise between the PCI and DC.

1974
Divorce referendum as a result of strong lobbying to repeal the 1967 law results in victory for pro-lobby. Terrorist bomb on Rome-Munich train kills 12 people.

1976
National elections see the Communists increase their share of the vote to a record high. The DC remains the largest party.

1977
The editor of *La Stampa* is shot dead by the left-wing terrorist group the Red Brigades. Former DC prime minister, Aldo Moro is kidnapped in Via Fani, Rome, and subsequently assassinated. His murder sends shockwaves

around the world. The Italian president, Giovanni Leone resigns after being involved in a scandal relating to military contracts.

1978
Abortion is legalized.

1980
Right-wing extremists plant a bomb at Bologna station killing 85 people.

1981
Italians vote in a referendum to support the 1978 abortion law. The P2 Masonic Lodge scandal breaks implicating leading politicians, business people and journalists. The DC prime minister, Forlani, publishes the entire list.

1982
The Mafia assassinate General Carlo Alberto Dalla Chiesa in Palermo, causing anti-Mafia protests across Italy.

1983
The first Italian Socialist government is formed under their leader Bettino Craxi. He would lead until 1988. The PCI finally break from the Communist Party in Moscow.

1984
The PCI win the European Parliament elections beating the DC into second place. The PCI leader Enrico Berlinguer dies.

1986
The Mafia 'Maxi' trial opens in Palermo. More than 300 mafiosi would eventually be convicted and sentenced.

1987
The DC makes sweeping gains to win national elections. A young Gianfranco Fini becomes leader of the neo-Fascist MSI Party, reforming it into a right wing political party and eventually changing its name to the *Alleanza Nazionale* or National Alliance. Fini would later serve as foreign minister and deputy prime minister under Silvio Berlusconi.

1989
The PCI, under its leader Achille Occhetto, votes to reform the party in response to changes brought about in the Soviet Union. The Berlin Wall would collapse one month later in December.

1991

The 'Segni' referendum results in Italians voting to abolish its electoral system. The PCI finally concludes reforms begun in 1989 by changing its name to the *Partito Democratico della Sinistra* (PDS). This causes hardliners to break away forming the *Rifondazione Comunista* party.

1992

The arrest of Socialist politician Mario Chiesa in Milan marks the beginning of the Bribesville or *Tangentopoli* corruption scandals. The Autonomist Party, the *Lega Nord* (the Northern League), wins 8 per cent at the national elections. Anti-Mafia judges, Giovanni Falcone and Paolo Borsellino, are assassinated by the Mafia in Sicily in May and June leading to unprecedented civil protests across Italy.

1993

A new electoral reform law is passed introducing a first-past-the-post style system. Italians hope the new system will lead to stronger government coalitions. Key PSI and DC leaders become embroiled in *Tangentopoli* scandals. Both parties dissolve and reform under new names. Splits occur within both parties. Bettino Craxi escapes to Tunisia to avoid arrest.

1994

Media mogul Silvio Berlusconi steps in to the political lacuna by forming the *Forza Italia* party. *Forza Italia* had previously been a national association of Milan, Berlusconi's football team. Coincidentally, Milan win that year's European Cup and within two months of forming *Forza Italia*, Berlusconi, backed up by a highly organized campaign team and a concerted media blitz, wins the national elections forming a coalition government with the Northern League under Umberto Bossi and Gianfranco Fini's National Alliance. The coalition lasts just eight months after the Northern League withdraws parliamentary support.

1995

The former Bank of Italy governor, Lamberto Dini, forms an interim Technocrat government with centre-left support, passing urgent reforms, including an austerity budget, prior to new elections.

1996

National elections see the centre-left Olive Tree alliance win an overall majority. The alliance is led by the economics academic and former DC minister, Romano Prodi.

1998

Despite tight economic and monetary conditions placed upon entry, Prodi succeeds in securing Italian membership of the euro and the process of

European monetary union, which would eventually start on 1 January 2002. But tensions within the centre-left government lead to the collapse of the Prodi government. The new prime minister is an ex-Communist, Massimo D'Alema. Prodi leaves Italian politics shortly afterwards to become president of the European Commission, but would reappear to lead the centre-left to victory in 2006.

1999

The former governor of the Bank of Italy and prime minster in the aftermath of the political scandals in 1993, Carlo Azeglio Ciampi, is elected Italian president.

2000

Bettino Craxi dies in exile in Tunisia. Further tensions in the centre-left coalitions see the collapse of the D'Alema government. The former Socialist, Giuliano Amato, forms an Independent government to take Italy through to national elections due in 2001.

2001

Prior to the 2001 national elections, the leading UK economic magazine, *The Economist*, launches a blistering attack on Silvio Berlusconi arguing that he is 'unfit to govern' due to his media interests. Despite this intervention, Berlusconi and his coalition win the national elections, defeating the centre-left alliance now led by Francesco Rutelli. Berlusconi loses the services of his foreign minister, Renato Ruggiero, who resigns in protest over the Eurosceptic views of cabinet colleagues. Italy's first constitutional referendum since 1946 sees a vote in favour of constitutional change, giving greater fiscal autonomy to the country's 20 regions as well as in education and environment policy.

2002

The euro replaces the lira as Italy's currency. Despite official denials, many Italians complain of sharp price rises in the aftermath of the change.

2003

Italy supports the US-led invasion of Iraq. Italian troops serve in Central Iraq until withdrawn by the centre-left government in 2006. In May, Berlusconi appears in Milan court on corruption charges. He reasserts that he is the victim of a conspiracy by politically-motivated magistrates. In July, Italy takes over the six-month presidency of the EU. Italy's presidency gets off to a disastrous start when Berlusconi refers (jokingly) to a German MEP, Martin Schultz, as a 'Nazi prison guard'. This creates a diplomatic incident with the European Parliament and Germany. Five days later matters get worse when one of Berlusconi's ministers, the Northern League's Stefano Stefani, claims that 'Germans are stereotypical blondes who eat our spaghetti and noisily invade our beaches'. Stefani resigns as a result of the ensuing diplomatic controversy. Berlusconi's presidency of the EU ends on a higher note with praise from Germany's Chancellor Schroeder and other leaders for his work on the European constitution. But a difficult year ends badly as 19 Italian servicemen are killed in a suicide bomb attack on their base in Iraq and then the president of Italy, Carlo Azeglio Ciampi, refuses to sign Berlusconi's new media law after raising numerous objections.

2004

The new media legislation finally passes into law after a number of modifications are made. Berlusconi is finally cleared of corruption after a four-year trial.

2005

The Italian Parliament ratifies new EU constitution but French and Dutch rejections means that it is shelved. The Berlusconi government resigns after suffering defeat in regional elections. Berlusconi forms a new government a few days later after receiving a presidential mandate.

2006

Berlusconi narrowly loses the national elections to his old foe, the centre-left Romano Prodi. Berlusconi demands a recount and refuses to accept defeat. The election result is confirmed by the Italian authorities and so Prodi forms a new government. His majority in the Italian Senate is only two and he relies on the ten votes of Italian Life Senators, former presidents and other distinguished Italians. A former Communist, Giorgio Napolitano, is elected the new Italian president by both Houses of Parliament. The head of the Sicilian Mafia, Bernardo Provenzano, is captured after more than 30 years on the run.

2007

Romano Prodi resigns after the government loses the Senate vote on foreign policy. President Napolitano asks him to stay on and Mr Prodi goes on to win confidence votes in both Houses of Parliament. New media law introduced into parliament.

NOTES

Chapter 4

1   In addition to this three-pronged strategy, many parts of Western Europe were also blessed with an economic revival that further promoted the idea of peace and stability. But the much-vaunted 'economic miracle' of the 1950s and 1960s occurred with the help of numerous one-off factors (Judt 1997: 25, 31–3). In the aftermath of the war, economic growth expanded as a result of American help in the form of Marshall aid which contributed 13 billion dollars to rebuild Western Europe's economic and social infrastructure. The economic boom of the 1950s and 1960s also constituted a 'catch-up' process, reestablishing the rate of industrial and agricultural production to pre-1913 levels after successive periods of economic stagnation, depression and war. For the southern European countries, including Italy, the postwar period saw rapid industrialization; a process which was made easier due to the fact that labour costs were relatively low after the war. Each European nation was therefore required to ensure that an economic, political and social infrastructure existed to fulfil the wider aims of the postwar settlement. This required the active participation of state institutions, social and political parties and commercial activity to secure the postwar peace. The restoration of state and society relations in many European countries, safeguarded by new democratic conventions (declarations, constitutions, statutes), constituted a unique opportunity to encourage greater civic and political democracy and economic and social equity. But for such relations to emerge and prosper required autonomous and public institutions, independent of state and market alike, in order to inform and promote active citizenry. One such public institution would be the media.

2   In fact the 'Mass Manipulation School' has always had an international line-up from C. Wright Mills and the Frankfurt School onwards. In Britain, Ralph Miliband declared that the mass media provided 'a crucial element in the legitimation of capitalist society' (1973: 197). In Italy, Giovanni Cesareo argued that the public service model of television had developed in line with the ruling bloc that created it. This system, he argued, increased the level of individualism of the consumer and atomized the audience (1974: 157); in America, Noam Chomsky long-held the view that broadcasters are too closely tied to state authorities and economic elites to afford any real independence (1994: 110).

Chapter 5

1   Although there was a common rationale of purpose behind public service – to provide information and to act as a forum for public debate – individual national systems developed in line with their own distinctive political, economic and social norms and institutional patterns. In pursuing these common objectives, each Western European country adopted its own variant of the public service ideal. In Italy a centralized and unitary system was promoted by the political authorities (and the Allied forces) to encourage greater social and political cohesion contrary to constitutional provisions

allowing for regional autonomy. In the Cold War era, Italy was too important to the West to be allowed to undergo social and political disintegration. In France, the governments of the Fourth Republic (1945–58) maintained a public monopoly but did very little to encourage broadcasting policy. Although television services began in 1947, there were still only a million viewers in 1958. Under de Gaulle's Fifth Republic, control of broadcasting was centralized further (Smith 1995: 68–9). In the Federal Republic of Germany, a federalized public monopoly was introduced partly to banish all traces of centralized dictatorship and partly to act as a bulwark against the future resurgence of centralized powers (Smith 1995: 78–9). In Britain, the ITV system provided some form of commercial and regional relief to act as counterweight to the centralized BBC (Curran and Seaton 1988: 179). Finally, some countries with multi-ethnic populations introduced multilingual public service broadcasting to cater for each ethnic group (in Belgium, Walloon and Flemish, and in Switzerland, German, French and Italian) within the national fold. Other countries also introduced limited provisions for their ethnic minorities (Siune and Treutzschler 1992: 102–3). There were public service monopolies in Austria, Ireland, the Netherlands and the Nordic countries (Denmark, Norway and Sweden) (Siune and Treutzschler 1992: 102–4).

2   Public service broadcasters in Western Europe were protected from commercial operators in part because of the scarcity of Hertzian frequencies. The broadcasting monopolies were legitimized because they were held ultimately accountable to democratic representatives and not to unaccountable state power or market forces. Where limited commercial operations were permitted (in Britain from 1955), they too were regulated to provide services for the whole community. Also, the dual system was harmonious to the extent that broadcasters competed for viewers but their sources of finance were kept separate, thus preventing cutbacks in service provision. Most public service broadcasters relied on some form of public funding, either through a licence fee only (Denmark, Norway and Sweden), a mixture of licence fee with some advertising revenue (Austria, Belgium, Finland, France, Germany, Greece, Ireland, Italy, the Netherlands, Portugal and Switzerland) or a dual system (Britain) (Siune and Treutzschler 1992: 103). Protected from commercial operators and with a guaranteed source of income, broadcasters could offer a universal service and target a unified audience, largely unrestrained by audience figures, commercial pressures, etc. Above all, governments sought to use broadcasting as a means by which to educate and inform society. In terms of education provision, broadcasters could, for instance, produce a whole body of documentaries for a general audience relating to a wide range of topics including science, the arts and nature. But education also extended towards dramatizing great literary works or presenting classic social dramas. Also, minority groups could be targeted for special broadcasting provisions. The obvious example to give is children's television but others include regional television or linguistic minority provision. In terms of information provision, broadcasting became the primary medium for political communication and electoral coverage. Political coverage was accompanied by guidelines to ensure that a range of public opinions were heard. Finally, public service broadcasting also included entertainment provision. Whether it was purer forms of entertainment (quiz shows, chat shows, soap operas, films) or more high-brow forms (fiction, drama, plays, documentaries), such shows could attract a general viewing audience and encourage citizens to talk to each other.

3   In the mainland North, between 3 and 8 per cent of the population were classed as illiterate; in the mainland South between 19 and 32 per cent; in Sicily, 25 per cent; in Sardinia, 23 per cent (see Forgacs 1990a: 18).

4   From the 1950s onwards, large parts of Western Europe experienced an economic upturn which created its own problems and had unintended side-effects. The large increase in social migration across the continent was one such effect. One consequence of the migratory flight towards economic hot-spots was the need for more social provision, more housing and better education. As a result of the economic boom, new patterns of social consumption began to emerge. The development of the modern privatized family, living in new urban tenements, increased the pressures for new cultural and leisure pastimes. A major cultural form was, of course, television. This form of broadcasting became the primary medium through which citizens could make sense of their lives and understand the nature of economic and social change affecting them. Other traditional forms of media were slowly relegated to a secondary role. The rapid fall in cinema attendance was one example although, and as discussed in the section on postwar Italian cinema, in some countries its presence continued to be felt until the late 1960s (Gundle 1990: 212). Television therefore acted as a unifying agent to maintain social cohesion and stability at a time when many countries were experiencing rapid economic expansion and social mobility.

5   The increasing affluence of Italians coupled with the greater choice and availability of broadcast services meant that television moved from being, in part at least, a communal activity watched in bars and other public places, to being a familial activity. The 1960s witnessed, therefore, an increasing differentiation of the audience. Many studies have also supported the argument of the students in highlighting the atomizing effects of the media, especially television in Italy. Cesareo (1974: 157), for example, argues that the development of a television system controlled by a capitalist ruling bloc promoted all things individual and atomistic. Ginsborg (1990: 242) also argues that although television was initially a collective pastime, with many people watching in bars and clubs, the effects of the 'miracle' atomized society and increased the tendency towards passive and familial use of leisure time, as more and more people could afford to buy their own sets. Yet, the theory that television has been directly responsible for the atomization of Italian society was, and remains, somewhat problematic. While there was undoubtedly a decline in communal pastimes in Italy, this argument ignores ways in which television may have helped to reintegrate and reinvigorate civil society. For example, Cavazza (1979: 94–6) points out that those who followed the telegiornale reports would have been struck by two conflicting impressions: first, the celebration of the achievements of the government, which helped those in power; second, the determination of the government to find solutions to serious problems of which the viewer had been, until then, hardly aware. The protests of 1968 were, at least in part, due to the failure of the centre-left coalitions to meet the needs of an increasingly dynamic society. The problem, as Ginsborg (1990: 98) points out, was that the political majority had done both too much and too little; they talked endlessly of reform, but left expectations unfulfilled. The argument that RAI fragmented Italian society in the 1960s is unproven, as Franco Monteleone (1992: 345) argues: 'RAI's strategic priorities were directed to increasing the production and consumption levels independently from any desired social demand. Under

the aegis of a broadcasting monopoly, the main principle was to control the cognitive process of socialisation, to satisfy the majority of viewers and gain consensus'.

6   The term in a literal translation means 'to divide into lots', 'to lot'. In its political sense it means patronage by the major parties. The term is normally associated with the tripartite partition of RAI in the mid-1970s. But the first recorded use of the word in this context was by Alberto Ronchey in 1968 (see Ortoleva 1994: 116).

7   The need for the *lottizzazione* of RAI resulted above all else from a wider political crisis. The advent of severe political violence in the early 1970s was a manifestation of wider economic and social instability affecting Italy. Gone were the days of Christian Democrat dominance, undermined as the Party was from within and without and forced to look elsewhere for electoral and coalition partners. Gone also were the days of heady economic growth which had, in part, hidden the manifest regional, social and economic disparities in Italy. The inclusion of the Communists as a 'sleeping partner' in successive coalition governments in the 1976–9 period was widely regarded as a 'Historical Compromise': the union of Catholics and Communists supporting the same government.

Chapter 6

1   As we have seen, the implementation of the postwar peace in Europe was greatly facilitated by this sustained period of economic growth. By the early 1970s, however, the period of continuous expansion had come to an end and much of Europe began to experience fluctuating economic cycles of boom, stagnation and bust. The economic crisis of the mid-1970s, precipitated as it was by the 1973 oil crisis, was the first sign of deeper structural problems for European economies. For many European governments, one possible solution to the economic ills was to commercialize those industries that had formally been under-utilized. A prime example of this was the telecommunications and broadcasting industries. These were not run on economic criteria but linked to political and cultural needs. European broadcasting systems were also national-based with no substantive international dimension to their opera-tions. As a result, broadcasting was uncommercial and remained largely untapped by business capital, except for hardware sales and advertising where permitted (Siune and Treutzschler 1992: 103). While European economies were buoyant in the postwar period, advertising and marketing opportunities were under-utilized. With the onset of economic troubles, this situation began to change. Furthermore, by the 1960s social conditions were evolving fast and this impaired the ability of governments to keep close control of the broadcasting industry. The postwar boom had produced very different social and economic conditions to those existing in the immediate postwar years. The 30 years from 1945 to 1975 saw massive social upheavals across Europe. The allocation of resources to fund welfare systems ensured that people, on the whole, were healthier and better educated. Economic growth had also led to a significant increase in living standards. In many ways, the public had simply matured, especially in their broadcasting tastes, and no one company could fulfil all their broadcasting needs (Richeri 1993: 52–4). In short, there were greater and greater demands being made on an industry which had been traditionally supply-led. In the meantime, halfway measures were taken to allow greater viewing choice while maintaining strict broadcasting standards and social cohesion. The decision to commence a second public service

channel in the early 1960s (in Britain, Italy and Germany) created greater segmentation of the audience and greater viewing choice, but in a controlled, complementary and coordinated manner. Therefore, by the 1970s there were numerous interlocking but distinct pressures in favour of broadcasting change: the advent of new distribution technologies; the reemergence of political thinking welcoming greater commercial intervention; the demands of the public for more programming and services; and the constant search for economic expansion and renewal. Broadcasters could have produced one or two counter-arguments; after all, limited commercial intervention did exist in most countries in the form of advertising and spare Hertzian capacity had allowed the advent of new public channels in the 1960s. But faced with so many compelling arguments for change, governments gradually dismantled the old broadcasting systems. With hindsight therefore it is hardly surprising that the public service monopolies would, one by one, succumb to a commercial logic that would dominate broadcasting policy for the next two decades.

2   The new Administrative Council consisted of 16 members, of whom 10 were elected by the parliamentary commission in charge of supervising broadcasting and 6 were elected by IRI.

3   It is interesting, however, to note that the Communists abstained in the final vote on the Bill and within two years of the vote were represented inside RAI.

4   The Italian case certainly denotes strong and distinct features that place it apart from many of its European rivals. Other European broadcasting companies chose the middle route between partial commercialization and partial maintenance of their public service commitments. The overall effects for all public service broadcasters across Western Europe were threefold: there was a renewed emphasis placed on audience figures; there was a net reduction in expensive programmes (especially drama); and these were substituted by more low-cost programming. At the same time, a series of measures were adopted to boost traditional income. The real value of the licence fee fell throughout the 1980s due to the steep increase in international programme costs and the failure to peg the fee to these costs rather than the more general inflation rate. All European public service broadcasting companies were therefore forced to look for new sources of income and ways in which to reduce their overheads. The first tactic was to alter the structure and organization of the schedules. A second related tactic involved shifting the focus of programme acquisitions. A third tactic involved extending the logic of maximizing financial and audience ratios to internal company structures. The advent of resource utilization schemes resulted in a complete internal reorganization of many public service companies. Such schemes are too numerous to list completely, but included: contracting out personnel and administration tasks to outside agencies; more efficient coordination of production resources (via computerization); tendering or sub-contracting programmes out to internal departments and external production companies in order to reduce costs; and finally, the commercialization of the back-catalogue of programmes and shows via increased video sales. The effect of this policy was to restructure public service broadcasting into commercial-style companies that relied less on big in-house production centres and more on external production companies (Burgelman 1997: 130).

Chapter 8

1   It is interesting to note, however, that after 20 years of liberalization and re-regulation of broadcasting markets in Western Europe, public service broadcasting still constitutes a central plank of national and European media policy. One might ask why this should remain so when the prevailing ideological wind is so anti-public service? This has also prompted renewed debate as to the relative merits or otherwise of public service broadcasting. In his submission to the Swedish Commission on the Future of Broadcasting in 1999, Richard Collins outlined the relative strengths and weaknesses of public service broadcasting. Arguably, there are at least four advantages of having an efficient, independent and well-managed public service broadcaster. Firstly, Collins argues that public service broadcasters can better supply a cheap 'table d'hôte' broadcasting service. Expanding on an argument developed by Graham and Davies (1997), he argues that free market economics recognizes the existence of goods which confer long-term benefits for all individuals and societies, but which are normally under-supplied by the commercial sector. These goods are called 'merit goods', and include things like a public education system, funding for the arts and academic research, etc. Collins argues that the current expansion of broadcasting does not necessarily solve the problem of the under-supply of certain forms of programming by the commercial sector. Hence, public service broadcasters are better placed to provide programme formats such as in-depth political coverage or regional programming. However, he also warns that these services can only succeed if they are widely consumed. In other words, public service broadcasters cannot be consigned to the margins of the marketplace, as in America (2000: 10). The second rationale for public service broadcasting is that it is better placed than commercial operators to ensure a universal service to all citizens. Public service broadcasters have, in coexistence with the stable nation-state, been traditionally mandated to provide two kinds of universal service: geographical and audience universality. In other words, public service broadcasting functions as a central institution of the Habermasian public sphere that offers the potential of including a general public rather than particular publics. As Paddy Scannell cogently argues: 'the fundamentally democratic thrust of broadcasting lay in the new kind of access to virtually the whole spectrum of public life ... made available to all' (1989: 140). However, the idea of a public sphere coexisting with the stable nation-state has been put under intense pressure due to the twin movements of greater European integration and more demands for regional autonomy. The complex nature of devolutionary pressures within many European nations has led some academics to question how political theorists might best take account of these new political and communicative spaces in Europe (Somalvico 1999; Schlesinger et al. 2001: 2–5) and to revise the idea of the public sphere as coterminous with the state. How can public service broadcasters best reconcile their loyalty to the nation-state on the one hand, and at the same time cater for new communicative demands coming from Europe, stateless nations and autonomous regions? There is no simple answer to this question and individual countries will inevitably adopt different strategies. The third advantage of public service broadcasting over commercial operators is that it can offer citizens information from which to make informed and rational decisions, in an industry increasingly dominated by multinational conglomerates. The main charge made against big business is that informed political coverage can sometimes be sacrificed for corporate

motives. Hence, it was possible for Rupert Murdoch to drop the BBC World Channel from his Asian satellite service in order to curry favour with the Chinese government. But while private media can provide a platform for the beliefs and opinions of their owners, public service broadcasters have also failed in the past to distance themselves from political meddling, and such interference still occurs routinely in some countries. The fourth advantage of public service broadcasters is that they often provide a benchmark or quality threshold for the industry as a whole. Many broadcasters, unlike some of their commercial rivals, have sought to maintain a large production base in the past 20 years, promoting high programme-making values. And although budgets for research and development of new programming formats have come under financial pressure, and despite the fact that all broadcasters are under intense pressure to gain high audience ratings, public service broadcasters still have more opportunities than their commercial rivals to experiment with new programme ideas. Another example of this quality benchmark is the innovative websites that have been developed in the past few years by public service broadcasters including ZDF and the BBC. It can be reasonably argued, therefore, that there is a strong case for maintaining a well-organized and independent public service broadcasting system. Nevertheless, the continuing success of commercial broadcasting places a question mark over the long-term viability of publicly-funded and owned television and radio channels. Collins argues that for public service broadcasters to provide an independent and universal service available to all, and which also provides a quality benchmark for the rest of the industry, broadcasters must be more accountable and efficient, and promote innovation and creativity within the sector. One way in which broadcasters could become more accountable is to have more 'open, explicit and accountable systems of broadcasting governance' (2000: 19). Another way is by outsourcing programming and promoting a vibrant independent production sector. Public service broadcasters have so far failed to stem the tide of money flowing away to the commercial broadcasting sector. Zenith Media calculate that public service broadcasters' share of advertising expenditure declined from 44 per cent in 1990 to 28 per cent in 1994 (quoted in Collins 2000: 14). Gambaro (2000: 8) observes that, in 1987, the licence fee constituted 45 per cent of total broadcasting income. By 1998 this figure had fallen to 25 per cent due to a combination of factors including the relative stagnation in the value of the licence fee and the sharp growth in advertising revenues (2000: 8). It should be noted, therefore, that public service broadcasters still face an uphill battle if they are to arrest the decline of their audience base and share of income. The Dutch broadcaster NOS has noted that: 'Public service broadcasting is associated with effort, commercial broadcasting with relaxation. Young people in particular are turning away from public broadcasters ... ' (quoted in Collins 2000: 17).

2   Interview with Paolo Murialdi, Milan, 19 June 1995.
3   Interview with Paolo Murialdi, Milan, 19 June 1995.
4   I have used an exchange rate of 2,500 Italian lira to £1 stirling.
5   The advertising ceiling has worked in various ways. From the late 1950s until the mid-1970s, advertising was severely restricted. Thereafter, two different 'advertising ceilings' have been used to restrict RAI's income. The first method was to restrict the total amount of income raised through advertising (i.e. a maximum figure). This was abolished at the end of 1993. The second method (which is still in force) is the more common 'quota system'. RAI can advertise a maximum of 12 per cent per hour (14 per cent in prime-time).

This is compared to commercial broadcasters (Mediaset) who can advertise a maximum of 18 per cent per hour (20 per cent in prime-time).

6   Interview with Claudio Demattè, Milan, 30 January 1996.

7   There are a number of other key institutions that help regulate Italy's media industries. Firstly there is the parliamentary commission that supervises radio and television services and investigates the general management of RAI with a view to ensuring that it promotes an adequate degree of political pluralism in its general and news programmes, despite the fact that AGCOM is also nominally charged with overseeing this (Andreano and Iapadre 2005: 99). Secondly, there is the Ministry of Post and Telecommunications that monitors the RAI/state convention and is also responsible for the distribution of frequencies (in line with AGCOM's National Frequency Distribution Plan) in the run up to digital switchover (digital terrestrial services began in 2004).

8   This would also allow the Italian government to tackle the thorny issue of the licence fee. Reducing RAI's dependence on licence fee money would allow the government greater freedom to amend the current system (see Somalvico 1999: 70–2).

9   In a European parliamentary debate in July 2003 to mark the start of the six-month Italian presidency of the EU, and when goaded by a German MEP, Martin Schulz, Berlusconi told him that he would be 'perfect' for the role of concentration camp guard in a forthcoming movie. The remarks caused much consternation across Europe and created embarrassment for Italian officials and parliamentarians (including his own coalition allies). A week later, Berlusconi's minister for tourism and Northern League party member, Stefano Stefani, unleashed a stream of vitriol against Germans (see Timeline). The comments of Berlusconi and Stefani created the biggest crisis in German-Italian relations in the postwar period. Moisés Naím (2003) summed up some of the European press comments: 'A crass buffoon [and] a man of very questionable integrity' is how The Economist described Berlusconi. He incarnates 'nepotism, corruption and dishonesty' said Denmark's Information, while Aftonbladet, a Swedish daily, dismissed him as 'an arrogant clown' and the Berliner Zeitung wrote that he was 'a shady deal-maker'. France's Libération concluded that he was a 'threat to liberal democracy'. The UK Financial Times argued that 'he lives in a media-bubble where his public gaffes and gratuitous insults go largely unreported at home at least until he goes abroad'. The war of words also extended to the quality of programmes on Italian television, when an article written by Tobias Jones and published in the Financial Times (2003), said the Italian television studio had replaced the Senate and soft porn has replaced hard news. The article was based on his book, The Dark Heart of Italy (2003).

10   This interview took place within the electoral period covered by Law No. 28 of February 2000 providing for equal access (Par Condicio) for parties to media during electoral campaigns. The actor's criticisms of Berlusconi were no worse however than many Emilio Fede 'sermons'.

11   For an excellent blow-by-blow account, see Biagi and Mazzetti (2005: 51–125).

Chapter 9

1   RAI derives 93 per cent of its revenue from two sources: a licence fee payable by all Italian households and spot and sponsored advertising. The company's total income in 2004 was 4,930 million euro. The licence fee which, in 2004, made up 53 per cent of RAI's total income, is the lowest in Europe (93.80

euros in 2002) and the most widely evaded (21 per cent of Italian households failed to pay their licence fee in 2004). Between 1994 and 2000 the licence fee grew by 2.4 per cent annually, compared to a 2.9 per cent annual rise in the cost of living.

2   It should also be mentioned that in September 2000, RAI executives expected advertising revenue for that year to exceed the amount of income from the licence fee and sundry sources for the first time in the company's history. This, as it turns out, was somewhat wishful thinking.

BIBLIOGRAPHY

Achille, Y. and Miege, B. (1994) The limits to the adaption of European public service broadcasting television, *Media, Culture and Society*, 16.

AGCOM (Communications Authority) (1998) Piano nazionale di Assegnazione delle Frequenze per la Radiodiffusione Televisiva: Relazione Illustrativa, 30 ottobre 1998, available at www.agcom.it/provv/pnf/relaz_.htm.

AGCOM (Communications Authority) (1999) Relazione Annuale sull'Attività Svolta e sui Programmi di Lavoro, available at www.agcom.it/rel_01/index.htm.

AGCOM (Communications Authority) (2000) Libro Bianco sulla Televisione Digitale Terrestre, available at www.agcom.it/provv/libro_b_00/librobianco.htm.

Allum, P. (1990) Uniformity undone: aspects of Catholic culture in postwar Italy, in Z.G. Baranski and R. Lumley (eds) *Culture and Conflict in Postwar Italy*. London: Macmillan.

Anderson, B. (1991) *Imagined Communities: Reflections on the Origin and Spread of Nationalism*. London: Verso.

Andreano, S. and Iapadre, P. (2005) Audio-visual policies and international trade: the case-study of Italy, in P. Guerrieri, P. Iapadre, P. Lelio and G. Koopman (eds) *Cultural Diversity and International Economic Integration: The Global Governance of the Audio-Visual Sector*. Cheltenham: Edward Elgar.

Angela, P. (1998) Togliamo la spazzatura dalla tv, *La Repubblica*, 31 December.

Balassone, S. and Guglielmi, A. (1993) *La brutta addormentata. La TV e dopo*. Rome/Naples: Theoria.

Baranski, Z.G. and Lumley, R. (eds) (1990) *Culture and Conflict in Postwar Italy*. London: Macmillan.

Barca, F. (1998) *Indies: Le società di produzione televisiva in Gran Bretagna*. Rome: RAI-ENI.

Barca, F. (1999) La televisione digitale in Italia. Scelte istituzionali orientamento delle imprese televisive, in *Economia della Cultura*, 3. Bologna: Il Mulino.

Barca, F. (2007) *Le TV invisibili. Storia ed economia del settore televisivo locale in Italia*. Rome: RAI/ERI (Zone series).

Bardi, L. and Rhodes, M. (1998) *Politica in Italia*. Istituto Carlo Cattaneo, Bologna: Il Mulino.

Barile, P. (1995) *Idee per il governo. Il sistema radiotelevisivo*. Bari: Laterza.

Barzanti, R. (1994) *I confini del visibile. Televisione e cinema senza frontiere nelle politiche dell' Unione Europea*. Milan: Lupetti.

Bechelloni, G. (1995) *Televisione come cultura*. Genoa: Liguori Editori.

Berlin, I. (1956) *The Age of Enlightenment: The Eighteenth-century Philosophers*. Oxford: Oxford University Press.

Bettetini, G. (1990) L'Italia televisiva chiama davvero l'Europa, in C.D. Rath *et al.* (eds) *Le televisioni in Europa*. Turin: Fondazione Giovanni Agnelli.

Biagi, E. (1994) Video delle mie brame (interview with the President of RAI, Letizia Moratti), *Panorama*, 2 December.

Biagi, E. (1995) *Il fatto*, transmitted on Raiuno, 30 May.

Biagi, E. and Mazzetti, L. (2005) *Era ieri*. Milan: Rizzoli.

Bobbio, N. (1987) *The Future of Democracy*. Cambridge: Polity Press.

Bocca, G. (1997) *Italiani strana gente*. Milano: Mondadori.

Braun, M. (1995) *L'Italia da Andreotti a Berlusconi. Rivolgimenti e prospettive politiche in un Paese a rischio*. Milan: Feltrinelli.

Briggs, A. (1961) *The History of Broadcasting in the United Kingdom. Volume One: The Birth of Broadcasting*. London: Oxford University Press.

Briggs, A. (1965) *The History of Broadcasting in the United Kingdom. Volume Two: The Golden Age of Wireless*. London: Oxford University Press.

Briggs, A. (1970) *The History of Broadcasting in the United Kingdom. Volume Three: The War of Words*. London: Oxford University Press.

Briggs, A. (1979) *The History of Broadcasting in the United Kingdom. Volume Four: Sound and Vision*. Oxford: Oxford University Press.

Briggs, A. (1995) *The History of Broadcasting in the United Kingdom. Volume Five: Competition*. Oxford: Oxford University Press.

Brunetta, G.P. (1995a) *Cent'anni di cinema italiano, 1, dalle origini alla seconda guerra mondiale*. Laterza: Bari.

Brunetta, G.P (1995b) *Cent'anni di cinema italiano, 2, dal 1945 ai nostri giorni.* Laterza: Bari.

Bruno, V. (1991) Punturine di Vespa (interview with Bruno Vespa), *Prima Comunicazione*, April.

Bruno, V. (1992) Non siamo replicanti (interview with Angelo Guglielmi), *Prima Comunicazione*, April.

Bruno, V. (1994) Ma poi la signora Moratti ... (interview with Alfio Marchini), *Prima Comunicazione*, November.

Bull, M. and Rhodes, M. (1997) Between crisis and transition: Italian politics in the 1990s, *Western European Politics*, 20(1).

Buonanno, M. (1999) *Indigeni si diventa: Locale e globale nella serialità televisiva.* Firenze: Sansoni.

Buonanno, M. (2006) *Le radici e le foglie. La fiction italiana, l'Italia nella fiction. Anno diciasettesimo.* Rome: RAI/ERI (Zone series).

Burckhardt, J. (1990) *The Civilization of the Renaissance in Italy.* Harmondsworth: Penguin.

Burgelman, J-C. (1997) Communication's policy in western Europe, in J. Corner *et al.* (eds) *International Media Research: A Critical Survey.* London: Routledge.

Burke, P. (1990) Introduction, in J. Burckhardt, *The Civilization of the Renaissance in Italy.* Harmondsworth: Penguin.

Burns, T. (1977) *The BBC: Public Institution and Private World.* London: Macmillan.

Capra, C. (1976) Il giornalismo nell'età rivoluzionaria e napoleonica, in V. Castronovo and N. Tranfaglia (eds) *La stampa italiana dal' 500 all' 800.* Laterza: Bari.

Carr, E. (1962) *What is History?* London: Pelican.

Cavazza, F. (1979) Italy: from party occupation to party partition, in A. Smith (ed.) *Television and Political Life.* London: Macmillan.

Cesareo, G. (1974) *La televisione sprecata.* Milan: Feltrinelli.

Chomsky, N. (1994) *Il potere dei media.* Florence: Vallecchi Editore.

Ciampi, C-A. (2002) Open letter to Parliament, reprinted in *La Repubblica*, 25 July.

Clark, M. (1984) *Modern Italy: 1871–1982.* London: Longman.

Collins, R. (2000) A future for public service broadcasting? Keynote speech given to the Public Service Broadcasting in a Digital Age Conference, Banff, University of Alberta, 8–10 June.

Connell, I. and Curti, L. (1985) Popular broadcasting in Britain and Italy: some issues and problems', in P. Drummond and R. Paterson (eds) *Television in Transition*. London: BFI.

Corner, J. *et al.* (1997) *International Media Research: A Critical Survey*. London: Routledge.

Curran, J. (1991) Rethinking the media as a public sphere, in P. Dahlgren and C. Sparks (eds) *Communication and Citizenship: Journalism and the Public Sphere*. London: Routledge.

Curran, J. and Gurevitch, M. (1991) *Mass Media and Society*. London: Edward Arnold.

Curran, J. and Seaton, J. (1988) *Power without Responsibility*, 3rd edn. London: Routledge.

D'Arma, A. (2007) Digital switchover in Italy: an analysis of government policies 1996–2006, paper presented to the Annual International Communications Association (ICA) Conference, San Francisco, 24–8 May.

Dagrada, E. (1996) Television and its critics: a parallel history, in D. Forgacs and R. Lumley (eds) *Italian Cultural Studies: An Introduction*. Oxford: Oxford University Press.

Dahlgren, P. (1995) *Television and the Public Sphere: Citizenship, Democracy and the Media*. London: Sage.

Dahlgren, P. and Sparks, C. (eds) (1991) *Communication and Citizenship: Journalism and the Public Sphere*. London: Routledge.

Dante Aligheri (1997) *Divina Commedia*. Rome: Newton Compton Editori.

De Vescovi, F. (1986) *Economia dell'informazione televisiva*. Rome: Editori Riuniti.

De Vescovi, F. (1997) *Il Mercato della televisione*. Bologna: il Mulino.

Del Debbio, P. (1991) *Il mercante e l'inquisitore. Apologia della televisione commerciale*. Milan: Il Sole 24 Ore Editori.

Dematté, C. (1993) Indirizzi programmatici per il piano di ristrutturazione della RAI, reprinted in *Gulliver – mensile politico sulle comunicazioni di massa*, October.

Diamanti, I. (1996) The Northern League: from regional party to party of government, in S. Gundle and S. Parker (eds) *The New Italian Republic: From the Fall of the Berlin Wall to Berlusconi*. London: Routledge.

Dickie, J. (1996) Imagined Italies, in D. Forgacs and R. Lumley (eds) *Italian Cultural Studies: An Introduction*. Oxford: Oxford University Press.

Doyle, G. (2002) *Media Ownership: The Economics and Politics of Convergence and Concentration in the United Kingdom and European Media.* London: Sage.

Doyle, G. and Hibberd, M. (2003) *Competition, Cultural Variety and Global Governance: The Case of the UK Audio-Visual System.* Hamburg: Hamburgisches Welt-Wirtschafts-Archiv. Republished in P. Guerrieri, P. Iapadre, P. Lelio and G. Koopman, G. (2005) *Cultural Diversity and International Economic Integration: The Global Governance of the Audio-Visual Sector.* Cheltenham: Edward Elgar.

Eco, U. (1990) A guide to the neo-television of the 1980s, in Z.G. Baranski and R. Lumley (eds) *Culture and Conflict in Postwar Italy.* London: Macmillan.

Elliott, P. (1982) Intellectuals, the 'information society' and the disappearance of the public sphere, *Media, Culture and Society,* 4.

Emiliani, V. (2002) *Affondate la RAI. Viale Mazzini, prima e dopo Berlusconi.* Milan: Garzanti.

Esposito, R. and Grassi, A. (1975a) The monopoly reformed: the new Italian Broadcasting Act (Part 1), *EBU Review,* 26(4): 42–7.

Esposito, R. and Grassi, A. (1975b) The monopoly reformed: the new Italian Broadcasting Act (Part 2), *EBU Review,* 26(5): 48–55.

Euromedia Research Group (1997) *The Media in Western Europe: The Euromedia Handbook,* 2nd edn. London: Sage.

European Task Force (1988) *Europe 2000: What Kind of TV?* Manchester: Manchester University Press.

Fleischner, E. and Somalvico, B. (eds) (2002) *La televisione diventa digitale. Scenari per una difficile transizione.* Milan: Angeli.

Fontanarosa, A. (2000) TV di Stato, ecco il piano per privatizzarle, in *La Repubblica,* 29 August.

Forgacs, D. (1990a) *Italian Culture in the Industrial Era, 1880–1980: Cultural Industries, Politics and the Public.* Manchester: Manchester University Press.

Forgacs, D. (1990b) The Italian Communist Party and culture, in Z.G. Baranski and R. Lumley (eds) *Culture and Conflict in Postwar Italy.* London: Macmillan.

Forgacs, D. and Lumley, R. (eds) (1996) *Italian Cultural Studies: An Introduction.* Oxford: Oxford University Press.

Frayling, C. (1981) *Spaghetti Westerns.* London: Routledge.

Freedom House (2006) *Map of Press Freedom*. Available at www-.freedomhouse.org, accessed 11 October 2006.

Frei, M. (1996) *Italy: The Unfinished Revolution*. London: Mandarin.

Galante Garrone, A. (1979) I giornali della Restaurazione, in V. Castronovo and N. Tranfaglia (eds) *La stampa italiana del Risorgimento*. Laterza: Bari.

Gambaro, M. (2000) La pubblicit come fattore di produzione per l'azienda e fonte di ricavo per la tv, in A. Grasso (ed.) *La scatola nera della pubblicità. Volume terzo. L'Economia*. Turin: SIPRA.

Gambaro, M. and Silva, F. (1992) *L'economia della Televisione*. Bologna: Il Mulino.

Garnham, N. (1986) The media and the public sphere, in P. Golding *et al.* (eds) *Communicating Politics: Mass Communications and the Political Process*. Leicester: University of Leicester Press.

Gellner, E. (1983) *Nations and Nationalism*. Oxford: Basil Blackwell.

Gellner, E. (1997) *Nationalism*. London: Weidenfeld & Nicolson.

Giacalone, D. (1992) *La guerra antenne. Televisione, potere e politica: i frutti del non governo*. Milan: Sterling & Kupler Editori.

Giddens, A. (1991) *Modernity and Self-Identity: Self and Society in the Late Modern Age*. Stanford, CA: Stanford University Press.

Ginsborg, P. (1990) *A History of Contemporary Italy: Society and Politics, 1943–1988*. London: Penguin.

Ginsborg, P. (1996) Explaining Italy's crisis, in S. Gundle and S. Parker (eds) *The New Italian Republic: From the Fall of the Berlin Wall to Berlusconi*. London: Routledge.

Ginsborg, P. (2003) *Berlusconi*. Turin: Einaudi. English edition (2005) *Silvio Berlusconi: Television, Power and Patrimony*. London: Verso.

Golding, P. (1990) Political communication and citizenship: the media and democracy in an inegalitarian social order', in M. Ferguson (ed.) *Public Communication: The New Imperatives. Future Directions for Media Research*. London: Sage.

Graham, A. and Davies, G. (1997) *Broadcasting, Society and Policy in the Multimedia Age*. Luton: Luton University Press.

Grasso, A. (1992) *Storia della televisione italiana*. Milan: Garzanti.

Grasso, A. (2004) *Storia della televisione italiana* (enlarged edition). Milan: Garzanti.

Gray, J. (1995) *Isaiah Berlin*. London: Harper Collins.

Greene, Sir Hugh (1969) *The Third Floor: A View of Broadcasting in the Sixties*. London: The Bodley Head.

Grenville, J.A.S. (1980) *A World History of the 20th Century. Volume One: Western Dominance 1900–1945*. London: Fontana.

Guglielmi, A. and Balassone, S. (1995) *Senza rete. Politica e televisione nell'Italia che cambia*. Milan: Rizzoli.

Gundle, S. (1990) From neo-realism to Luci Rosse: cinema, politics and society, 1945–1985, in Z.G. Baranski and R. Lumley (eds) *Culture and Conflict in Postwar Italy*. London: Macmillan.

Gundle, S. (1996) Fame, fashion and style: the Italian star system, in D. Forgacs and R. Lumley (eds) *Italian Cultural Studies: An Introduction*. Oxford: Oxford University Press.

Gundle, S. and Parker, S. (eds) (1996) *The New Italian Republic: From the Fall of the Berlin Wall to Berlusconi*. London: Routledge.

Habermas, J. (1989) *The Structural Transformation of the Public Sphere*. Cambridge: Polity Press.

Hallamore Caesar, A. (1996) Postwar Italian narrative: an alternative account, in D. Forgacs and R. Lumley (eds) *Italian Cultural Studies: An Introduction*. Oxford: Oxford University Press.

Hallin, D. and Mancini, P. (2004) *Comparing Media Systems: Three Models of Media and Politics*. Cambridge: Cambridge University Press.

Hearder, H. (1983) *Italy in the Age of Risorgimento*. London: Longman.

Hearder, H. and Waley, D.P. (eds) (1963) *A Short History of Italy*. Cambridge: Cambridge University Press.

Hibberd, M. (2001a) The reform of public service broadcasting in Italy, *Media, Culture and Society*, 23(2): 233–52.

Hibberd, M. (2001b) Public service broadcasting in Italy: historical trends and future prospects, *Modern Italy*, 6(2): 153–70.

Hibberd, M. (2002a) Il sistema radiofonico in Gran Bretagna: identità e prossimità, in E. Menduni (ed.) *La radio. Percorsi e territori di un medium mobile e interattivo*. Bologna: Baskerville.

Hibberd, M. (2002b) La televisione digitale conviene sia pubblica? Il caso della Gran Bretagna, in E. Fleischner and B. Somalvico (eds) *La televisione diventa digitale. Scenari per una difficile transizione*. Milan: Angeli.

Hibberd, M. (2003a) E-participation, broadcasting and democracy in the UK, *Convergence*, IX(1).

Hibberd, M. (2003b) La TV pubblica nel Regno Unito: 1936–1976, *Giornale di storia contemporanea*, VI(2).

Hibberd, M. (2004a) Italian democracy gone mad? The privatisation of public service broadcasting in Italy, *Trends in Communication*, XII(1).

Hibberd, M. (2004b) RAI under the centre-right: wither 50 years of public service television? in S. Fabbrini and V. Della Sala (eds) *Politics in Italy: Italy between Europeanization and Domestic Politics*. Oxford: Berghahn.

Hibberd, M. (2004c) La TV digitale nel Regno Unito: 1998–2004, in G. Frezza and M. Sorice (eds) *La TV che non c'è: scenari dell'innovazione televisiva in Europa e nel mediterraneo*. Salerno: Edizioni 10/17.

Hibberd, M (2006) *Il grande viaggio della BBC*. Rome: RAI/ERI.

Hibberd, M (2007) Conflicts of Interest and Media Pluralism in Italian Broadcasting, in *West European Politics*, Vol. 30, No. 4, PP 881–902, September.

Hibberd, M., Kilborn, R., McNair, B., Marriott, S. and Schlesinger, P. (2000) *Consenting Adults?* London: Broadcasting Standards Commission.

Hine, D. (1979) Italy, in F.F. Ridley (ed.) *Government and Administration in Western Europe*. Oxford: Martin Robertson.

Hine, D. (1993) *Governing Italy: The Politics of Bargained Pluralism*. Oxford: Oxford University Press.

Hobsbawm, E.J. (1990) *Nations and Nationalism Since 1780: Programme, Myth, Reality*. Cambridge: Cambridge University Press.

Humphreys, P. (1994) *Media and Media Policy in Germany: The Press and Broadcasting Since 1945*, revised edn. Oxford: Berg.

Ignazi, P. and Katz, R. (1995) *Politica in Italia*. Bologna: Il Mulino.

Iseppi, F. (1980) The case of the RAI, *Media, Culture and Society*, 2.

Iseppi, F. (1998) La via italiana al servizio pubblico, *Problemi dell'informazione*, 23, September.

Jacobelli, J. (1996) *Letizia Moratti. Io e la RAI*. Milano: Rizzoli.

Jensen, K.B. and Jankowski, N.W. (eds) (1991) *A Handbook of Qualitative Methodologies for Mass Communication Research*. London: Routledge.

Joll, J. (1983) *Europe Since 1870: An International History*. London: Pelican.

Jones, T. (2003) *The Dark Heart of Italy: Travel Through Time and Space Across Italy*. London: Faber & Faber.

Judt, T. (1994) Nineteen eighty-nine: the end of which European era? *Daedalus* 123, Summer.

Judt, T. (1995) The future of Europe. Lectures given to Johns Hopkins University, Bologna, Italy, 29 and 30 May. These lectures were subsequently published in Judt, T. (1997).

Judt, T. (1997) *A Grand Illusion? An Essay on Europe.* Harmondsworth: Penguin.

Katz, R.S. and Ignazi, P. (eds) (1996) *Italian Politics: The Year of the Tycoon.* Boulder, CO: Westview Press.

Keane, J. (1991) *The Media and Democracy.* Cambridge: Polity Press.

Landy, M. (2000) *Italian Film.* Cambridge: Cambridge University Press.

Lane, D. (2004) *Berlusconi's Shadow: Crime, Justice and the Pursuit of Power.* London: Allen Lane.

Lepschy, G. (1990) How popular is Italian? in Z.G. Baranski and R. Lumley (eds) *Culture and Conflict in Postwar Italy.* London: Macmillan.

Levi, C. (1945) *Cristo sì fermato a Eboli.* Torino: Einaudi.

Losurdo, D. (1994) *La seconda repubblica. Liberalismo, federalismo, postfascismo.* Turin: Bollati Boringhieri Editore.

Lumley, R. (1990) *States of Emergency: Cultures of Revolt in Italy, 1968 to 1978.* London: Verso.

Lumley, R. (1996) Peculiarities of the Italian newspapers, in D. Forgacs and R. Lumley (eds) *Italian Cultural Studies: An Introduction.* Oxford: Oxford University Press.

Macchiatella, C. (1985) *Il gigante nano. Il sistema radiotelevisivo italiano: dal monopolio al satellite.* Torino: ERI.

Machiavelli, N. ([1513] 1991) *Il principe.* Milan: Rizzoli Libri.

Mack Smith, D. (1985) *Cavour.* London: Weidenfeld & Nicolson.

Mack Smith, D. (1996) *Mazzini.* New Haven, CT: Yale University Press.

Maltese, C. (2005). RAI, la strana coppia Petruccioli-Meocci, *La Repubblica*, 30 July.

Mammì, O. (1992) Introduction to D. Giacalone, *La guerra antenne. Televisione, potere e politica: i frutti del non governo.* Milano: Sterling & Kupler Editori.

Mancini, P. (1991) The public sphere and the use of news in a 'coalition' system of government, in P. Dahlgren and C. Sparks (eds) *Communication and Citizenship: Journalism and the Public Sphere.* London: Routledge.

Marano, A. (1995) *La tv che verrà. Nuove technologie e federalismo per una riforma del sistema della comunicazione*. Rome: Edizioni SEAM.

May, T. (1997) *Social Research: Issues, Methods and Process*. Buckingham: Open University Press.

Mazzoleni, G. (1993) La comunicazione politica alla vigilia della seconda Repubblica, *Problemi dell'Informazione*, 18(4).

Mazzoleni, G. (1995a) The RAI: restructuring and reform, in C. Mershon and G. Pasquino (eds) *Italian Politics: Ending the First Republic*. Boulder, CO: Westview Press.

Mazzoleni, G. (1995b) Towards a videocracy? Italian political communication at a turning point, *European Journal of Communication*, 10(3).

Mazzoleni, G. (2000) The Italian broadcasting system between politics and the market', *Italian Journal of Modern Studies*, 5(2): 371–94.

Mazzoleni, G. (2004) Italy, in M. Kelly, G. Mazzoleni and D. McQuail (eds) *The Media in Europe*. London: Sage.

Mazzoleni, G. and McQuail, D. (eds) (2004) *The Media in Europe*. London: Sage.

McQuail, D. (1991) Mass media in the public interest: towards a framework of norms for media performance, in J. Curran and M. Gurevitch (eds) *Mass Media and Society*. London: Edward Arnold.

Menduni, E. (1993) L'autunno della televisione (tre anni dalla legge Mammì), *Problemi dell'Informazione*, 18(4).

Menduni, E. (1996) *La più amata dagli Italiani: La televisione tra politica e telecomunicazioni*. Bologna: Il Mulino.

Menduni, E. (ed.) (2002) *La radio. Percorsi e territori di un medium mobile e interattivo*. Bologna: Baskerville.

Mershon, C. and Pasquino, G. (eds) (1995) *Italian Politics: Ending the First Republic*. Boulder, CO: Westview Press.

Miliband, R. (1973) *The State in a Capitalist Society*, 2nd edn. London: Quartet Books.

Monteleone, F. (1980) *Storia della RAI dagli alleati alla DC*. Bari: Laterza.

Monteleone, F. (1992) *Storia della radio e della televisione in Italia. Società, politica, strategie, programmi 1922–1992*. Venezia: Marsilio.

Murialdi, P. (1993) Nelle mani del parlamento, *Problemi dell'Informazione*, 18(3).

Murialdi, P. (1994a) *Maledetti professori. Diario di un anno alla RAI*. Milano: Rizzoli.

Murialdi, P. (1994b) l'Italia sotto i riflettori: Berlusconi e la RAI, *Problemi dell'Informazione*, 19(4).

Murialdi, P. (1997) Per una ricerca storica sulla *lottizzazione, Problemi dell'Informazione*, 22(1).

Murialdi, P. (2000) *Storia del giornalismo italiano*. Bologna: Mulino.

Murialdi, P. (2003) *Storia della stampa italiana dal 1945*. Bologna: Mulino.

Naím, M. (2003) Berlusconi could learn a thing from Nixon, *Financial Times*, 23 July.

Nowell-Smith, G. (1990) Italy: tradition, backwardness and modernity', in Z.G. Baranski and R. Lumley (eds) *Culture and Conflict in Postwar Italy*. London: Macmillan.

Ortoleva, P. (1994) La TV tra due crisi – 1974–1993, in Castronovo and Tranfaglia (eds) *La stampa italiana nell'eta della TV: 1975–1994*. Bari: Laterza.

Ortoleva, P. (1995) *Mediastoria: comunicazione e cambiamento sociale nel mondo contemporaneo*. Parma: Pratiche Editrice.

Ortoleva, P. (1996) A geography of the media since 1945, in D. Forgacs and R. Lumley (eds) *Italian Cultural Studies: An Introduction*. Oxford: Oxford University Press.

Pilati, A. and Richeri, G. (2000) *Le fabbrica delle idée: Il mercato dei media in Italia*. Bologna: Baskerville.

Pinder, J. (1991) *European Community: The Building of a Union*. Oxford: Oxford University Press.

Pini, M. (1978) *Memorie di un lottizzatore*. Milan: Feltrinelli.

Pinto, F. (1980) *Il Modello Televisivo*. Milan: Feltrinelli.

RAI Annual (1993–2006) *RAI Annuario, 1992–2005*. Torino: Nuova ERI.

RAI (1998) *Nuova Raitre e Piani Aziendali Coordinati: Linee Guida*. Torino: Nuova ERI.

Rath, C-D. (1990) *Le televisioni in Europa*. Torino: Fondazione Giovanni Agnelli.

Reith, J. (1949) *Into the Wind*. London: Hodder & Stoughton.

Richeri, G. (1990) Hard times for public service broadcasting: RAI in the age of commercial competition, in Z.G. Baranski and R. Lumley (eds) *Culture and Conflict in Postwar Italy*. London: Macmillan.

Richeri, G. (1993) *La TV che Conta: Televisione come Impresa*. Bologna: Baskerville.

Ricolfi, L. (1997) Politics and the mass media in Italy, *Western European Politics*, 20(1).

Rizza, N. (1989) *Costruire Palinsesti: Modalità logiche e stili della programmazione televisiva tra pubblico e privato*. Turin: Nuova ERI.

Rizza, N. (1990) Il palinsesto come fattore di produzione, *Problemi dell'Informazione*, 15(4).

Rositi, F. (1994) Sette televisioni nazionali e quasi ventimila casi, *Problemi dell'Informazione*, 19(3).

Sartori, C. (1989) *La Grande Sorella*. Milan: Mondadori.

Sartori, C. (1993) *La qualità televisiva*. Milan: Bompiani.

Sassoon, D. (1986a) Politics and market forces in Italian broadcasting, *European Journal of Politics*, 3(2): 67–83.

Sassoon, D. (1986b) *Contemporary Italy: Politics, Economy and Society since 1945*. London: Longman.

Scannell, P. (1989) Public service broadcasting and modern public life, *Media, Culture and Society*, 11(2).

Scannell, P. and Cardiff, D. (1982) Serving the nation: public service broadcasting before the war, in B. Waites (eds) *Popular Culture Past and Present*. London: Croom Helm.

Scannell, P. and Cardiff, D. (1991) *A Social History of British Broadcasting, Volume One: The Pre-War Years*. London: Macmillan.

Schlesinger, P. (1990) The Berlusconi phenomenon, in Z.G. Baranski and R. Lumley (eds) *Culture and Conflict in Postwar Italy*. London: Macmillan.

Schlesinger, P. (1991) *Media, State, and Nation: Political Violence and Collective Identities*. London: Sage.

Schlesinger, P. (1992) Europeanness: a new cultural battlefield? *Innovation*, 5(1).

Schlesinger, P. (1997) From cultural defence to political culture: media, politics and collective identity in the European Union, *Media, Culture and Society*, 19(3).

Schlesinger, P., Miller, D. and Dinan, W. (2001) *Open Scotland? Journalists, Spin Doctors and Lobbyists*. Edinburgh: Polygon.

Schudson, M. (1991) Historical approaches to communication studies, in K.B. Jensen and N.W. Jankowski (eds) *A Handbook of Qualitative Methodologies for Mass Communication Research*. London: Routledge.

Seton-Watson, C. (1968) *Italy from Liberalism to Fascism*. London: Methuen.

Siune, K. and Truetzschler, W. for the Euromedia Research Group (1992) *Dynamics of Media Politics: Broadcast and Electronic Media in Western Europe*. London: Sage.

Smith, A. (ed.) (1979) *Television and Political Life*. London: Macmillan.

Smith, A. (ed.) (1995) *Television: An International History*. Oxford: Oxford University Press.

Smith, A.D. (1991) *National Identity*. Harmondsworth: Penguin.

Smith, H.W. (1975) *Strategies of Social Research: The Methodological Imagination*. New York: Prentice Hall.

Somalvico, B. (1998) Per un autentico federalismo radio-televisivo, in *AA.VV., RAI. Idea e progetto. Comunicazione per il XXI secolo*. Roma: Licorno.

Somalvico, B. (1999) L'evoluzione del concetto di servizio pubblico nel sistema televisivo europeo, *Rivista Italiana della Comunicazione Pubblica*, 1(2), June.

Sorice, M. (2002) *Lo specchio magico. Linguaggi, formati, generi, pubblici della televisione italiana*. Rome: Riuniti.

Sorlin, P. (1996) *Italian National Cinema*. London: Routledge.

Sorrentino, C. (1997) The Italian media system, in L. d'Haenens and F. Saeys (eds) *Media Dynamics & Regulatory Concerns in the Digital Age*. Berlin: Quintissenz.

Sorrentino, C. and Hibberd, M. (2007) Italy, in d'Haenens L. and Saeys, F. *Western Broadcast Models: Structure, Conduct and Performance*. New York: Mouton de Gruyter.

Spotts, F. and Wieser, T. (1986) *Italy: A Difficult Democracy*. Cambridge: Cambridge University Press.

Stephens, M. (1988) *A History of News: From the Drum to the Satellite*. Harmondsworth: Penguin.

The Economist (2001) Fit to run Italy? Editorial, 21 April.

Tracey, M. (1983) *A Variety of Lives: A Biography of Sir Hugh Greene*. London: Bodley Head.

Venice Commission (2005) *On the Compatibility of the Laws 'Gasparri' and 'Frattini' of Italy with the Council of Europe Standards in the Field of Freedom of Expression and Pluralism of the Media*. Strasbourg: Council of Europe.

Vespa, B. (2002) *L'Italia di Berlusconi. L'Italia dei Girotondi*. Rome: RAI/Mondadori.

Wagstaff, C. (1996) Cinema, in D. Forgacs and R. Lumley (eds) (1996) *Italian Cultural Studies: An Introduction*. Oxford: Oxford University Press.

Weymouth, T. and Lamizet, B. (eds) (1996) *Markets and Myths: Forces for Change in the European Media*. London: Longman.

Willan, P. (2002) Berlusconi stokes new row in TV bias, *Observer*, 22 April.

Williams, R. (1959) *Culture and Society, 1780–1950*. London: Chatto & Windus.

Williams, R. (1976) *Keywords*. London: Fontana.

Wolf, M. (1990) The evolution of television in Italy since regulation, in Z.G. Baranski and R. Lumley (eds) *Culture and Conflict in Postwar Italy*. London: Macmillan.

Wood, M. (1994) Views from the Italian front: changing industrial patterns in the Italian film and media industries. Paper presented to Turbulent Europe: Conflict, Identity and Culture, EFTSC, 1994.

Wood, M. (2005) Italian Cinema. Oxford: Berg.

INDEX OF MAIN TERMS AND KEY NAMES